New Trends in Banking and Finance

Çağatay Başarır, Burak Darıcı &
Hasan Murat Ertuğrul (eds.)

New Trends in Banking and Finance

PETER LANG

Bibliographic Information published by the Deutsche Nationalbibliothek
The Deutsche Nationalbibliothek lists this publication in the Deutsche Nationalbibliografie; detailed bibliographic data is available online at http://dnb.d-nb.de.

Library of Congress Cataloging-in-Publication Data
A CIP catalog record for this book has been applied for at the Library of Congress.

Cover illustration: istock/lovelyday12

ISBN 978-3-631-77986-6 (Print)
E-ISBN 978-3-631-78057-2 (E-PDF)
E-ISBN 978-3-631-78058-9 (EPUB)
E-ISBN 978-3-631-78059-6 (MOBI)
DOI 10.3726/b15343

Peter Lang – Berlin · Bern · Bruxelles · New York · Oxford · Warszawa · Wien

This publication has been peer reviewed.

www.peterlang.com

Preface and Acknowledgements

Banking sector is one of the main building blocks of the financial systems of country economies. With the invention of money, the banking sector also started to develop and every passing day led to innovations in the financial sector. In this context, as a part of the banking sector that renews its technology continuously, development of the financial markets that the sector is involved with becomes important. The banking sector, constantly having an active role in the financial markets, has to renew itself regularly.

In recent years, rapid technological, social, and economic changes have effects on financial sectors in the unlimited world of globalization and increasing competition. Especially after the 2008 global crisis, it is revealed that all the financial markets, starting with the banking sector, face more risks than in the past. Therefore, the importance of the financial sector is reiterated one more time. This book presents the latest trends in the banking and financial sectors in the light of these developments.

In this book, developments both in the financial markets and banking sector are discussed by the academicians and practitioners, who are experts in their fields, from different viewpoints. The book consists of sixteen parts that discuss the developments in financial markets theoretically and empirically. While some parts of the book analyze the banking sector in the viewpoint of financial standards, financial analysis, and also marketing analysis, other parts emphasize the insurance sector which is an inseparable part of the financial markets.

We would like to thank all the authors and researchers, who are experts in their field, for their devotion and diligence, and hope this work will be of help to our readers. We also offer our endless gratitude to the families and children of our authors, who have been the source of motivation for our authors with their patience and support during the making of this valuable work. And also we would like to thank Professor Süleyman ÖZDEMİR, Rector of Bandırma Onyedi Eylül University for his contributions and support.

Editors: Asst. Prof. Çağatay Başarır Prof. Burak Darıcı
& Assoc. Prof. Hasan Murat Ertuğrul

Contents

List of Contributors 9

Zehra Civan
1 Systemic Risk, Causes and Precautions 11

Pınar Fulya Gebeşoğlu
2 Implications for a Macro Prudential Policy Framework: Systemic Risk and Shadow Banking Operations in Insurance Sector 27

Mesut Türkay
3 A Historical Analysis on the Recycling of Petrodollars 39

Onur Akkaya
4 The Reaction of the Bank of England to the US Dollar Exchange Rate 53

Özlem Ayvaz Kızılgöl
5 Analyzing the Relationship between Cryptocurrencies and Exchange Rates 61

Özlem Akın and S. Mehmet Özsoy
6 Global Trends in Liquidity Creation: The Role of the Off-Balance Sheet 77

Çiğdem Kurt Cihangir and Seçil Öztürk
7 Green Banking in Turkey 95

Özer Yılmaz
8 The Relationship Marketing Approach to Creating Competitive Advantage in the Banking Sector 115

Nimet Varlık
9 Macroeconomic Factors Affecting Non-Performing Loans in the Turkish Banking Sector 129

Tuba Derya Başkan
10 Analyzing the Relationship between the Valuation Method Used within the Scope of TFRS-9 Financial Instruments Profitability and Capital Structure of the Turkish Banking Sector 145

Gülçin Gürel Günal and Ertuğrul Deliktaş
11 The Market Structure of the Turkish Banking Sector That Changed with the Crisis in 2001: Merger and Acquisition Effect 157

İbrahim Murat Bicil and Çağatay Başarır
12 The Relationship between the Real Sector Confidence Index and Financial Indicators 173

Ömer Faruk Biçen and Kumru Türköz
13 The Effects of Financial Development on the Real Sector in Turkish Economy 183

Umut Uyar and Özlem İnce
14 Examining the Relationship between Market Information and Buy-Sell Decisions by PIN Values 197

Sezer Bozkus Kahyaoğlu
15 Generalized Autoregressive Score (Gas) Model: An Applied Analysis on the BIST 100 Index 217

Haşim Bağcı and Burhan Günay
16 The Effect of Basel Accords on Economic Value Added and Market Value Added 233

List of Figures 245

List of Tables 247

List of Contributors

Özlem Akın
Asst. Prof., Ozyegin University, ozlem.akın@ozyegin.edu.tr

Onur Akkaya
Dr., Kilis 7 Aralık University, onurakkaya@kilis.edu.tr

Özlem Ayvaz Kızılgöl
Asst. Prof., Bandırma Onyedi Eylül University, okizilgol@bandirma.edu.tr

Haşim Bağcı
Asst. Prof., Aksaray University, hasimbagci@aksaray.edu.tr

Çağatay Başarır
Asst. Prof., Bandırma Onyedi Eylül University, cbasarir@bandirma.edu.tr

Tuba Derya Başkan
Asst. Prof., Kırıkkale University, tBaşkan@kku.edu.tr

İbrahim Murat Bicil
Asst. Prof., Balıkesir University, muratbicil@balikesir.edu.tr

Ömer Faruk Biçen
Asst. Prof., Balikesir University, ofbicen@balikesir.edu.tr

Sezer Bozkus Kahyaoğlu
Assoc. Prof., İzmir Bakırçay University, sezer.bozkus@bakircay.edu.tr

Çiğdem Kurt Cihangir
Asst. Prof., Hitit University, kurt_cigdem@yahoo.com

Zehra Civan
Dr., Vakıfbank, İstanbul, Turkey, civanzh@gmail.com

Ertuğrul Deliktaş
Prof., Ege University, ertugrul.deliktas@ege.edu.tr

Pınar Fulya Gebeşoğlu
Ph.D., The Ministry of Treasury and Finance, fulya.ozorhan@hazine.gov.tr

Gülçin Gürel Günal
Res. Asst., Dr., Ege University, gulcin.gurel@ege.edu.tr

Burhan Günay
Asst. Prof. Yıldırım Beyazıt University, bgunay@ybu.edu.tr

Özlem İnce
Ph.D. Candidate, Pamukkale University, ozlemince@hotmail.com

S. Mehmet Özsoy
Asst. Prof., Ozyegin University, mehmet.ozsoy@ozyegin.edu.tr.

Seçil Öztürk
Asst. Prof., Çanakkale Onsekiz Mart University, secilozturk@comu.edu.tr

Mesut Türkay
Ministry of Treasury and Finance, Ph.D. Republic of Turkey, Ankara, Turkey
mesut.türkay@hazine.gov.tr

Kumru Türköz
Res., Asst., Balikesir University, kumru.turkoz@balikesir.edu.tr

Umut Uyar
Asst. Prof., Pamukkale University, uuyar@pau.edu.tr

Nimet Varlık
Asst. Prof., Kırıkkale University, nvarlik@kku.edu.tr

Özer Yılmaz
Asst. Prof., Bandirma Onyedi Eylül University, oyilmaz@bandirma.edu.tr

Zehra Civan

1 Systemic Risk, Causes and Precautions[1]

Abstract: There are several ongoing studies on systemic risks and related preventive measures that have been one of the most popular topics after the 2008 financial crisis. This chapter researches the concept of systemic risks and gives definitions of systemically important financial institutions, and global and domestic systemically important banks, as well. This study includes the reasons for systemic risks and the necessary precautions to be taken to reduce them. It differs from other studies with respect to the overall general concept of systemic risks.

Keywords: Systemic Risk, Financial Crisis, Precautions, financial Institutions

1 Introduction

Financial institutions subject to systemic risks and economic damages caused by them, as well as the reasons for systemic risks, have become the most often discussed topics in the academic and financial environment due to the last economic crisis that started in 2007 and was distributed to all financial markets in 2008.

Systemic risk which has become one of the most discussed issues in the literature since the 2008 financial crisis has no single definition. Instead, there are many alternative definitions highlighting the systemic risk in the literature. Some of these are given below.

BIS (Bank for International Settlements) defines systemic risk as the risk emerging when the failure of a financial institution to meet its obligations creates a chain reaction and affects other institutions negatively, leading to financial difficulties in a broad sense. This definition emphasizes the domino effect of systemic risks (BIS, 1994: 177).

Rochet and Tirole (1996: 733) define it as the propagation of a bank's economic distress to other economic agents linked to that bank through financial transactions.

G-10 defines systemic risk as follows in the report on Consolidation in the Financial Sector published in 2001:

---

1 The views expressed in this chapter are those of the author and do not necessarily represent the views of VakifBank, Turkey.

Systemic financial risk is the risk that an event will trigger a loss of economic value or confidence in, and attendant increases in uncertainly about, a substantial portion of the financial system that is serious enough to quite probably have significant adverse effects on the real economy. Systemic risk situations can occur suddenly and unexpectedly, or the possibility of systemic risk occurs when there are no appropriate political arrangements. Negative economic impacts resulting from systemic risks are generally seen as the disruption of the payment system and credit flows and the disappearance of asset values. (G-10, 2001: 126)

Kaufman and Scott (2003: 371) define systematic risk as the risk or probability of breakdowns in an entire system, as opposed to breakdowns in individual parts or components, and is evidenced by comovements (correlation) among most or all the parts.

ECB (European Central Bank) defines systemic risk as the risk in which financial instability becomes so widespread that it impairs the functioning of a financial system to the point where economic growth and welfare suffer materially (ECB, 2009: 135).

Erdem Başçı, who was the Central Bank Governor of Turkey from April 2011 to April 2016, highlighted the contagious effect of systemic risk in the opening speech he made at the G-20 conference titled "Financial Systemic Risk" held in Istanbul on September 27, 2012. He emphasized the interdependence among financial institutions while explaining the concept of systemic risk.

As stated by *Smaga (2014: 2)*, systemic risk is much more than a single risk affecting financial institutions. Risks such as credit risks, liquidity risks, and operational risks, etc., directly affect the relevant institutions while systemic risk occurs indirectly.

Some of the studies in the literature on systemic risk are about definitions of systemic risk while others are aimed at measuring the systemic risks. Studies aimed at preventing systemic risks also show what can be done to reduce these risks. This part first gives a summary of the literature including studies on measurement of systemic risks and then mentions systemically important financial institutions (SIFIs), reasons for systemic risks, and precautions that can be taken to prevent such risks.

2 Literature Summary

The literature including theoretical and empirical studies on systemic risks is expanding each passing day. This section has been limited to studies on systemic risks. There is no single or standard method used to measure systemic risks revealed by the literature review. This risk is measured with different approaches in the relevant literature. It is not clearly known which one reflects this risk correctly.

The leading studies in the literature on measurement of systemic risks are briefly mentioned below:

Lehar (2005: 2582) defined systemic risks using the model developed by Merton (1974) and the default probabilities of financial institutions in the study that was based on asset returns and liabilities. In this way, the possibility of financial institutions' failure to make payments was calculated.

Huang et al. (2009: 2039) suggested the distress insurance premium technique as a systemic risks measurement method that tries to predict the asset-return correlation and is based on calculation of insurance premiums of banks using banks' default probabilities for possible financial crisis situations.

Segoviano and Goodhart (2009: 16–17) have created a banking stability index that is aimed at measuring interconnectedness of banks and their impacts on each other during an economic crisis using credit default swap data and tries to predict the systemic risks.

Adrian and Brunnermeier (2008: 1–2) suggested the CoVaR method to measure systemic risks. They defined CoVaR as the value-at-risk (VaR) of the financial system conditional on a financial institution being under distress. In this method, the contribution of a financial institution to the systemic risks of the system is shown with ΔCoVaR.

Acharya et al. (2010: 2–3) suggested the MES (Marginal Expected Shortfall) method. Using this method, they concluded that a bank with higher MES value made a bigger contribution to the systemic risks. Afterwards, *Brownless and Engle (2012: 2–3)* suggested the Systemic Risk (SRISK) method, which is related to MES. This method aims to predict the capital amount that will be needed by the financial institution in the next economic crisis.

Tarashev and Zhu (2011: 130–132) developed a new measurement based on portfolio credit risk and network analysis to measure the systemic risks. They argued that the contribution of a bank to the systemic risks mainly depended on its role in the financial sector and relationship with other banks.

Lahmann and Kaserer (2011: 4–7) used a new measurement technique called *Expected Systemic Shortfall (ESS)* in their study. The possibility of a systemic situation and the tail loss, i.e., the maximum shortfall in case of a systemic risk, are measured with ESS.

Cao (2013: 2–5) tried to determine the systemic importance of each institution operating in a financial sector. Considering that all institutions in the financial sector constitute the financial system, he measured a systemic risk in two steps: (i) calculating the total systemic risk of the financial system, (ii) measuring the contribution of each financial institution to the total systemic risks using the "Multi-CoVaR" method and the "Sharpley Value" criterion, respectively.

3 Systemically Important Financial Institutions (SIFIs)

Many institutions led by G-20 initiated efforts to determine systemically important financial institutions and reduce risks after the 2008 financial crisis. First, the financial Stability Board (FSB) prepared a report which was released on October 20, 2010, and it was accepted at the G-20 Leaders Summit in November 2010. The FSB made suggestions about reducing the ethical risks caused by systemically important financial institutions in this report. The suggestions are as follows (FSB, 2010: 2)[2]:

- Take necessary precautions to ensure that all financial institutions can be resolved safely, quickly, and without destabilizing the financial system and exposing the taxpayer to the risk of loss;
- Especially global systemically important financial institutions that pose greater risks to the global financial system have higher loss absorbency capacity;
- More intensive supervisory oversight for financial institutions which may pose systemic risk;
- Robust core financial market infrastructures to reduce contagion risk from the failure of individual institutions;
- Other supplementary precautions as determined by the national authorities.

Afterwards, the G-20 leaders asked FSB to prepare a policy framework to reduce and prevent systemic and moral risks caused by systemically important financial institutions. The framework that was prepared by FSB and published on November 4, 2011 includes a timeline and processes to prevent systemic and ethical risks. The timeline that was approved by the G-20 leaders aimed to initiate the precautions in 2012 and complete them by 2019. The process started in 2012 and still continues.

The report includes a description of systematically important financial institutions (SIFIs). SIFIs are defined as financial institutions that cause serious deterioration of the financial system and economic activities when they get into trouble and cannot perform their activities due to their size, complexity, and systemic interdependence (FSB, 2011: 1)[3].

---

2 FSB, October 20, 2010, "Reducing the moral hazard posed by systemically important financial institutions: FSB recommendations and time lines," page 2.

3 FSB, November 4, 2011, "Policy measures to address systemically important financial institutions," page 1.

Basel Committee on Banking Supervision (BCBS) has divided SIFIs into two categories: global systemically important banks (G-SIBs) and domestic systemically important banks (D-SIBs). It took into account the magnitude of the loss that would result from bank failures while making this distinction.

3.1 Global Systemically Important Banks (G-SIBs)

The early studies on systemically important financial institutions (SIFIs) were on banks. BCBS published a report on G-SIBs in November 2011. The report contains the method for determining global systemically important banks and details related to the additional capital liability to be imposed on determined banks (BCBS, 2011). FSB determined twenty-nine banks as global systemically important banks (G-SIBs) based on the method included in this report and announced their names. It was decided that FSB would update the list in November every year. Some banks can be added while some can be removed from the list as it is updated. BCBS made it compulsory for the banks included in the G-SIB list to have additional capital in accordance with their systemic importance as of 2016.

BCBS suggests that negative impacts of a bank failure on the global financial system and economy must be measured instead of considering the bank's bankruptcy individually. The committee developed a method based on indicators that are considered to make banks systemically fragile in order to determine global systemically important banks. The indicators are related to sizes, complexities, interdependencies, substitution, and cross-border activities of banks.

Each one of these five indicators and their sub-indicators are equally weighted in this indicator-based method developed by BCBS. The measurement is given in Tab. 1.1

Scores are calculated for each bank included in the study while determining G-SIB in this indicator-based measurement method used by BCBS. In addition, a threshold is determined by BCBS. The score calculated for each bank is compared with the threshold determined by BCBS, and if it exceeds the threshold, this bank is regarded as G-SIB by BCBS. BCBS identified four equal score ranges. Banks are distributed to these four groups according to their calculated scores. The systemic significance level of each group is considered to be different and the additional capital liabilities differ accordingly. The additional capital requirement for banks in the group with the highest systemic risks is 2.5 percent of the risk weighted assets. This rate is 1 percent for the lowest group. There is also a fifth group with a capital buffer rate of 3.5 percent that is left blank (BCBS, 2013: 8–13).

Tab. 1.1: Indicator-Based Measurement Method. Source: Basel Committee on Banking Supervision (BCBS, 2013: 6)

Category (and weighting)	Individual indicator	Indicator weighting
Cross-jurisdictional activity (20%)	Cross-jurisdictional claims	10%
	Cross-jurisdictional liabilities	10%
Size (20%)	Total exposures as defined for use in the Basel III leverage ratio	20%
Interconnectedness (20%)	Intra-financial system assets	6.67%
	Intra-financial system liabilities	6.67%
	Securities outstanding	6.67%
Substitutability/financial institution infrastructure (20%)	Assets under custody	6.67%
	Payments activity	6.67%
	Underwritten transactions in debt and equity markets	6.67%
Complexity (20%)	Notional amount of over-the-counter (OTC) derivatives	6.67%
	Level 3 assets	6.67%
	Trading and available-for-sale securities	6.67%

3.2 Domestic Systemically Important Banks (D-SIBs)

BCBS evaluated the magnitude of the potential impact of a bank failure in terms of domestic and global economy while defining SIBs. According to this evaluation, G-SIBs and D-SIBs were separated. BCBS argues that a globally non-systemic bank may have systemic significance for the local financial markets and the local economy.

The framework created for G-SIBs was expanded in 2012 to include D-SIBs. In October 2012, BCBS published the framework including the guidelines of the method to be used to determine D-SIBs. This framework is both compatible with the G-SIB framework and entitles national authorities to take other precautions for D-SIBs depending on the conditions of the country (BCBS, 2012: 1–6)[4].

4 Basel Committee on Banking Supervision, October 2012, "A framework for dealing with domestic systemically important banks," pages 1–6.

4 Reasons for Systemic Risks

The last economic crisis made it necessary to evaluate systemic risks caused by banks that constitute a vast majority of the financial markets. Although the literature contains many ways a problem or crisis faced by a bank can spread to other banks, they can be divided into three groups (Bijlsma, Klomp, and Duineveld, 2010: 10–11):

The first one is the case in which a bank faces a big problem, and it causes assets of another bank to lose value. The distress experienced by a bank can affect another bank directly or indirectly. The direct impact results from mutual agreements such as derivative agreements made by two or more banks. Agreements made by the bank in distress lose value and this decreases the value of the assets owned by the institution that is the other party of the agreement. The indirect impact results from the fact that both banks work with the same customers, i.e., common depositors and debtors.

The second one is the case in which the ability of a bank to procure liquidity is negatively affected even though the assets of this bank are not affected by the situation of the bank in crisis. Banks usually meet their short-term funding needs from the interbank market. If a bank in the interbank market goes into trouble, this will have a negative impact on the funding amount and conditions offered to the interbank market, and shrink or even eliminate the fund procurement capability.

Thirdly, crises can spread from one bank to another through information flow. When a bank is in distress and the relevant information spreads in the market rapidly, customers will withdraw their money from the bank and encourage other customers to do the same. In this way, there will be a significant amount of fund outflow from banks, liquidity shortage will emerge, and this will have a negative impact on the operation of the financial system.

Many reasons creating the systemic risk emerge when an institution fails to fulfill its obligations towards parties with which it is cooperating (Murphy, 2012: 2). The size, interconnectedness, domino effect, and contagion effect of financial institutions are listed among reasons causing systemic risks in almost all studies. These three reasons are examined below.

4.1 Too Big to Fail

The "Too Big to Fail" means that relevant authorities usually try to save institutions that are considered to have systemic importance and pose risks for the whole financial system and financial stability if they have a financial distress situation.

The issue of "Too Big to Fail" turned into a big problem for countries especially after the 2008 financial crisis. Under normal circumstances, an organization that does not fulfill its obligations should be in the process of liquidation. Banks, which are also financial institutions, are expected to enter into the liquidation process when they fail to fulfill their obligations. However, allowing banks that have mutual interdependence with many large and complex institutions or sectors that are important for the financial system and therefore the national economy to enter the normal liquidation process can have negative consequences in terms of financial stability. Therefore, it becomes mandatory for the relevant national authorities to take special precautions regarding large-scale banks in financial distress, especially during periods of crisis for the sake of financial stability (FSA, 2009: 96–97). Big state interventions were performed on banks in countries such as the USA, England, Spain, Germany, Iceland, Belgium, France, the Netherlands, etc., to build trust in the markets, protect rights of savers, prevent economic routs caused by failure of banks in distress, and prevent the distress from spreading from one financial institution to another and making the crisis contagious, with the aim of maintaining financial stability in the last global financial crisis.

Relevant authorities damage the market discipline by preventing large financial institutions from going bankrupt through public guarantees. Such institutions trust overt and covert public guarantees, take more risks in the market due to their increased appetite for risk, increase the capital shortfall in the whole market by getting more loans with less capital, and destroy the competitive environment for small institutions. Furthermore, incentives in the form of guarantee or direct funding provided by states in order to save large banks have negative social impacts as they are paid from the taxes paid by citizens (Bernanke, 2009).

Although bank sizes have increased in the last twenty years, their productivity has decreased whereas the risks related to loans, the market, and liquidity have increased. Studies have revealed a negative correlation between bank sizes and productivity. Although it is argued that these banks get cost advantages resulting from scale economy, studies have proven otherwise. It was thought before the 2008 financial crisis that the bigger a bank was, the better it was. It was thought that being a large bank provided banks with an advantage in the international arena. However, the last crisis turned large-scale banks or financial institutions into a problem that must be kept under control in terms of national economies for authorities regulating the financial system.

4.2 Domino Effect and Interconnectedness

Banks transfer some of their risks to other financial institutions through derivative transactions such as swap, hedge, etc., in order to reduce their macroeconomic risks. These financial institutions create a chain by transferring some of their risks to other institutions in the same way as with derivative products. As a result, banks have become dependent on each other with derivative agreements among themselves. This new situation is called counter party risk. In this way, a financial problem faced by one of the parties can propagate very rapidly by spreading to other financial institutions in a short time (Murphy, 2012: 9–11).

This financial network between them creates a domino effect and therefore a trouble faced by a financial institution has a small or large negative impact on other financial institutions. After the last financial crisis, this has been called interconnectedness or mutual dependence, and it is regarded as one of the reasons for systemic risk.

The liquidity risk caused by the trust issues between banks creates a systemic risk by creating a domino effect and spreading to other banks. For example, whether a bank is bankrupt or not, if it refuses to give a loan to another bank, this will create trust and liquidity risks between the banks. As a result, it can cause the interbank market and short-term repo market to crash, as well as create liquidity squeeze and panic in the financial sector. This way, it causes a liquidity-induced systemic risk affecting the vast majority of the financial system (Adrian and Boyarchenko, 2013: 1–2).

As a result of insurance agreements and arrangements made between banks, these banks become interconnected due to the deposits of the same customers in each other's balance sheets, derivative contracts, or loans obtained from the interbank market. It is questioned why banks choose interconnectedness, i.e., mutual dependence.

- First of all, to procure enough liquidity in order to remain liquid against the possibility that depositors can withdraw their deposits,
- In order to protect themselves against the risk that debtors may fail to repay their loans,
- For new investment opportunities,
- There is a close relationship between them in order to protect themselves against decreases in asset prices.

The abovementioned cases have a negative impact on liquidities of banks. A bank's capital can be very insufficient. In this case, the bank usually tries to make up this deficiency by getting loans from the interbank market. Although this network provides significant support for banks, it can also cause a problem or crisis in a bank to spread to others. A trouble faced by a bank can cause the other bank or banks to lose money due to agreements between them. The bankruptcy of a bank decreases the asset prices of other related banks, and this reduces the capital of the bank whose asset prices decrease, which leads to bankruptcy of the other bank. Interconnectedness brings about the contagion effect (Adrian and Boyarchenko, 2017: 26–27).

4.3 Contagion Effect

When an institution or a group of financial institutions that have systemic importance for the financial sector gets into trouble, this has a negative impact on other financial participants in terms of the critical financial goods and services they offer to the economy. This is called a negative externality and poses a danger for the whole financial system. Negative externality is one of the propagation channels of the contagion effect. The criteria used in the literature to describe the contagion are given below (Constancio, 2012: 111).

- Presence of more spillover effects than those that can be explained by economic factors,
- The contagion effect is completely different from normal circumstances,
- Incidents causing the contagion have negative extremities,
- The contagion is sequential, so it can pass from one to another.

The contagion effect results from insufficiencies of institutions and affects all financial institutions. It affects not only those with weak financial conditions but also strong ones due to the domino effect and changing financial market conditions. A systemically important institution going into trouble, significantly reduced trust in the financial system, sudden decreases in the market liquidity, fire sales due to a lack of trust or liquidity problems, etc., can be given as examples of the contagion effect.

The contagion effect refers to propagation of systemic risks through various channels. These channels can be summarized as follows (Smaga, 2014: 10);

- Credit risks and liabilities included in balance sheets, risks not included in balance sheets (derivative contracts, etc.), and mutual commercial agreements such as import/export agreements,
- Market; trust and behavior factors (moral risk, information flow), fire sales, crash of the whole market due to a negative external crisis, etc.,
- Structural; similar structures of assets and liabilities, risk management techniques and methods,
- Global; foreign banks (refraining from providing loans, i.e., not funding the other party in times of crisis), exposure of the domestic financial system to external shocks, procuring financing from global financial markets, large capital outflows, etc.,

- Product; using derivative and movable goods (mutual independence in the financial system results in using leverages more than necessary),
- Payment systems; the link between payments and exchange systems (direct or indirect).

The contagion effect resulting from the systemic risks affects especially the banking sector. Therefore, it damages the entire financial system and the macro economy significantly. The banking sector is vulnerable to the risks posed by the contagion effect and precautions need to be taken by the relevant authorities.

5 Precautions to Reduce the Systemic Risks

It is still a matter of debate how the last financial crisis happened, how it evolved, and why it spread rapidly. Ben Bernanke, who was the former chairman of FED (Federal Reserve System), defined the last crisis as the worst financial crises faced by the world since the 1930s and said that the main reasons for the crisis were still controversial in his speech on March 10, 2018 The 2008 financial crisis caused a severe collapse in the global economy. He pointed out that the 2008 crisis was global while the crises in the 1990s were regional.

There are many suggestions for reducing the systemic risk, and they can be summarized by dividing into four categories: being too big to fail, strengthening the financial infrastructure, procyclicality in the audition system, and foundation of a systemic risk authority (Bernanke, 2009).

(i) Too Big to Fail or Too Interconnected to Fail:
Ben Bernanke (2009) referred to large-scale financial institutions as a problem by using the expression "too big to fail or too interconnected to fail." A crisis caused by such large-scale institutions can have a negative impact on the whole financial system, even the global economy by spreading to other economies at a global level. In order to prevent this, it is necessary to restrict the activities and size of the financial institution which is regarded as a risk for the financial market by the regulatory authorities and to prevent excessive risk taking.
Large complex institutions must be monitored on a regular basis and audited more effectively. First of all, the institutions that are weak in terms of capital adequacy, liquidity, and risk management should be identified by auditing authorities. An institution that is considered to create a systemic risk should be enabled to increase its capital adequacy and liquidity ratios compared to other institutions. As a matter of fact, additional capital requirement was imposed on banks with Basel III. Not only banks but also all financial

institutions should be followed more closely by rules and regulations. It is necessary to facilitate liquidation of bankrupt companies and reduce the costs they inflict on the macro economy.

(ii) Strengthening the Financial Infrastructure:
The financial infrastructure must be strengthened in order to ensure proper operation of the financial system, rules and agreements regulating the trade, payments, barters and collections in financial markets in any crisis situation as well. Relevant authorities must take necessary steps so that banks can meet the capital and liquidity requirements by shortening maturity dates and increasing liquidity. In order to prevent a similar crisis in the future, the financial system should be considered as a whole, not individually (Bernanke, 2009).

(iii) Procyclicality in the Audit System:
The financial system is procyclical thanks to capital ratio standards, accounting principles and other regulations. The greatest impact of procyclicality on financial institutions is that they act more freely during loan provision and expansion periods whereas they reduce the loan amount in times of crisis although the credit worthiness of the debtor does not change significantly.
The capital ratios of the bank are required to maintain a minimum ratio through the regulations on capital adequacy ratio. It is thought that banks will be more reliable and robust in this way. As it is not possible for banks to raise capital during an economic crisis, they are expected to achieve the capital ratios demanded in normal periods. Increasing capitals during crises may lead to a reduction in the amount of loans given by banks. Financial markets must be supported by achieving higher capital ratios in good times in order to prevent such situations that can affect the macro economy negatively.
Deposit insurances, which are another source of cyclicality, must be rearranged. Deposit insurance rates and durations had to be increased by the countries affected from the last economic crisis and that placed an additional burden on the economy. Risky banks must be enabled to pay more premiums than others in normal periods in order to ease such burdens on the economy (Bernanke, 2009).

(iv) Foundation of a Systemic Risk Authority:
Although auditing banks on a regular basis is necessary to reduce the systemic risk, it is not enough by itself. The financial infrastructure needs to be strengthened in terms of rules, regulations, accounting principles, and payment systems in order to prevent a crisis, at large institutions that are too big to fail, from spreading to the whole financial system. A "systemic risk authority" is needed to prevent such sudden ups and downs in crisis periods. This authority should monitor the systemic risk, detect

interconnected institutions, take necessary precautions in time, and offer consultancy services to the financial system if necessary (Bernanke, 2009). The systemic risk authority should:

a) Monitor large and rapidly increasing loans not only in a certain company or sector but also in all companies and markets,
b) Determine changes in the financial markets or products increasing the systemic risk, deficiencies in risk management such as increases in the financial leverage ratios, and potential risks,
c) Analyze the potential contagion effect between financial institutions or companies and markets, as well as determine interconnected institutions that carry out a lot of mutual transactions,
d) Make sure that loopholes in regulations aimed at protecting the whole financial system, customers, and investors are detected and corrected.

Conclusion and Recommendations

There are ongoing studies on systemic risk and related preventive measures that have been one of the most popular topics due to the 2008 financial crisis. The studies suggest that first systemically important institutions must be analyzed individually and their individual financial structures must be strengthened in order to prevent the systemic risk. Strengthening the entire financial system against crises should not be the sole objective, also it must be aimed to ease the moral risk that may arise from organizations that are too big to fail.

In order to determine the systemic risk in advance and to take the necessary measures, first a unit that will monitor the systemic risk should be established. This unit should be able to gather the necessary data from financial institutions and financial markets in order to monitor the systemic risk. However, there are some obstacles preventing access to required data such as different accounting standards in countries, limited disclosure of requested information to the public, differences in reporting times, etc. The systemic risk monitoring authority should be able to solve these problems. In addition to having national authorities take the necessary steps for solution of the problems, cooperation among institutions in the international arena must be aimed. Finally, a global financial stability early warning system should be established (ECB, 2009: 132) and a global risk map must be prepared.

References

Acharya, V.V., Pedersen, L.H., Philippon, T., and Matthew, R. (2010), "Measuring Systemic Risk," https://pages.stern.nyu.edu/~tphilipp/papers/Systemic.pdf, April 8, 2016.

Adrian, T. and Boyarchenko, N. (2017), "Liquiditiy Policies and Systemic Risk," https://www.newyorkfed.org/medialibrary/media/research/staff_reports/sr661.pdf, 22 November 2017.

Adrian, T. and Brunnermeier, M.K. (2008), "CoVaR," http://citeseerx.ist.psu.edu/viewdoc/download?doi=10.1.1.458.9323&rep=rep1&type=pdf, January 10, 2017.

Bank for International Settlements (1994), 64th Annual Report. Access link https://www.bis.org/publ/arpdf/archive/ar1994_en.pdf[2] .

Başçı, E. (2012), "Financial Systematic Risk - G-20 Conference Opening Speech," G-20 Conference, September 27–28, 2012, İstanbul.

Basel Committee on Banking Supervision. (2011), A Framework for Dealing with Domestic Systemically Important Banks, https://www.bis.org/publ/bcbs224.pdf, September 6, 2017.

Basel Committee on Banking Supervision. (2012), Global Systemically Important Banks: Assessment Methodology and the Additional Loss Absorbency Requirement, https://www.bis.org/publ/bcbs207.pdf, September 6, 2017.

Basel Committee on Banking Supervision. (2013), Global Systemically Important Banks: Updated Assessment Methodology and the Higher Loss Absorbency Requirement, https://www.bis.org/publ/bcbs255.pdf, September 6, 2017.

Bernanke, B.S. (2009), "Financial Reform to Address Systemic Risk," The Council on Foreign Relations, March 10, 2009, Washington D.C.

Bijlsma, M., Klomp, J., and Duineveld, S. (2010), *CPB Document: Systemic risk in the Financial Sector*, https://www.cpb.nl/sites/default/files/publicaties/download/systemic-risk-financial-sector-review-and-synthesis.pdf, November 14, 2017.

Brownlees, C.T. and Engle, R. (2012), Volatility Correlation and Tails for Systemic Risk Measurement, https://bfi.uchicago.edu/sites/default/files/research/SSRN-id1611229.pdf, February 25, 2017.

Cao, Z. (2013), Multi-CoVaR and Shapley Value: A Systemic Risk Measure, http://risk2015.institutlouisbachelier.org/uploads/440754460_Cao_systemic_risk_measure_Risk_forum.pdf, 3 February 2017.

Constancio, V. (2012), "Contagion and the European Debt Crisis," *Banque de France Financial Stability Review*, 16: 109–121.

European Central Bank, Financial Stability Review December 2009: A Concept of Systemic Risk, https://www.ecb.europa.eu/pub/pdf/other/financialstabilityreview200912en.pdf, December 5, 2017.

European Central Bank, Financial Stability Review: The Concept of Systemic Risk, https://www.ecb.europa.eu/pub/pdf/other/financialstabilityreview200912en.pdf, November 14, 2017.

Financial Services Authority, The Turner Review: A Regulatory Response to the Global Banking Crisis, http://www.ecgi.org/tcgd/2009/FSA_Turner_Report_on_Financial_Crisis_2009.pdf, November 14, 2017.

Financial Stability Board, Policy Measures to Address Systemically Important Financial Institutions, http://www.fsb.org/wp-content/uploads/Policy-Measures-to-Address-Systemically-Important-Financial-Institutions.pdf, September 6, 2017.

Financial Stability Board, Reducing the Moral Hazard Posed by Systemically Important Financial Institutions: FSB Recommendations and Time Lines, http://www.fsb.org/wp-content/uploads/r_101111a.pdf, September 6, 2017.

Group of Ten (2001), Report on Consolidation in the Financial Sector, https://www.imf.org/external/np/g10/2001/01/Eng/pdf/file3.pdf, November 16, 2017.

Huang, X., Zhou, H., and Zhu, H. (2009), "A Framework for Assessing the Systemic Risk of Major Financial Institutions," *Journal of Banking and Finance*, *33*(11):2036–2049.

Kaufman, G.G. and Scott, K.E. (2003), "What Is Systemic Risk, and Do Bank Regulators Retard or Contribute to It?," *The Independent Review*, *VII*(3):371–391.

Lahmann, W. and Kaserer C. (2011), The ESS-Indicator: A New Measure of Systemic Risk Applied to the European Financial Sector, https://papers.ssrn.com/sol3/papers.cfm?abstract_id=1906682, January 22, 2017.

Lehar, A. (2005), "Measuring Systemic Risk: A Risk Management Approach," *Journal of Banking and Finance*, 29(10):2577–2603.

Merton, R. C. (1974). On the pricing of corporate debt: The risk structure of interest rates. The Journal of finance, 29(2), 449–470.

Murphy, E.V. (2012), What Is Systemic Risk? Does It Apply to Recent JP Morgan Losses?, https://digital.library.unt.edu/ark:/67531/metadc87231/m1/1/high_res_d/R42545_2012May24.pdf, November 17, 2017.

Rochet, J. C., and Tirole, J. (1996). Interbank lending and systemic risk. Journal of Money, credit and Banking, 28(4), 733–762.

Segoviano, M. and Goodhart, C. (2009), Banking Stability Measures, https://www.imf.org/external/pubs/ft/wp/2009/wp0904.pdf, October 9, 2017.

Smaga, P. (2014), The Concept of Systemic Risk, http://eprints.lse.ac.uk/61214/1/sp-5.pdf, November 16, 2017.

Tarashev, N. and ve Zhu, H. (2011), "Specification and Calibration Errors in Measures of Portfolio Credit Risk: The Case of the ASRF Model," *International Journal of Central Banking*, 4(2):129–174.

Pınar Fulya Gebeşoğlu

2 Implications for a Macro Prudential Policy Framework: Systemic Risk and Shadow Banking Operations in Insurance Sector

Abstract: This chapter explores the implications for a macro prudential policy framework with respect to the management of systemic risk that may arise from shadow banking operations in the insurance sector. Risks inherent in shadow banking are discussed and the conditions that may lead to systemic risk in the insurance sector are investigated.

Keywords: Systemic Risk, Shadow Banks, Insurance Sector, Macro Prudential Policy

1 Introduction

Shadow banking has been drawing increasing attention recently with the latest developments in securitization that emerged as a natural outcome of growing global interlinkages between the banking and capital markets sector. Securitization has certain advantages such as enabling transfer of credit risk and helping capital markets develop and deepen. However sophisticated securitization techniques triggered excessive risk-taking in financial markets which produced repercussions and contagion through interlinkages and threatened financial stability in the global financial crisis of 2008. Hence the aftermath of the global financial crisis provided regulatory and supervisory authorities with the motivation to implement more stringent macro prudential measures targeting shadow banking.

The shadow banking operations may possibly create systemic risk either indirectly through transmission channels by affecting the banking sector or directly via risks taken by engaging in banking sector risks such as liquidity, maturity, excess leverage (FSB, 2018). The Financial Stability Board (FSB) monitors recent developments in the shadow banking system as risks emerging in the shadow banking sector might deteriorate financial stability.

The phenomenon of "too big to fail" in response to the failure of the AIG and huge bailout packages financed through taxpayers' rights and benefits engendered vehement support for imposing more onerous regulations on financial institutions that are considered as "systemically risky." The debate on the extent of systemic risk in the insurance sector has not yet achieved a consensus. Although it is widely accepted that the source of the credit crises were mainly banks but not the core insurance activities, bank-like operations of insurance companies undeniably played a crucial role both in inflating the asset price bubble during the pre-crisis period and also in deepening the loss during the crisis through interconnectedness of the insurance sector with other financial institutions.

Insurance corporations and pension funds together have 17.7 percentage share of total global financial assets as of 2016 (FSB, 2018:11). Also the share of the insurance and private sector has been rising steadily since the Global Financial Crisis of 2008–2009. As insurance and private pension sectors play an important role in the financial sector, the interconnectedness between the insurance and private pension sectors with banks and other financial intermediaries warrant the emphasized attention of the supervisory authorities.

As the global trends incline toward non-bank financing that provide a viable alternative for diversification of credit, unforeseen vulnerabilities emerge which threaten financial stability in case of financial distress. This chapter explores the implications for a macro prudential policy framework with respect to the management of systemic risk that may arise from shadow banking operations in the insurance sector. Risks inherent in shadow banking are discussed, and the conditions that may lead to systemic risk in the insurance sector are investigated. The regulatory framework for shadow banking operations in the insurance sector is perlustrated. An outline of future prospects to establish a macro prudential policy framework regarding systemic risk in the insurance sector that may arise due to shadow banking operations is presented in the Conclusion.

2 Systemic Risk in the Insurance Sector

The systemic risk can be defined as the risk of failure of a part or parts of the financial system as a whole that has potential negative implications on the real economy via spillovers.

The emphasis on the crucial role expected out of macro prudential regulatory and supervisory frameworks hinges on the perception of systemic risk in the insurance sector. The general consensus regarding the systemic risk in the insurance sector states that the business model of insurance and reinsurance companies is fundamentally different compared to other financial institutions such as banks.

The three essential criteria used by the FSB for the assessment of the systemic risks are size, substitutability, and interconnectedness (FSB, 2009). The IAIS (International Association of Insurance Supervisors) recommended addition of time that is measured as the speed of loss transmission to third parties. The IAIS recommendation distinguishes the long-term nature of the insurance business where obligations are not instantly translated into immediate cash outflows unlike the banking sector (IAIS, 2009).

The Geneva Association published a special report on systemic risks in insurance sector and argued that core insurance activities do not create systemic risks when assessed on the basis of the FSB criteria. The criterion of size is found to be misguiding, as it is the level of diversification of risk that determines the systemic risks and the typical large insurer has more potential to be diversified over a wider range of insurance lines and jurisdictions. The nature of interconnectedness matters most in terms of systemic risks and yet reinsurance which is a common form of interconnectedness in the insurance business is expected to mitigate the systemic risks compared to CDS transactions, which constitute another form of interconnectedness and hence expected to aggravate the systemic risks.

The insurance sector is regarded as a highly substitutable sector considering that the sector is efficiently competitive which enables continuity of coverage in case of a possible failure (IAIS, 2011). Also insurance claims span a larger time horizon compared to claims on banks which allow time to adjust to unforeseen risks. Therefore it is concluded that only the non-core activities engaged by the insurers such as derivatives trading on non-insurance balance sheets and mismanagement of securitization activities may lead to systemic risk if conducted on huge scales (Geneva Association, 2010).

The recommendation that only the insurers engaging in banking activities should be subject to additional scrutiny is based on analysis of post-crisis data. For instance more than 90 percent of the state support provided to the insurance sector in the United States during the course of the global financial crisis included few insurers engaging in bank-like activities. Yet, this approach of focusing on ex-post data may be misleading, as it has a narrow scope reflecting only the specific characteristics of the 2008 global financial crisis. There exists probability of incurring an unprecedented sort of crisis constituting an unforeseen case and contributing to the formation of a whole new narrative.

For instance, Schwarez and Schwarez (2014) highlight that insurers undertake a huge role in financial intermediation and capital accumulation process as one of the major institutional investors despite the common view that insurance sector does not pose a significant systemic risk. The insurance business model depends on collection of premiums in return for provision of protection against insurable risks which by nature span a longer-term horizon and enable the insurer to act as a critical source of funding for various sectors including financial, corporate, and real estate sectors. Hence the authors argue that the potential for insurance business to raise systemic risks is limited neither to the size and scale of certain insurers that are regarded as systemically important insurers nor to certain kinds of activities such as derivatives trading and shadow banking operations engaged in the sector. Instead, Schwarez and Schwarez (2014) point out that structural interconnections between insurers and the rest of the financial sector may as well create a source of systemic risk through simultaneity, correlated actions, and contagion. Hence common exposures of the insurance sector emerge as a potential source of systemic risks independent of the entity- and activity-based approaches (Schwarez and Schwarez, 2014).

Albeit seldom a failure of a reinsurer due to an unexpectedly large catastrophe allows time for rearrangement of investment portfolios due to long tail liabilities in the insurance sector. Also the procedures involving resolution, winding up, and liquidation are not expected to produce systemic risks in the insurance sector as in a run-on bank crisis. Hence even the catastrophic risks are not expected to pose systemic risks considering the low frequency, limited size of loss, reinsurance coverage provided, and relatively slow pace of claims settlement process. Insurance policies with redemption options are also evaluated as not systemically risky, since these are usually accompanied by lapse penalties or surrender charges.

A possible financial distress might potentially spillover through different channels of transmission considering the level of interconnectedness between the insurance and private pension sectors and other financial institutions including both banks and non-bank financial institutions. For instance, the available data as of 2016 for twenty-nine jurisdictions gathered in the FSB 2017 report indicate that funding provided to other financial institutions from insurance and pension companies together exceed funding from banks. Hence, if flow of funding from insurance and pension companies deteriorates unexpectedly there exists potential for contagion via available funds to other financial institutions and to banks subsequently (FSB, 2017).

The increasing risk of longevity along with rising sensitivity to low interest rate environment led insurers to become more actively involved in the capital markets, which translated into another source of potential systemic risks posed by life insurance companies. Promised rates of return embedded in various life products challenge the business model of life insurers and provide incentive for pursuing higher yield. Hence the supervisory authorities should lay special emphasis on product design process and tailor the regulatory framework to motivate insurers to avoid excessive risk-taking by offering minimum return guarantees.

3 Shadow Banking Operations in the Insurance Sector

Shadow banking or "market based finance" frequently used as a substitute term can be defined as credit intermediation activities of financial institutions that reside beyond the scope of the regular banking sector. Securitization-based credit intermediation represents 10 percentage of the narrow measure of shadow banking which involves non-bank financial entities that engage in shadow banking operations with potential risk to financial stability (FSB, 2018).

Banking activities that remain beyond the scope of core balance sheet activities are mainly composed of derivatives such as swaps, options, futures and forward contracts, and securitized assets and financial guarantees.

The lines of business insurers engage in affect their investment strategies. For instance, insurers operating mostly in property and casualty branches tend to focus more on fixed income assets with shorter-term liability durations and hence need to balance their investment strategies more conservatively compared to insurers with more illiquid liabilities. Insurance companies focusing on annuities, life products, and private pension companies are usually endowed with more options to diversify their portfolios in order to align their investment strategies with the maturity and liquidity of their liabilities. On the other hand the insurers that suffered financial hardship during the global financial crisis were neither life insurers nor property and casualty insurers but rather were mainly comprised of monoliners engaging in financial guarantees and CDSs (Credit Default Swaps).

Insurance companies engage in shadow banking activities in order to manage their portfolios. Also some insurance companies are involved in direct lending or securitization activities through their subsidiaries. The European Commission stated that these kinds of shadow banking activities that are subject to the Solvency II framework do not pose systemic risks to the wider financial sector (European Commission, 2013).

Securitization activities engaged by the insurance sector serves as reinsurance and offer the investors to diversify their risks as insurance-related risks are mostly independent of the business cycle. Also the volume of insurance-linked securities is quite low in comparison with outstanding asset backed securities which further scales down the potential risk expected. In addition to the acyclicality of insurance-related risks and low scales involved insurance, supervisory and regulatory frameworks impose additional capital requirements on insurers investing in insurance-linked securities such as cat bonds (Insurance Europa, 2014).

Regulatory reforms realized in the aftermath of the global financial crisis contributed to restoration of financial stability. The July 2017 Assessment of Shadow

Banking Risks conducted by the FSB upon request from the G-20 indicates that priorly addressed aspects of shadow banking that were thought to contribute to the financial crisis do not pose systemic risks (FSB, 2017). Still recent developments in fintech and innovations that foster credit expansion indicate emerging need for additional regulatory precautions. Therefore, ensuring that transparency standards are restored at international level is crucial in monitoring potential risks that might arise from shadow banking operations in non-insurance balance sheets.

4 Implications for Regulatory Framework

The regulatory and supervisory legislation for the insurance sector evolved into a risk-based capital adequacy framework that focused on reserve requirements and establishment of guarantees to protect the rights and benefits of insurers over the years. This trend starting with Canada in 1992 was followed by the United States, Australia, Switzerland, etc., inclined toward market-based accounting principles, which led to valuation of risky assets to be determined by credit spreads (IMF, 2016).

The insurance regulatory framework imposed by Switzerland, which includes the Swiss Solvency Test and a set of principle based regulatory regimes, is a risk-based capital regime like the Solvency II, whereas the US insurance regulatory framework includes both rule-based and principle-based approaches (Geneva Association, 2010). In the aftermath of the Global Financial Crisis, the Federal Insurance Office (FIO) was established under the US Treasury by the Dodd-Frank Wall Street Reform and Consumer Protection Act. The FIO is vested with the authority to monitor all aspects of the insurance sector and to represent the USA on prudential aspects of international insurance matters. The EU-US Insurance Dialogue Project which was initiated by the US FIO and the National Association of Insurance Commissioners (NAIC) in partnership with the European Commission and the European Occupational Pensions Authority aims to analyze and compare the insurance regulatory regimes of the EU and the United States from several dimensions and enhance more effective supervision to promote business opportunities and consumer protection. The agenda for 2018 includes group supervision with a special focus on intragroup transactions. Intragroup transactions are recognized as potential sources of contagion in case of financial distress, and hence should be addressed specifically within an integrative approach by various supervisory authorities.

The scope of Solvency II that provides a supervisory ladder of intervention in case of a possible breach is expected to mitigate the speed of possible contagion in case of potential insurer failures. Also, speculative derivatives transactions are subject to higher capital requirements in accordance with risks involved at the group level within the Solvency II framework. Similarly the Swiss Solvency Test covers activities on non-insurance balance sheets in insurance groups. Hence the regulatory regimes currently in force address activities that are identified as systemically risky fairly well to the extent that group-wide supervision is handled with caution.

Although the insurance regulatory regimes that are currently in force adequately address risks that might arise out of core insurance activities, it was argued that the regulatory and supervisory frameworks failed in detecting the systemic risks that may arise out of quasi banking operations of insurers following the aftermath of the global financial crises (Harrington, 2009).

Considering the interlinkages among the insurance companies, banks, and other non-bank financial institutions, the need for group-wide supervision is crucial. In addition to ensuring the coordination between supervisory authorities of various financial sectors, cross-border cooperation and information-sharing agreements are required as systemically important insurers operate in several jurisdictions across the globe. Further harmonization of accounting and reporting rules and legislation regarding the insurance sector should prove useful in terms of timely and effective regulatory intervention.

Monoline insurance companies which are often referred to as *monoliners* have a different business model compared to traditional insurers because the nature of their business is based on assuming credit risk. The credit risk assumed evolved into a more risky business as financial guarantees became associated with more complex financial products such as credit default swaps. For instance, credit default swaps that were not subject to insurance regulation by definition turned out to be a crucial source of systemic risk. Hence, the need for further regulation targeting financial guarantee insurance is highlighted (Geneva Association, 2010). As the nature of business is fundamentally different to core insurance activities, additional regulatory precautions are needed to target the systemic risks arising from monoliners.

Since insurance sector is not regarded as systemically risky with respect to core insurance activities but rather deemed to be a potential source of risk only in case of underregulated non-core activities engaged by the insurers, the regulations targeting financial stability and systemic risks are proposed to be designed on activity basis (Insurance Europa, 2014; IAIS, 2018). Instead of approaching each and every non-core insurance activity as systemically risky, the volume of the activities engaged in and the interconnections within financial institutions should be taken into account.

As the insurance regulatory frameworks currently in force tend to emphasize capital requirements, the regulatory regimes should be balanced in favor of enhancing liquidity risk management, especially in case of short-term shadow banking operations engaged in massive scales. Provision of financial guarantees and writing credit default swaps are not subject to insurance regulatory framework in many jurisdictions because these are not categorized as insurance core activities. Hence issuance of financial guarantee insurance and securitization activities should also be treated within a macro prudential insurance supervisory framework. Some jurisdictions restrict insurers' trading in derivatives as a precaution although derivatives play a crucial role in risk management strategies of insurers.

Efforts should be made to tackle the problem of lack of standardization at international level such as different valuation standards adopted in balance sheet items and adoption of internal models in calculating solvency capital. The Common Framework developed by the IAIS for the supervision of internationally active insurance groups envisages more detailed requirements than the insurance core principles (ICPs).

Conclusion

Being an effective risk management tool to finance and protect business initiatives, insurance is crucial for sustainable growth in any modern economy. Moreover insurance sector takes off a noteworthy portion of the burden on government budgets by acting as a major contributor to social protection via life insurance and private pension products. Non-life insurance branches enable economic activities in various sectors by committing to financial compensation against professional and general liability, natural catastrophes, accidents, etc.

Unlike risks specific to the banking sector such as maturity, default and liability risks, insurance risks maintain their independence outside the business cycle. Yet, the global financial crisis of 2007–2008 had indeed proved that insurance sector is not entirely immune from the complicities of the business cycle and may in fact act as an underlying source of a potential systemic risk and pose a significant threat to financial stability.

The most widely accepted explanation in the literature addresses the quasi bank operations of the insurance sector such as engaging in shadow banking activities, providing sophisticated financial guarantees, and trading with complex derivatives as potential sources of threat to financial stability. The developments in fintech and innovations in securitization motivated insurers to go one step further and set up subsidiaries that engage in trading complex financial instruments instead of merely hedging assets in direct relationship with core insurance activities.

The traditional regulatory and supervisory framework targeting the insurance and reinsurance sectors historically focused on capital adequacy standards, which proved to be insufficient in the unprecedented case of the AIG failure in 2008.

Monoline insurers that engage in provision of financial guarantees face risks that are similar to the risks faced by the banking sector. Therefore the regulatory framework targeting monoline insurers should be differentiated in such a manner as to display consistency with the regulatory framework of the banking sector (Geneva Association, 2010).

Growing share of non-bank financial intermediation signals potential for emerging vulnerabilities that may threaten financial stability if left unregulated. Macro prudential regulation of shadow banking is recommended to manage possible systemic risk.

Also, regulatory gaps should be clarified and it should be ensured that subsidiaries of large financial conglomerates do not evade regulatory domain, and they are indeed subject to comprehensive regulation and supervision. For instance, the AIG Financial Products which was established as a subsidiary of the AIG Holding Company with the aim to engage in capital markets operations in 1987 managed to escape the scope of UK's Financial Services Authority despite being domiciled in London. The privilege provided to the subsidiary at the time was justified on the ground that the AIG Holding Company was already registered with the US Office of Thrift Supervision under the US Department of the Treasury, which was regarded as an equivalent regulator[1].

As the structure of the balance sheet of insurers is fundamentally different than that of banks, the regulatory framework designed for banks such as Basel III would not be proper in addressing the specific needs of the insurance sector. For instance, imposing excessive capital requirements on the insurance sector by reflecting the regulatory models designed for the banking sector would produce adverse consequences such as raising costs and insurance premiums with no justification of mitigating possible risks as the nature of the risks faced by the insurers and banks differ fundamentally. Hence insurance regulatory framework targeting risky activities of insurers should be designed to comply with the capital requirements and risk profiles of the insurance sector. Moreover, in order to assess potential risks the authorities should make an effort to gather more granular data that enables measuring interconnectedness between sectors and systemically risky companies or activities.

In response to the complications addressed, the FSB identified a list of globally systemically important insurers (G-SIIs) in consultation with the IAIS and national supervisory authorities. An integrated set of policy measures to manage the systemic risks associated with the G-SIIs are published and updated annually. For instance, higher loss absorbency requirements (HLA), implementation of systemic risk management plans and liquidity management plans, and resolvability assessment process to be applied by the senior regulators taking part in the crisis management groups are among the internationally agreed standards to be applied to the G-SIIs. However, this approach has been subject to criticism because designating a number of financial institutions as systemically important and imposing specific regulations on these institutions implies that these institutions are perceived as too big to fail, and hence creates moral risk and deteriorates fair competition (FSB, 2010; Ötker et al. 2011).

In conclusion cross-border cooperation and information sharing among supervisory authorities and group-wide supervision at a consolidated level including shadow banking operations on non-insurance balance sheets should prove as useful precautionary measures to mitigate potential sources of systemic risks. Regulation of monoliners should be tailored in line with their specific business model, which differs from traditional insurers' business model.

Notes

1. The OTS was merged with other agencies including the Office of the Comptroller of the Currency, the Federal Deposit Insurance Corporation (FDIC), the Federal Reserve Board of Governors, and the Consumer Financial Protection Bureau (CFPB) in 2011.

References

Adrian, T., and Shin, H.S. (2009), "The Shadow Banking System: Implications for Financial Regulation," *Staff Report*, Federal Reserve Bank of New York, No. 382, Federal Reserve Bank of New York, New York, NY.

Cummins J.D., and Weiss, M.A. (2014), "Systemic Risk and the U.S. Insurance Sector," *The Journal of Risk and Insurance, Vol.81*, No.3, pp. 489–527.

European Commission (2013), *Shadow Banking - Addressing New Sources of Risk in the Financial Sector*. Brusselsi, September 2013. https://eur-lex.europa.eu/legal-content/EN/TXT/PDF/?uri=CELEX:52013DC0614&from=LV

FSB (2009), “Guidance to Assess the Systemic Importance of Financial Institutions, Markets and Instruments: Initial Considerations,” *Report to G20* finance *Ministers and Governors* (October), Financial Stability Board.

FSB (2010), “Reducing the Moral Hazard Posed by Systemically Important Financial Institutions,” Financial Stability Board.

FSB (2017), “Assessment of Shadow Banking Activities, Risks and the Adequacy of Post Crisis Policy Tools to Address financial Stability Concerns,” Financial Stability Board, July 2017.

FSB (2018), “Global Shadow Banking Monitoring Report 2017,” Financial Stability Board.

Geneva Association (2010), “Systemic Risk in Insurance, an Analysis of Insurance and Financial Stability,” *Special Report of the Geneva Association Systemic Risk Working Group.*

Harrington, S.E. (2009), “The financial Crisis, Systemic Risk and the Future of Insurance Regulation,” *The Journal of Risk and Insurance, Vol.76*, No.4, 785–819.

International Association of Insurance Supervisors (2009), *Systemic Risk and the Insurance Sector* (October 25th), p.6.

IAIS (2011), Insurance and Financial Stability.

IAIS (2018), Activities Based Approach to Systemic Risk.

IMF (2016), The Insurance Sector –Trends and Systemic Risk Implications.

Insurance Europa (2014), Why Insurers Differ from Banks.

Ötker, I., Narain, A., Ilyina, A., and Surti, J. (2011), The Too Important to Fail Conundrum: Impossible to Ignore and Difficult to Resolve; IMF Staff Discussion Note.

Schwarez, D., and Schwarez S.L. (2014), “Regulating Systemic Risk in Insurance,” *The University of Chicago Law Review, Vol. 81*, No.4, pp.1569–1640.

Mesut Türkay

3 A Historical Analysis on the Recycling of Petrodollars

Abstract: This chapter provides a historical investigation on how OPEC countries recycle their oil revenues. This investigation is important because the results enable us to understand how they use petrodollars and be able to analyze the effects of petrodollars on major economic indicators and the global economy.

Keywords: Oil Price, Petrodollars, Macroeconomic Variables, OPEC Countries

1 Introduction

Oil price movements have attracted attention of large segments of the society, especially since the oil crisis of the 1970s when prices skyrocketed. The reason why oil price has always been on the forefront of the agenda is that changes in the price affect every economic unit, from exporters and importers of the product to corporations and ordinary citizens. Higher oil prices lead to redistribution of income from importers to exporters. Oil exporters accumulate a windfall of revenues called *petrodollars* while importers lose their purchasing power. Rising prices contribute to global imbalances by increasing current account surplus and deficits of exporters and importers. At the same time, as it is an important input of production, cost of production goes up and therefore price pressures emerge. Since it constitutes an important part of the household budget, almost everyone is more or less interested with the price of oil.

Rising oil price has led to the accumulation of petrodollars in the hands of oil exporters. This revenue can basically be spent or saved. Increasing imports, investing more in infrastructure, and raising wages are some options to spend oil revenue. On the other hand, accumulating foreign reserves, depositing money in foreign banks, paying down external debt, and purchasing foreign assets such as firms in other countries, equities and debt securities abroad, are alternative ways of saving petrodollars. How oil exporters recycle their revenues has very important implications for exporters, importers, and the global economy. This is one leading motivation of this chapter. We believe that it is useful to analyze the way exporters recycle petrodollars and its effects.

This chapter investigates how oil exporters, specifically OPEC countries[1], have recycled their petrodollar revenues in a historical perspective starting from 1970s. We analyze the similarities and differences about the spending and saving behavior of OPEC countries in certain periods of oil price increases. Specifically, the periods we are interested in are two oil shocks in the 1970s and the periods before and after the global economic crisis of 2008.

The chapter proceeds as follows. Second section describes the impact of petrodollars on various economic indicators and the global economy. Third section provides a historical analysis of oil price movements and petrodollar revenues starting from 1970s until today. In the fourth section, we explain the major recycling channels of petrodollars. More specifically, we investigate the historical trends in the use of petrodollars through trade and financial channels. Finally, fifth section concludes.

2 Macroeconomic Effects of Petrodollars

There is a large and growing literature on the macroeconomic and financial effects of oil price movements. Most of the existing literature focuses on the impact of oil prices on major macroeconomic indicators and asset prices. Our purpose is not to get into details but just to present a brief overview of the literature.

Bruno and Sachs (1985), Hamilton (1996), Kilian (2008), and Morana (2017) are some studies on macroeconomic effects of oil price shocks. Accordingly, oil price movements cause redistribution of income from importers to exporters. Since higher oil prices lower purchasing power in oil-importing countries, it is a drag on growth. On the other hand, oil exporters spend part of the petrodollars on imports, and this reduces the negative effect on growth. Recycling of petrodollars through investments in international capital markets provides necessary funding for oil importing countries indirectly. As oil is an important input of production, higher prices increase cost of production, lower corporate profitability, and lead to inflation pressures. At the same time, higher prices reduce disposable income and domestic demand in oil importing countries. A rise in oil prices worsens trade and current account balances and deteriorates net foreign asset position in importing countries. On the other hand, increasing revenues improves budget balance of oil exporters and debt stock declines. As a result of higher oil prices,

1 Algeria, Angola, Ecuador, Equatorial Guinea, Gabon, Iran, Iraq, Kuwait, Libya, Nigeria, Qatar, Saudi Arabia, Venezuela, and the United Arab Emirates. Congo became member in 2018 and is not included in the study.

aggregate global demand is likely to fall. Mohaddes and Pesaran (2017) find that falling oil prices have positive real output effects for the global economy.

Another strand of the literature focuses on the impact of oil prices on asset prices. Most of the studies in this field analyze how movements in oil prices affect interest rates and equity prices. Huang et al. (1996) developed theoretical framework for how oil prices impact equity values. According to the study, rising oil price increases cost and reduces cash flows of corporations. As stock prices are basically discounted values of expected cash flows, declining cash flows leads to lower stock prices. The impact on a specific stock depends on whether the company is a net customer or producer of oil. Nandha and Faff (2008) found that rising oil prices have a negative effect on equity prices for all sectors except mining, oil and gas industries. In general, higher oil prices reduce asset prices in oil-importing countries and raise them in oil-exporting countries (Bhar and Nikolova, 2009). According to Ready (2017), the impact of oil price movements on stock markets depends on whether oil price change is driven by supply or demand. Demand shocks are positively correlated with equity prices and economic growth, whereas supply shocks have negative correlation.

With the rise of oil prices, a windfall of export revenue accumulates in the hands of oil exporters. This leads to global saving glut and part of that is invested in international capital markets. Increasing demand for debt securities and equities puts downward pressure on interest rates and raises equity prices (Rebucci and Spatafora, 2006). Ahrend et al. (2006) argue that one important reason of low long-term interest rates is excess global savings due to high oil prices. Warnock and Warnock (2009) state that foreign purchases of US government bonds lower long-term interest rates. Since part of petrodollars are used to buy debt securities, rising oil prices contributed to the fall of interest rate all around the world.

3 Oil Prices and Revenues

Oil prices first attracted significant attention in 1970s when there was a huge jump in prices (Fig. 3.1). After the OPEC embargo in late 1973, oil prices quadrupled from $3 a barrel to almost $12 a barrel in March 1974. Second oil crisis occurred in 1979 due to falling production in Middle East, specifically Iran. Global oil supply declined only by 4 percent, but since demand is inelastic, prices jumped from about $14 a barrel in 1978 to $37 a barrel in 1980. After 1980, oil prices began a twenty-year decline, except for a rebound during the Gulf War.

Prices started to increase again in 1999. This time the rise was more gradual and long lasting. Oil prices climbed from about $18 a barrel in 1999 to $97 a barrel on average in 2008. In July 2008, prices reached all-time high of $144 a

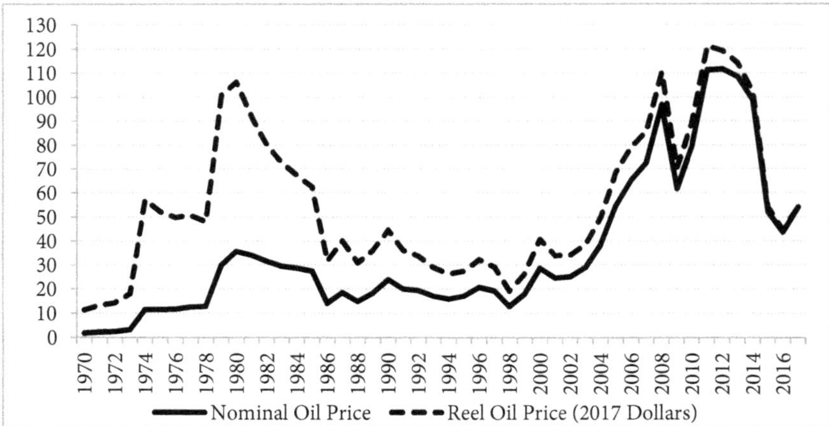

Fig. 3.1 Nominal and Real Oil Prices ($/Barrel). Source: US Energy Information Administration

barrel. That time, both nominal and real prices of oil surpassed the level seen in 1970s. The main reason behind this dramatic rise in oil prices was surging demand in emerging market economies, especially China and India. Another important reason was tight global supply conditions at that time and supply outages in some oil producers.

Oil prices collapsed to below $40 a barrel at the end of 2008 because of global economic crisis and declining demand. Governments and central banks around the world implemented unprecedented economic measures to tackle global recession and support recovery. Another increase in prices started with economies recovering from the crisis and rising demand. Oil prices averaged about $110 a barrel between 2011 and 2013. In the middle of 2014, oil prices started to fall due to a significant surge in shale production in USA and moderating demand in the emerging market economies. As a result of this oil glut, the price fell below $30 a barrel in February 2016. Since then, prices recovered somewhat due to improving demand and OPEC policies to limit supply. The average price of oil was about $54 a barrel in 2017.

With rising oil prices, oil exporting countries accumulated ample amount of export revenues. OPEC countries oil exports increased from $23 billion in 1972 to $116 billion in 1974 (Fig. 3.2). With the second oil shock, export revenue jumped from $130 billion in 1978 to $265 billion in 1980. The term *petrodollars* had become very popular at that time and it had crucial effects. Some of these

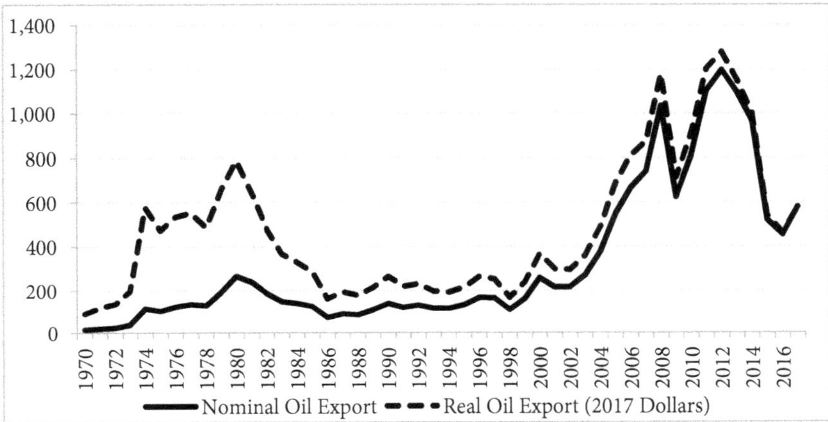

Fig. 3.2 OPEC Oil Exports (Billion Dollars). Source: OPEC Annual Statistical Bulletin

funds were deposited with banks in advanced countries. These were then lent to emerging market economies, especially Latin America. The credit boom related with oil price increase is seen as one important reason of Latin American debt crisis (Wiegand, 2008).

Oil price increase that started in 2003 led to a dramatic rise in export revenue of OPEC countries. Export revenue surged almost fivefold from \$215 billion in 2002 to \$1033 billion in 2008. Cumulative windfall of export revenue coming from oil between 2003 and 2008 was about \$3.6 trillion. Both nominal and real oil export income of OPEC countries exceeded the amount recognized in two oil shocks in 1970s. After the global economic crisis of 2008, recovering oil prices again boosted export revenue. The cumulative exports between 2010 and 2013 have been \$4.2 trillion. The peak in oil exports was seen in 2012 when the revenue reached \$1.2 trillion. With falling prices, OPEC oil exports were realized as \$578 billion in 2017.

The dramatic rise in oil revenues raises the natural question of how oil exporters have recycled their petrodollars. The next section provides the answer.

4 Channels for the Recycling of Petrodollars

There are two major channels through which oil exporters recycle their petrodollar revenue. First, the windfall can be used for imports of goods and services (the trade channel) and second it can be used to purchase foreign assets which improves their net asset positions (the financial channel).

Starting with the trade channel, we aim to analyze the trends in exports and imports of OPEC countries. One important question we want to answer is what percentage of export windfall is spent on imports in periods when oil prices surge and whether the spending behavior changes over time. In this analysis, an important point to consider is that together with oil exports, non-oil exports of OPEC countries also rise. Since oil exports constitute more than 90 percent of total exports in 1970s, non-oil exports can be ignored in this period. However, they are particularly important after 2002. While oil export revenue increased from $294 billion in 2002 to $1277 billion in 2012 using 2017 prices, non-oil exports rose from $94 billion in 2002 to $538 billion in 2012. Part of the increase of non-oil exports come from higher sales of natural gas and other minerals. Among OPEC countries, Iran, Qatar, Nigeria, and Algeria are important natural gas exporters. Another reason of rising non-oil exports of OPEC countries in this period is the diversification of exports from oil and related products to other sectors such as chemicals, manufactured goods, and machinery in some countries. This is particularly visible in United Arab Emirates and to some extent in Iran and Saudi Arabia according to *Harvard Atlas of Economic Complexity*.

In our analysis, we follow Ruiz and Vilarrubia (2006) and Higgins et al. (2006) and use total exports instead of oil exports for two reasons. First, practically and analytically, it is not possible to distinguish how oil and non-oil export revenue are deployed. Second, prices of many export goods such as natural gas and chemicals are highly correlated with oil price. Therefore, rising oil price also leads to increasing non-oil exports.

Fig. 3.3 demonstrates total exports and imports of OPEC countries in 2017 dollar prices. It is seen that exports surged in two oil shocks in 1970s and the period after 2002. OPEC exports increased from $151 billion in 1972 to $602 billion in 1974 and then $818 billion in 1980. Another striking rise in exports materialized after 2002. That time, thanks to the rise in oil prices, export revenue jumped from $392 billion in 2002 to $1.5 trillion in 2008 and then, after falling temporarily during the global crisis, to $1.8 trillion in 2012.

Through an overall and quick analysis of Fig. 3.3, we can say that OPEC countries have spent some portion of their export revenues on imports. Import spending follows export revenues and is smoother compared to exports. The proportion of exports that is spent on imports is mainly determined by the persistence of additional revenue and the gradualism of the increase in exports (Ruiz and Vilarrubia, 2006). If the rise in exports is thought to be permanent, its impact on consumption and imports will likely be higher compared to the case when increase is perceived as temporary. In 1970s, price of oil and hence exports increased sharply due to supply shocks. At first sight, rising export revenue was

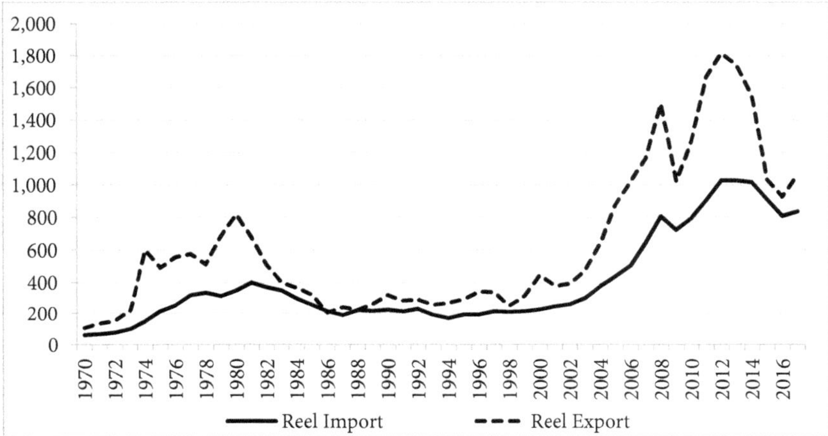

Fig. 3.3: OPEC Real Export and Imports (2017 Dollars). Source: OPEC Annual Statistical Bulletin

Tab. 3.1: Recycling of Exports Windfall (In 2017 Dollars). Source: OPEC Annual Statistical Bulletin

Period	ΔExport	ΔImport	% Recycling via Imports
1973–1976	991.4	314.7	31.7
1978–1981	644.4	53.5	8.3
1973–1981	3163.0	1541.0	48.7
2002–2008	3325.0	1504.5	45.2
2009–2013	2402.8	862.2	35.9
2002–2013	8873.6	4673.1	52.7

thought to be temporary and since the countries budgeted lower oil prices, it took time for them to adjust and increase imports. On the other hand, oil price increase after 2002 has been more gradual and was perceived to be more permanent since the rise in prices was mainly due to higher demand. Therefore, the proportion of export revenue recycled through imports seems to be higher after 2002 compared with the 1970s. Imports constituted about 55 percent of exports on average between 2003 and 2008, in contrast to 46 percent on average between 1974 and 1980.

In order to compare the importance of trade channel in different price surge episodes, Tab. 3.1 shows the exports windfall and the recycling through imports.

In each period considered, export windfall is defined as the additional export revenue with respect to the first year, which is the base year. For instance, the base year is 1973 in the first period and cumulative additional export windfall between 1974 and 1976 was $991.4 billion. Of that additional revenue, $314.7 billion was spent on imports. That is to say, 31.7 percent of additional export windfall was spent on imports in the first period. In the second oil shock, only 8.3 percent of extra export revenue was recycled through imports. If first and second oil shocks in 1970s are considered as one period, the analysis shows that 48.7 percent of additional export windfall was spent on imports. As the length of the period considered increases, recycling through imports goes up. That is because it takes time for countries to adjust to higher oil prices and import spending follows export revenue with some lag.

According to our analysis, between 2002 and 2008, about 45 percent of additional export revenue was spent on imports. The amount recycled via imports goes down to 36 percent after the global crisis of 2008. Considering the period between 2002 and 2013, about 53 percent of total additional export windfall was recycled via imports. If we compare the recycling of export revenue via imports in different periods, we find out that a higher percentage of additional export windfalls were recycled through imports after 2002. That is probably because oil price increases after 2002 were more gradual and considered as more permanent compared to 1970s. In addition, the improvement of trade infrastructure enabled OPEC countries to adjust faster and spend export revenue in imports.

Our estimates for recycling of additional export revenue via imports are similar to other studies in the literature. Among them, IMF (2005) estimated that about 50 percent of additional export revenue was spent in imports between 2002 and 2005. OECD (2005) analyzed the period between 1997 and 2004 and found that 60 percent of additional export revenue is recycled via imports in the next two years. Ruiz and Vilarrubia (2006) investigated and compared trade and financial channels in different periods. They found that recycling of export revenue through imports is about 50 percent between 2002 and 2005 and is higher compared to 1970s.

Second channel through which oil export revenue is recycled is the financial channel. According to this channel, part of export windfall can be used to improve net asset position of the country. There are several ways to increase net asset position and among them the most important ones are foreign reserve accumulation, depositing funds in foreign financial intermediaries, foreign direct investment, and investing in equities and debt securities abroad.

Basically thinking, net financial investment in the rest of the world is equal to current account surplus of the country. Fig. 3.4 presents current account

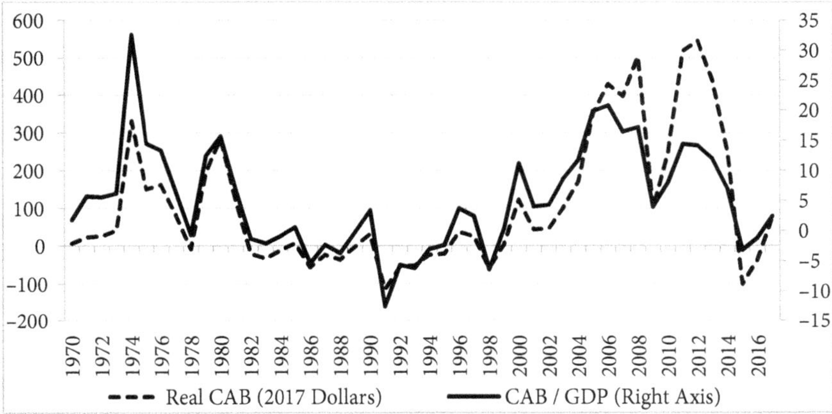

Fig. 3.4: OPEC Current Account Balance (2017 Dollars). Source: OPEC Annual Statistical Bulletin

balance of OPEC countries in 2017 dollars and in percent of GDP. Current account surplus reached 30 percent of GDP in the first oil shock in 1970s and about 20 percent of GDP before global financial crisis of 2008. In 2017 dollars, current account surplus rose to about $300 billion in 1974 and 1980. Total cumulative current account surplus between 1973 and 1981 has been about $1.4 trillion in 2017 dollars. Current account surplus reached $500 billion in 2008 and 2012. Cumulative current account surplus between 2002 and 2014 was about a record high of $4.1 trillion.

How OPEC countries used current account surpluses accumulated during high oil prices is the key question we want to answer. Analysis of trade channel is pretty straightforward; however, financial channel is much more complex for several reasons. First of all, published data is limited. We do not have detailed and time series data going back to 1970s for every country and different investment instruments. Second, the complexity of financial markets and rising financial integration make it hard to analyze where and how petrodollars are being invested. Many OPEC countries purchase foreign securities through other countries such as United Kingdom or offshore centers. For instance, some of the US debt securities purchases from UK are executed by using petrodollars deposited in UK financial institutions by oil exporters. It is extremely difficult to detect these details. Third, with financial globalization petrodollars are invested more diversely geographically and across asset classes. There is some evidence that some of the petrodollars are invested in regional stock and bond markets in the

Tab. 3.2: Current and Financial Accounts Windfall (Billion Dollars, 2017 Prices). Source: OPEC Annual Statistical Bulletin

Period	CAB	Direct	Portfolio	Other	Reserve	Error
1974–1976	644.7	16.8	109.7	98	167.4	252.7
1979–1981	598.1	0.8	158.4	181.9	83.8	173.2
2003–2008	1955.2	-132.7	292.3	434.9	804.7	636.3
2010–2013	1753.0	-18.7	124.0	505.0	470.8	681.5

Middle East, hedge funds and private equity funds around the world (McGuire and Tarashev, 2005). According to McGuire and Tarashev (2005), Bank for International Settlements (BIS) was unable to account for about 70 percent of the petrodollars accumulated between 1999 and 2005 by OPEC countries. It was 50 percent between 1978 and 1982. As the financial system and instruments become more complex, it is harder to detect how and where the funds are invested.

In order to investigate how petrodollars are used by OPEC countries, we analyze current account and financial accounts. Components of financial account are direct investment, portfolio investment, other investments, reserve accumulation, and net error and omissions. Tab. 3.2 presents these items in different periods under consideration.

The periods we analyze are two oil shocks in 1970s and the periods before and after the global crisis of 2008 when oil prices had been high and OPEC countries accumulated large current account surpluses. It is important to note that we have some missing data which affects our analysis. We have all the data for current account balances but for the components of financial account some are missing. Data for United Arab Emirates is missing for the whole period under consideration and some years of the data are missing for important countries such as Iran, Iraq, Nigeria, and Qatar. In our analysis, all the missing data are added to the error and omission component under financial account. Therefore, error and omissions include all the missing data and therefore are much higher than normal. They constitute on average 35 percent of total current surplus in the periods under study. Missing data of United Arab Emirates alone explains about 30 percent of error and omissions. Due to high error and omissions, it is better to analyze financial account items excluding error and omission.

During the first oil shock, excluding error and omissions item, about 43 percent of current account surplus was accumulated as reserves, 25 percent was deposited into foreign banks (other item), and 28 percent was used to purchase

Fig. 3.5: OPEC International Reserves (2017 Dollars). Source: Worldbank

foreign securities. During the second oil shock, the proportion of reserve accumulation declined to about 20 percent, while bank deposits and portfolio investment each constituted about 40 percent of current account surplus. In the period between 2003 and 2008, current account surplus of OPEC countries surged significantly. In this period, error and omission constitute about 30 percent of current account surplus. Excluding this item, about 60 percent of the remaining surplus was accumulated as foreign reserves. Around 30 percent was deposited into foreign banks and 20 percent was channeled into portfolio investments. OPEC countries received foreign direct investment in this period. In the period after global crisis of 2008, the use of petrodollars shifted away from reserve accumulation and portfolio investment toward bank deposits. Around half the current account surplus excluding error and omissions was deposited in foreign banks and 44 percent was accumulated as foreign reserves.

Fig. 3.5 shows international reserves of OPEC countries in 2017 dollars. International reserves rose from $90 billion in 1973 to $302 in 1980. Reserves exploded after 2002 since a higher proportion of current account surpluses were accumulated as reserves. International reserves went up from $191 in 2002 to a record high of $1.6 trillion in 2013. There has been some fall since then.

Compared with 1970s, the data shows that a higher proportion of petrodollars were used to accumulate foreign reserves after 2002. Bank deposits have remained an important vehicle to invest petrodollars. The proportion of current account surplus used as portfolio investment seems to have declined after 2002 compared to 1970s. However, this must be interpreted with caution. First, we do not have enough data to correctly determine where the petrodollars have been channeled.

We do not have detailed data of United Arab Emirates, Iran, and Nigeria for the period after 2002. Another crucial point to emphasize is that part of international reserves is also invested in foreign securities. Therefore, the proportion of portfolio investment is most likely more than our analysis shows.

It is of utmost importance how countries use international reserves. Most of the OPEC countries have Sovereign Wealth Funds (SWF) that invest international reserves in different financial assets. According to the Sovereign Wealth Fund Institute, total assets of these funds are $7.8 trillion as of 2017 and that is twice the size of what it was in 2007. The most important source of the funds is oil revenue. Among OPEC countries, United Arab Emirates, Kuwait, Saudi Arabia, and Qatar have funds with total assets of about $3 trillion. These funds make public investments, aim to stabilize government and export revenues, and save for the future generations. They usually make long-term investments in equities, government bonds, and foreign direct investment (FDI). In addition, they also invest in alternatives such as hedge funds, private equities, and real estate.

Conclusion

Changes in oil prices have substantial economic and financial effects. Especially times when prices move rapidly and by a big amount are worth analyzing. The most important periods to study are the two oil shocks in 1970s and the periods before and after the global economic crisis of 2008. In these periods, huge jumps in oil prices led to a windfall of export revenues that can be spent or saved in many alternative ways. Primary aim of this chapter is to investigate how and where the petrodollars are deployed.

In this chapter, we first provide a brief literature survey about the impact of oil price movements on economic and financial variables including growth, inflation, and asset prices. Then, we give a background about the changes in oil prices and export revenue of OPEC countries starting from 1970s. Afterwards, we investigate how petrodollars are recycled through trade and financial channels. Trade channel implies that part of the additional export windfall was spent on imports and the proportion changes over time. According to our analysis, about half of the additional export revenue was spent on imports and the percentage spent on imports increased after 2002 compared to 1970s for OPEC members. That is mainly because oil price increase after 2002 was more gradual and was perceived as more permanent. Financial channel is much more difficult to analyze due to missing data and complex global Financial system. We find out that the proportion of current account surplus used to accumulate reserves went up after 2002 compared to 1970s. Recycling petrodollars via foreign bank deposits have kept its importance throughout the period of the study. Percentage of portfolio investments seems to have declined but it is important to note that there is widespread evidence that international reserves are mostly invested in foreign securities such as bonds and equities. Thus, recycling of petrodollars via portfolio investment is most likely more than the numbers show.

In addition to its significant impact on major macroeconomic variables, oil price is an important determinant of international liquidity and higher prices create abundant amount of liquidity that is a major source of funding for emerging market economies. A fall in oil prices may create substantial risks for emerging markets by drying up that source. Especially countries that rely on international bank flows become much more fragile against oil price movements. Therefore, for these countries it is crucial to reduce financing needs and diversify sources of funding.

References

Ahrend, R., Catte, P., and Price, R. (2006), "Factors Behind Low Long-Term Interest Rates." OECD Working Paper No. 2006/18.

Bhar, R. and Nikolova, B. (2009), Oil Prices and Equity Returns in the BRIC Countries. *World Economy*, *32*(7), 1036–1054.

Bruno, M. and Sachs, J. (1985), *Economics of Worldwide Stagflation*. Cambridge, MA: Harvard University Press.

Hamilton, J. (1996), "This Is What Happened to the Oil Price Macroeconomic Relationship." *Journal of Monetary Economics*, *38*(2), 215–220.

Higgins, M., Klitgaard, T., and Lerman, R. (2006), "Recycling Petrodollars." *Current Issues in Economics and Finance*, *12*(9).

Huang, R.D., Masulis, R.W., and Stoll, H.R. (1996), "Energy Shocks and Financial Markets." *Journal of Futures Markets: Futures, Options, and Other Derivative Products*, *16*(1), 1–27.

IMF (2005), *Middle East and Central Asia Regional Economic Outlook*, September.

Kilian, L. (2008), "The Economic Effects of Energy Price Shocks. *Journal of Economic Literature*, *46*(4), 871–909.

McGuire, P. and Tarashev, N. (2005), "The International Banking Market." *BIS Quarterly Review*, December, 15–30.Mohaddes, K. and Pesaran, M.H. (2017), "Oil Prices and the Global Economy: Is It Different This Time Around?." *Energy Economics*, *65*, 315–325.

Morana, C. (2017), Macroeconomic and Financial Effects of Oil Price Shocks: Evidence for the Euro Area."

Economic Modelling, *64*, 82–96.

Nandha, M. and Faff, R. (2008), "Does Oil Move Equity Prices? A global view." *Energy Economics*, *30*(3), 986–997.

OECD (2005), *Economic Outlook 78*, December.

Ready, R.C. (2017), "Oil Prices and the Stock Market." *Review of Finance*, *22*(1), 155–176.

Rebucci, A. and Spatafora, N. (2006), "Oil Prices and Global Imbalances." *IMF World Economic Outlook*, 4, 71–96.

Ruiz, J. and Vilarrubia, J. (2006), "International Recycling of Petrodollars." University Library of Munich, No. 429.

Warnock, F.E. and Warnock, V.C. (2009), "International Capital Flows and US Interest Rates. *Journal of International Money and Finance*, *28*(6), 903–919.

Wiegand, M.J. (2008), "Bank Recycling of Petro Dollars to Emerging Market Economies during the Current Oil Price Boom" (No. 8–180). International Monetary Fund.

Onur Akkaya

4 The Reaction of the Bank of England to the US Dollar Exchange Rate

Abstract: This chapter focuses on the relationship between the Federal Reserve Bank and the Bank of England. It researches the dynamic reaction of the exchange rate on the monetary policy shocks in the form of a variation of the long-term interest rate differential. Overall, the conclusion is that the Bank of England is bonded to the evolution of the exchange rate according to the Federal Reserve Bank's monetary policy actions.

Keywords: Exchange Rate, Bank of England, Federal Reserve Bank, Monetary Policy

1 Introduction

The Great Britain (hereafter GB) joined the European Union in 1973. In 2016, its decision to withdraw from the membership of the European Union (hereafter EU) was accepted in the GB[1]. In this context, we see that the Bank of England (hereafter BoE) has taken independent, but parallel, decisions/actions from the central bank of the European Union. So, is the BoE, which is economically out of system, affected by decisions taken by the Federal Reserve Bank (hereafter FED), as seen in the European Central Bank (hereafter ECB)? In this study, we aim to find an answer to this question. To do so, the time-series data are operated quarterly, which is a seasonally unadjusted data from 1990:Q1 to 2016:Q3. The main purpose of this chapter is to investigate the dynamic reaction of the exchange rate on the monetary policy shocks in the form of a variation of the short-term interest rate differential.

This condition is called Taylor Rule[2] defined by Taylor (1993).We conduct a literature review on this subject. However, I selected some special paper, which is nearly same as our case and/or topic, in the literature. The first paper I selected, Barnett et al. (2016), includes the merger-theoretical Divisia monetary aggregate, which is a higher monetary measure. The paper confirms the effectiveness of the simultaneous restraint of Kim and Roubini (2000), specially adapted to the Indian economy, especially when compared to recursion and recurring damage

1 This period is called "Brexit."

2 Our topic is known as "Taylor Rule", which Taylor (1993) was firstly descript this relationship, in economy theory.

to the exchange rate structure. Brüggemann and Lütkepohl (2005) analyzed short and long-term interest rates by focusing on United State of America and Eurozone system. According to the hypothesis, interest rates should be based on spreading and unexciting interest rates. Long-term interest rates in the Eurozone should also remain constant. When all four interest rates are integrated, we expect to find three linearly independent cointegration relationships in the four interest rate series system. Hoffman (2013) reviewed the FED and the ECB on foreign exchange markets from 1979 to 2009. Greenspan[3] played a role in US monetary policy in stock markets. The ECB played a role in monetary policy decisions. The next section gives the data and empirical strategy and presents the findings. Final section concludes with remarks.

2 Background

At the basis of this research, we assume that the central bank and the BoE have an ultimate goal to achieve long-term price stability. The important question is whether BoE's monetary policy is determined by interest rate rule as described by Taylor (1993), or by other domestic market conditions? This is actually an interesting and partially answered question. However, another interesting question could be that has the FED influenced the monetary policies of BoE relatively? To better understand the study period, Fig. 4.1 reports the interest rate, exchange rates, and inflation rates of the USA and the UK. The situation is presented [Tab. 4.2] in terms of correlation coefficients. In addition, Tab. 4.2 lists the important events during the study period.

Between the 1990s–2010s, the economy of the UK experienced kind of problems hit by severe economic crises in 1994, 1997, and 2008. One of the biggest economic crises in the UK has occurred in 2008. As a result of this crisis, UK's economy went through structural economic reforms. The monetary policies of the BoE devoted on great moderation in monetary policy to address great inflation rates following the 2008 crisis. This enabled us to implement Taylor (1993) rules for the relationship between the FED and the BoE.

In this context, the negative correlation with consumer price index that totals all items for UK is given in Tab. 4.2. Similarly, positive relationship with the exchange rate turns into Tab. 4.2. The correlation is not surprising in the political independence of the BoE. The BoE has become more integrated with the world

3 The old president of FED.

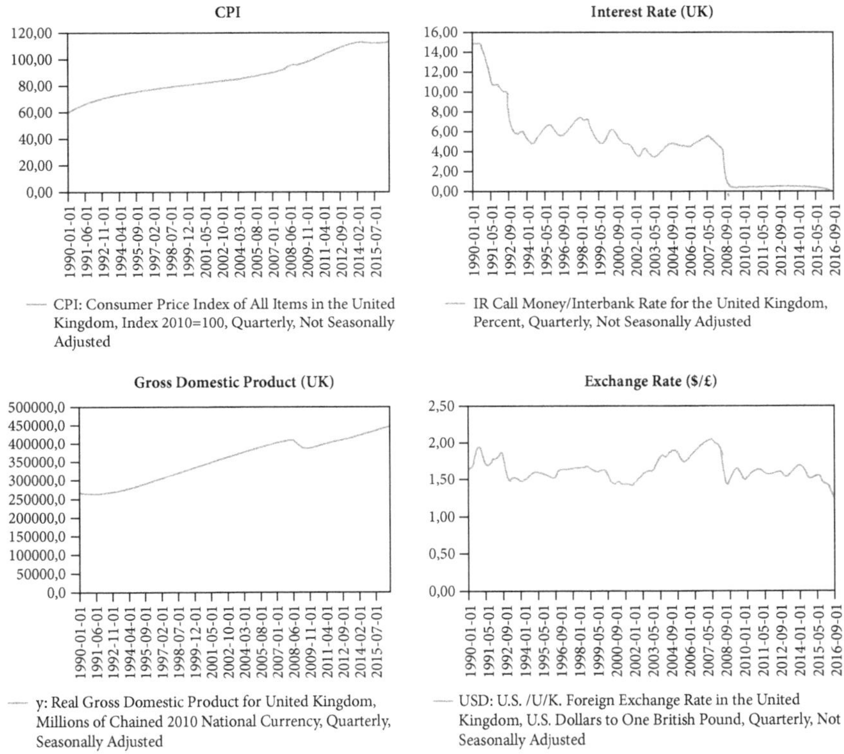

Fig. 4.1: Levels of time series

and seems to take into account the policies of the FED. Therefore, we analyze the great inflation, the great moderation, and the great integration period of the BoE.

3 Data

The time-series data are operated quarterly, which is a seasonally unadjusted data from 1990:Q1 to 2016:Q3. The UK short-term rate; IR_t is measured by discount rate. The Δp_t is consumer price index that totals all items for UK. The y_t is Gross Domestic Product for United Kingdom, quarterly adjusted, not seasonally[4]. The

4 The price index, the GDP, the United Kingdom short-term ınterest rate, and the nominal £/$ exchange rate are provided by the Federal Reserve Bank of ST. Louis Economic Database.

Tab. 4.1: Results of Unit Root Tests

Variable	Deterministic Terms	Lag Order	Test	Value of Test Stat.
IR_t	C	n(SIC)=12	ADF	-2.86
	c,t	n(SIC)=12	ADF	-3.67(*)
Δp_t	C	n(SIC)=14	ADF	0.55
	c,t	n(SIC)=14	ADF	-2.25
e_r	C	n(SIC)=12	ADF	-2.07
	c,t	n(SIC)=12	ADF	-2.07
y_t	C	n(SIC)=14	ADF	-0.28
	c,t	n(SIC)=14	ADF	-2.11
		n(SIC)=14	ADF	2.11
d(IR_t)	C	n(SIC)=12	ADF	-6.98 (*)
	c,t	n(SIC)=12	ADF	-7.10 (*)
$d(\Delta p_t)$	C	n(SIC)=14	ADF	-2.93 (*)
	c,t	n(SIC)=14	ADF	-2.99
$d(y_t)$	C	n(SIC)=14	ADF	-4.69 (*)
	c,t	n(SIC)=14	ADF	-4.67 (*)
de_r	c	n(SIC)=14	ADF	-8.48(*)
	c,t	n(SIC)=14	ADF	-8.52(*)

n(SIC) indicate the lag orders suggested by Schwarz Info Criterion, respectively, when the maximum lag order equals 14. ADF denotes the Augmented Dickey-Fuller test and (*) indicates that the null hypothesis of a unit root is rejected at the 10 %, 5 %, and 1 % levels, respectively.

Tab. 4.2: Correlation Coefficients

	IR (United Kingdom) Towards USD	Δp_t
1990–2000	0,760	-0,834
2001–2016	0,496	-0,868
1990–2016	0,397	-0,886

Tab. 4.3: Rank of Cointegration Tests

Test Type	None No Intercept No Trend	None Intercept No Trend	Linear Intercept No Trend	Linear Intercept Trend	Quadratic Intercept Trend
Trace	1	1	1	1	3
Max-Eig	1	1	1	1	1

USD (United States Dollar) is natural currency to US dollar exchange rate that average of daily rates for United Kingdom. Tab. 4.1 presents the result of unit roots for all of the variables.

4 Empirical Evidence

Tab. 4.3 shows that the trace tests are by (Johansen, 1995). A vector error correct model (VECM) used is ("k" is the lag order, "l" represents lags, and "r" represents cointegrating vectors):

$$\Delta Y = \varphi\left[\frac{Y_{t-1}}{Trend_{t-1}}\right] + \sum_{j=1}^{k-l} \tau \Delta Y_{l-j} + \vartheta D_t + u_t$$

Tab. 4.4 displays the value of VECM coefficients. Our expectation is that the error correct mechanism (ECM) coefficient has a negative of sign and statistical significance. If it has all of them, we conclude that there is a strong relationship between short-term dynamics equation and long-term equation.

In the following pages, equations in empirical result are estimated according to Taylor (1993). We analyzed the relationship between the BoE and the FED in order to measure the reaction of the BoE on the monetary policies of the FED[5]. Also, interest rate and inflation coefficients are not statistically significant.

The [Equation1] operated framework allows us to test restrictions in the long run:

$$\begin{gathered} \boldsymbol{IR_t} = -0{,}165\Delta \boldsymbol{p_t} + 11.555\boldsymbol{USD_t} - 0.083\boldsymbol{Trend}_t, \\ \{-17.631\} \quad \{22.957\} \quad \{-8.341\} \\ (0.0) \quad (0.0) \quad (0.0) \end{gathered} \tag{Eq.1}$$

In the event of decrease in inflation and a depreciating exchange rate, the equation resembles an interest rate which implies a contraction of the policy

5 Taylor (1993).

Tab. 4.4: The BoE and the FED Short-Term Dynamics Equation Result for the Period 1990:Q1 to 2016:Q3

Variable	Coefficient	t-Statistic	Prob.
ECM	*-0.108*	*-2.202*	*0.030*
dIR_{-1}	0.143	1.142	0.256
$dUSD_{-1}$	-2.086	-1.997	0.048
$d\Delta p_{EU_{-1}}$	-0.098	-0.969	0.335
C	-0.031	-0.404	0.686

stance. The inflation coefficient is statistically different from that suggested by Taylor (1993). Furthermore, the USD exchange rate coefficient has the positive sign as expected so that an increase, i.e., depreciation, causes an increase in the short-term rate. More specifically, in the Equation 1, therefore, it will take a bit less than three months to return to target path [Tab. 4.4].

$$y_t = \begin{matrix} 1.856\Delta \boldsymbol{p}_t + & 8.294\boldsymbol{USD}_t + & 1.036\boldsymbol{Trend}_t, \\ \{11.691\} & \{9.733\} & \{9.736\} \\ (0.0) & (0.0) & (0.0) \end{matrix} \qquad \text{(Eq.2)}$$

As for the model-2 (Equation 2), in particular, positive reactions are observed in both the output and the inflation rate in response to a rise in the interest rate[6]. Furthermore, both responses are big in magnitude and significant and immediate response of the inflation rate is actually positive. In summary, it is demonstrated that the BoE followed the developments of the US economy closely, but devoted itself to the long-standing policy of price stability.

The reactions to a shock on the short-term interest rate which is reported in the first row of Fig. 4.2 are pragmatic. We see that both the consumer price index and the exchange rate are negatively increased with the interest rate. In respect to the exchange rate, the development in the policy situation creates a gradual change that follows the improvement in the policy rate, while reducing the interaction rate. This finding is consistent with the Dornbusch overshooting hypothesis. When we look at the second row of the table, which presents the consumer price index and the short-term interest rate is negatively associated with

6 This supports the Philips Curve relationship in our sample.

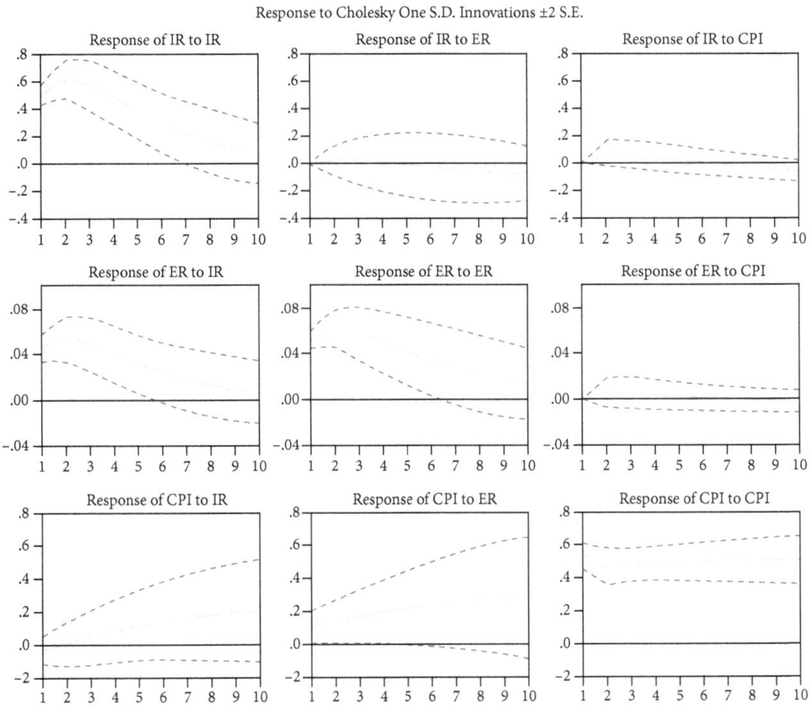

Fig. 4.2: Impulse responses for the model-1 (1990:Q1–2016:Q3)

Tab. 4.5: Ramsey Reset Test for the Model-1

F-statistic	17.44325	Prob. F(1,104)	0.0001
Log likelihood ratio	16.59101	Prob. Chi-Square(1)	0.0000

the exchange rate. The short-term interest rate has been drastically decreased in all of the time periods. But, the consumer price index is slightly negatively associated with the exchange rate. Finally, in the third row of the table, the consumer price index has an inevitable association with the consumer price index and the exchange rate. Both variables have positively increased in all of the time periods.

To investigate the stability situation for the model-1, we use the Ramsey reset test. The results show that the model-1 has stability for F-statistic and log likelihood ratio [Tab. 4.5].

Conclusion

At the basis of the research, we assumed that the central bank and the Bank of England have an ultimate goal to achieve long-term price stability. The main objective of this research is to determine whether BoE's monetary policy is determined by interest rate rule as described by Taylor (1993), or by other domestic market conditions. Indeed, this is an interesting and partially answered question. Overall, the findings suggest that the BoE devoted to the long-standing policy of price stability although it kept an eye on the development of the US economy at all times.

References

Brüggemann, R. and Lütkepohl, H. (2005), "Uncovered Interest Rate Parity and the Expectations Hypothesis of the Term Structure: Empirical Results for the US and Europe, SFB 649 discussion paper, No. 2005,035, SFB 649," *Economic Risk*, Berlin.

Eleftheriou, M. (2009), "Monetary Policy in Germany: A Cointegration Analysis on the Relevance of Interest Rate Rules." *Economic Modelling*, *26*, 946–960.

Hoffmann, A. (2013), "Did the Fed and ECB React Asymmetrically with Respect to Asset Market Developments?." *Journal of Policy Modelling*, Elsevier, *35*(2), 197–211.

Johansen, S. (1995), *Likelihood-Based Inference in Cointegrated Vector Autoregressive Models*. Oxford: Oxford University Press.

Kim, S. and Roubini, N. (2000), "Exchange Rate Anomalies in the Industrial Countries: A Solution with a Structural VAR Approach." *Journal of Monetary Economics*, *45*, 561–586.

Taylor, J.B. (1993), "Discretion versus Policy Rules in Practice." *Carnegie-Rochester Conference Series on Public Policy*, *39*, 195–214.

William, B., Soumya, S.B., and Taniya, G. (2015), "An SVAR Approach to Evaluation of Monetary Policy in India: Solution to the Exchange Rate Puzzles in an Open Economy." *Working Papers Series*. In Theoretical and Applied Economics 201503, University of Kansas, Department of Economics, revised Aug 2015.

Özlem Ayvaz Kızılgöl

5 Analyzing the Relationship between Cryptocurrencies and Exchange Rates

Abstract: This chapter aims to analyze the long-term relationship between exchange rates and cryptocurrencies in consequence of the increased use of cryptocurrencies and the fact that they are regarded as an investment tool. In this regard, an empirical analysis was conducted on the relationship of exchange rates with Bitcoin and Ethereum cryptocurrencies.

Keywords: Cryptocurrencies, Exchange Rates, VAR Model, Relationship

1 Introduction

When the historical development of money is examined, it is seen that it has taken various forms. Initially valuable objects were used but banknotes started to be used later. Today virtual currencies in the form of digital currencies represent the final form of money. (Koçoğlu, Çevik, and Tanrıöven, 2016: 79). They are called cryptocurrencies. They are also called virtual money, cryptographic money, electronic money, digital money, or e-money.

Cryptocurrency is a peer to peer (P2P) electronic money system that is created with algorithms and based on the blockchain technology (Vockathaler, 2015: 1). Although there are other cryptocurrencies, Bitcoin is the first, most well-known and preferred cryptocurrency. Bitcoin was initially used to a great extent only in online game platforms and then its popularity increased and it evolved into an ecosystem consisting of some components after it started to be accepted as a payment method by many sellers (Dulupçu, Yiyit, and Genç, 2017: 2241).

Bitcoin is a decentralized monetary system and currency that enables online payments to be made from any place in the world to any person and cannot be controlled by any state, company, or authority (Rosinach and Raventos, 2012: 4; Bilir and Çay, 2016: 24). The fact that Bitcoin emerged as a reaction to financial policies aroused interest and made it spread in a short time. Although Bitcoin was created as a reaction to intermediary institutions such as banks within a financial system and policies enforced by the state, it does not have a centralized structure. The financial freedom created by Bitcoin recently and the fact that it started to gain worldwide recognition very rapidly has increased its value each passing day. It draws attention with the extreme increases in its price rather than the innovations it is likely to offer. After the global economic crisis in 2008, incidents such as the decline in trust in institutions and banks that control the flow of money and the freezing of bank accounts in European countries have increased the interest in Bitcoin and caused it to be preferred by investors more, each passing day (Dulupçu et al., 2017: 2245).

The fact that cryptocurrencies have remained on the agenda in recent years and the increase in the number of people and institutions making big investments in cryptocurrency production have made it necessary for states to make efforts to regulate this structure. However, some countries have recognized, understood, and made legal arrangements related to this currency, while some countries tried to solve the problem by rejecting it altogether (Aslantaş Ateş, 2016: 351). Bitcoin is widely used in developed countries such as Japan, Canada, the United States of America, Germany, France, England, etc. There are Bitcoin ATMs in Japan and Ireland. The first Bitcoin ATM in the world was used in Canada. The first Bitcoin ATM in Turkey was installed in Istanbul Atatürk Airport. On the other hand, Australia, New Zealand, Finland, Norway, Korea, China, Russia, and Israel stated that Bitcoin did not fit the definition of money (Malhotra and Maloo, 2014: 3; Hepkorucu and Genç, 2017: 48).

The theoretical background of cryptocurrencies was first brought up in 1998 by Wei Dai who suggested a currency created and operated using the encryption science instead of a centralized system (Koçoğlu et al., 2016: 79). The technical system constituting the infrastructure of such currencies was established with the article titled "Peer to Peer Electronic Cash System" published by a person or group using the Satoshi Nakamoto nickname on the Internet in late 2008. It came to life in the virtual world after it was used by Satoshi Nakamoto for the first time (Sönmez, 2014: 2; Eross, McGroarty, Urquhart, and Wolfe, 2017: 2).

The first Bitcoin transaction was performed in January 2009 by the system's founders. The first usage of Bitcoin in the real economy was a pizza order placed on May 22, 2010. The pizza that cost 25 American Dollars at the time was later known as the most expensive pizza in the world (Yermack, 2013: 5, Sovbetov, 2018: 2). Using Bitcoin as an instrument of payment has been recognized more and more in the business world since 2010. Major companies such as DISH Network, Microsoft, Dell, Expedia, com, Shopify, Steam, Save the Children, (https://koinbulteni.com/odemeleri-bitcoinle-kabul-eden-8-buyuk-firma-4991.html) PayPal, WebMoney, Newegg, Greenpeace, and Tiger Direct's acceptance of payments with Bitcoin has played an important role in the increased popularity of Bitcoin. Bitcoin can transform into other currencies through stock exchanges, and Bitcoin can be purchased with other currencies. Bitcoin can be purchased in many ways such as cash, Paypal, bank transfer, Bitcoin ATM, etc. (Koçoğlu et al.,

2016: 82). The Mt. Gox platform that was located in Japan was the first stock exchange where Bitcoin could be traded in 2010 (Yermack, 2013: 5). Mt. Gox was considered to one of the most important stock exchanges in the Bitcoin market from 2010 until it went bankrupt in 2014. Today there are many stock exchanges such as Binance, Kucoin, cex.io, Hitbtc, Bitfinex, Bittrex, Bitstamp, Localbitcoins.com, Coinmama, Bitflyer, etc., where Bitcoin can be purchased and sold with various currencies (https://bitcoinlerim.com/en-iyi-bitcoin-borsalari/). Bitcoin value has increased significantly after 2016 in parallel with its popularity. The highest Bitcoin value witnessed so far is 19,498 USD. The total market value of Bitcoin was about 162 billion dollars as of May 2018 (http://www.tepav.org.tr/tr/blog/s/6195/Bitcoinin+toplam+piyasa+degeri+160+milyar+dolari+asti). Although its transaction volume is low in Turkey, the BTC/TL exchange rate is displayed in real time.

This chapter aims to analyze the long-term relationship between exchange rates and cryptocurrencies in consequence of the increased use of cryptocurrencies and the fact that they are regarded as an investment tool. Many studies in the academic literature discuss the technical (related to the computer science and mathematics) aspects of these currencies, whereas the number of studies analyzing the financial aspect is limited. In this regard, an empirical analysis was conducted on the relationship of exchange rates with Bitcoin and Ethereum cryptocurrencies with the aim of contributing to literature.

2 Literature Review

Various samples of empirical studies on cryptocurrencies are evaluated in this part of the study. There are few studies conducted on this matter in Turkey. They can be summarized as follows: Atik, Köse, Yılmaz, and Sağlam (2015) analyzed the correlation between daily exchange rates of Bitcoin and the most circulated cross exchange rates in the world from 2009 to 2015 using the Granger causality analysis. They found out a lagged correlation between Bitcoin and Japanese Yen and detected a one-way causality relationship from Japanese Yen to Bitcoin. Koçoğlu et al. (2016) studied Bitcoin pricing and analyzed the effectiveness, liquidity, and volatility of Bitcoin stock exchanges. They analyzed eight different Bitcoin stock exchanges between June 2, 2014 and June 2, 2015. The analysis revealed that there was no significant correlation between Bitcoin and other currencies. They concluded that Bitcoin was unreliable and prone to speculative usage due to extreme variations in prices, and it was a currency with very high volatility, i.e., high risks. Hepkorucu and Genç (2017) investigated the stationarity of prices using Bitstamp values based on American Dollar and the data related to the period between September 2011 and August 2017 by taking non-linear factors into account. For this purpose, they analyzed the series with Fourier ADF and standard ADF tests and determined that the series was not stationary. They found out that the similarity of the results of the unit root tests accepting and rejecting the presence of structural changes proved the series to have unit roots. They stated that product prices were set by shocks in the market. Dulupçu et al. (2017) analyzed the hypothesis that the increases in Bitcoin prices resulted from speculative transactions in direct proportion with its popularity rather than its real value with Variance Decomposition Analysis and Granger causality test. The tests revealed that direction of causality was from the popularity to the price of Bitcoin. They stated that the current price of Bitcoin was a result of speculative movements rather than its own value. Dirican and Canoz (2017) analyzed the relationship between Bitcoin and stock markets with the ARDL Bounds Test using the data set consisting of 206 weekly observations from 24.05.2013 to 05.11.2017. They included the Bitcoin prices, five large stock exchanges with the highest transaction volumes in the world, as well as the S&P500 and BIST100 indexes in their analysis. They determined a cointegration relationship between the Bitcoin prices and the USA and China stock exchange indexes. They could not detect any correlations with the London FTSE100, Tokyo NIKKEI 225, and Istanbul BIST100 indexes.

The empirical studies conducted on cryptocurrencies in the world can be summarized as follows: Yermack (2013) investigated whether Bitcoin was a currency. He observed that the Bitcoin exchange rate volatility between 19.07.2010 and 29.11.2013 was higher than the volatilities of widely used currencies. Furthermore, he found out that there was almost zero correlation between Bitcoin and Pound, Frank, Euro, and Yen exchange rates and gold prices. Baek and Elbeck (2014) compared the volatilities of Bitcoin and daily S&P500 index and tried to explain the relationship between them using monthly data related to the period between 2010 and 2014. They also examined the variables affecting Bitcoin returns. They found out that Bitcoin was twenty-six times more volatile than the S&P500 index. They concluded that the monthly changes in the difference between the highest and lowest daily prices of Bitcoin was the only variable affecting the Bitcoin prices in the regression model they set up using the economic variables affecting the Bitcoin returns. They obtained findings showing that the Bitcoin market was speculative. Bouoiyour and Selmi (2014) tried to answer the following questions: What does Bitcoin look like? Is it a safe haven or a speculative trap? Is it a business income? Is it a short-term hedge? Is it a long-run promise? Is it a good idea to invest in Bitcoin? Is it a long-term promise? They regressed the Bitcoin prices to the investor's attractiveness, the exchange-trade ratio, the monetary velocity of Bitcoin, the estimated output volume, hash rate, gold price, and the Shangai index. They conducted the ARDL Bounds Test, Variance Decomposition Analysis, Impulse Response functions, and VEC Granger causality test using the daily value related to the period between 05.12.2010 and 14.06.2014. They found out that Bitcoin could be used for economic reasons, but it was not a safe haven or a long-term promise. They pointed out that Bitcoin had a speculative nature. Glaser, Zimmermann, Haferkorn, Weber, and Siering (2014) researched whether people used Bitcoin as an instrument of transaction or an investment tool in the period from 01.01.2011 to 08.10.2013 using the GARCH method. They found strong evidence showing that Bitcoin was not an instrument for buying goods and services but a speculative investment tool for users. Cheung, Roca, and Su (2015) researched the presence of bubbles in the Bitcoin prices at the Mt. Gox stock exchange using the method developed by Phillips, Shi, and Yu (2013). They analyzed data of 1307 days between 2010 and 2014. In addition to determining short-term bubbles, their most important finding was three long-term price bubbles. They pointed out that the bursting of those price bubbles was one of reasons for the collapse of the Mt. Gox stock exchange. Dyhrberg (2015) aimed to explain the capacity of Bitcoin to offer protection against price changes. She used the GARCH method with data of 1769 days between 19.06.2010 and 22.05.2015. The study revealed that Bitcoin could be used as a hedge against stocks in the Financial Times Stock Exchange Index (FTSE) and the US Dollar in the short term. She stated that Bitcoin possessed some of the same hedging abilities as gold and could be included in the variety of tools available to market analysts to hedge market-specific risk. Georgoula, Pournarakis, Bilanakos, Sotiropoulos, and Giaglis (2015) analyzed the relationship between the Bitcoin prices and fundamental economic variables, technological factors, and measurements of collective mood derived from Twitter feeds using the time-series analysis method. They determined a positive correlation between the Twitter sentiment ratio and Bitcoin prices through a short-term regression analysis. Furthermore, they found out that the number of Wikipedia search queries and the hash rate had a positive effect on Bitcoin prices. On the contrary, they stated that the value of Bitcoin was negatively affected by the exchange rate between the USD and the Euro. They used a vector error-correction model (VECM) to investigate the existence of long-term relationships between cointegrated variables. This model revealed that the Bitcoin price was positively associated with the number of Bitcoins in circulation and negatively associated with the S&P500 stock market index. Vockathaler (2015) set two main objectives in his study. Firstly, he reviewed the previous studies and evaluated whether their findings were based on facts. Secondly, he investigated the long-term factors affecting Bitcoin prices. He observed that the results obtained from some previous studies differed to a great extent when they were tested again after the results were published. In addition, he found out that most of the volatility of Bitcoin resulted from unexpected shocks, and he determined the impacts of these shocks using the GARCH model. He concluded that unexpected shocks made the greatest contribution to Bitcoin price fluctuations. Kristoufek (2015) analyzed potential drivers of Bitcoin prices, ranging from fundamental sources to speculative and technical ones. Furthermore, he contributed to the debates on Bitcoin by analyzing the potential influence of Bitcoin prices on the Chinese market. He analyzed the period from 14.09.2011 to 28.02.2014. Despite being a speculative asset, it was concluded that main factors such as commercial use, supply, and changes in price levels affected Bitcoin prices in the long term. He decided that Bitcoin was both a standard financial asset and an asset with speculative qualities. Eswara (2017) investigated the volatility of the Bitcoin value against five global currencies (Dollar, Euro, Pound, Yen, and Yuan) along with Indian Rupee and analyzed the impact of these five currencies on the Bitcoin prices in Indian Rupee, as well as the relationship between them. He used cryptocurrency logarithms and conducted a time-series analysis with 105 daily observations in the period between 04.04.2017 and 21.07.2017 using the ARCH and GARCH models. He proved that the other cryptocurrencies had a significant impact on the Bitcoin value in Indian Rupees. He found out that the Rupee value of Bitcoin was affected positively by its value in Dollars and negatively by its value in Pound and Yuan. Sovbetov (2018) analyzed the factors affecting the prices of the five most common cryptocurrencies (Bitcoin, Ethereum, Dash, Litcoin, and Monero) with the ARDL method using weekly data related to the period between 2010 and 2018. He found out that cryptomarket-related factors such as market, trading volume, and volatility were significant determinants for all five cryptocurrencies both in the short and long run. He showed that attractiveness of cryptocurrencies was subject to the time factor. He revealed that the S&P500 index had a negative impact on cryptocurrencies other than Bitcoin in the short term while it had a weak positive impact on Bitcoin, Ethereum, and Litcoin in the long term.

3 Empirical Analysis

3.1 Data Set and Variables

This study aims to conduct an empirical analysis of the relationship between cryptocurrencies and exchange rates. The data included in the study is weekly data from the period between 10.08.2015 and 04.12.2017. The data was obtained from

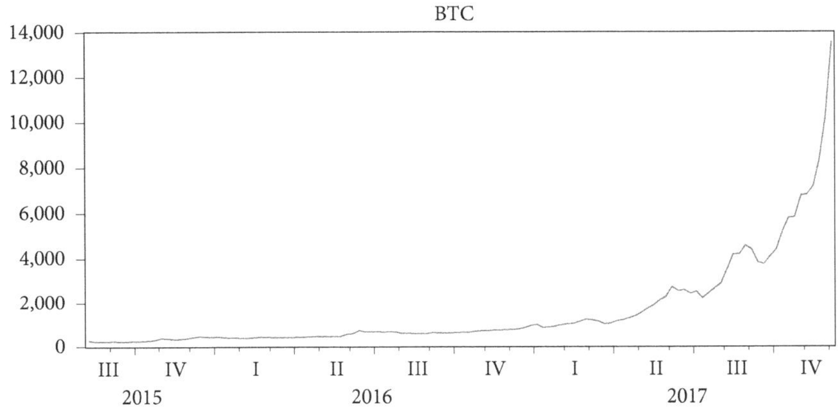

Fig. 5.1 The Bitcoin-USD exchange rates time series

the https://tr.investing.com website. Bitcoin and Ethereum cryptocurrencies, Euro, Japanese Yen, Pound Sterling, and Swiss Franc that are currencies with the highest circulation (https://www.ceifx.com/news/400/Top-10-Most-Traded-Currencies-in-the-World) in the world were chosen as variables along with the Turkish Lira which was chosen in order to make a comparison with these currencies. The cross exchange rates of Bitcoin and Ethereum are denominated in US Dollar. Fig. 5.1 shows the weekly Bitcoin-USD exchange rates between 2015 and 2017.

Fig. 5.1 shows that there were little changes in 2015 and 2016, and Bitcoin prices started to increase as of the first quarter of 2017. This increase reached a very high level by the end of 2017.

In the study, logarithmic forms of data were used instead of raw data. The Continuous Compounds of all variables were found as follows (Atik et al., 2015: 254).

$$\ln\left(\frac{Y_t}{Y_{t-1}}\right) \tag{1}$$

TRY, CHF, GBP, EUR, JPY, BTC, and ETC represent Turkish Lira, Swiss Franc, Pound Sterling, Euro, Japanese Yen, Bitcoin, and Ethereum, respectively, in the analyses. Tab. 5.1 shows the correlation matrix between the variables.

According to Tab. 5.1, it can be said that there is a positive and strong correlation between CHF and EUR and a moderate and positive correlation between CHF and JPY.

Tab. 5.1: The Correlation Matrix between the Variables

	TRY	CHF	GBP	EUR	JPY	BTC	ETC
TRY	1						
CHF	0.233	1					
GBP	0.194	0.320	1				
EUR	0.252	0.866	0.436	1			
JPY	0.254	0.624	-0.048	0.511	1		
BTC	0.130	-0.028	-0.006	-0.078	-0.050	1	
ETC	0.095	0.060	-0.023	0.028	0.083	0.167	1

3.2 Empirical Results

The empirical analyses of the study were conducted with unit root tests, the Granger causality test, Impulse Response Functions, and Variance Decomposition Analysis. Initially, the Augmented Dickey-Fuller (ADF), Phillips-Perron (PP), Kwiatkowski-Phillips-Schmidt-Shin (KPSS), and Ng-Perron unit root tests were executed on the variables included in the study. According to the unit root test results, all variables are stationary at level. While determining the optimal lag length for VAR analysis, the optimal lag lengths were found as 0 for FPE, SC, and HQ; 8 for LR; and 12 for AIC information criteria. The prerequisites needed for the VAR model are that the inverse roots of the model remain within the unit circle (lower than 1) and the error terms do not have autocorrelation. The 8th and 12th lags were checked for autocorrelation and the LM statistic was determined to be 92.410 (prob: 0.0002) at the 8th lag and 54.388 (prob: 0.277) at the 12th lag. Consequently, the H_0 hypothesis is not rejected at the 12th lag, i.e., there is no autocorrelation problem. It was checked whether the requirement to keep the inverse roots within the unit circle at this lag length was met, and the result is shown in Fig. 5.2. It can be seen that the inverse roots of the model were within the unit circle at the 12th lag length. As a result, the optimal lag length was determined as 12.

After the VAR model was observed to be stable, the causality relationship between the variables was determined through the Granger causality test. Tab. 5.2 shows the results of the Granger causality test.

According to the results in Tab. 5.2, there is a causality relationship from CHF, EUR, and GBP to BTC. But there is no exchange variable that is the reason for ETC. No causality relationship was determined between BTC and ETC. The results of the Impulse Response Functions and Variance Decomposition Analysis are sensitive to the order of the variables within the system and can

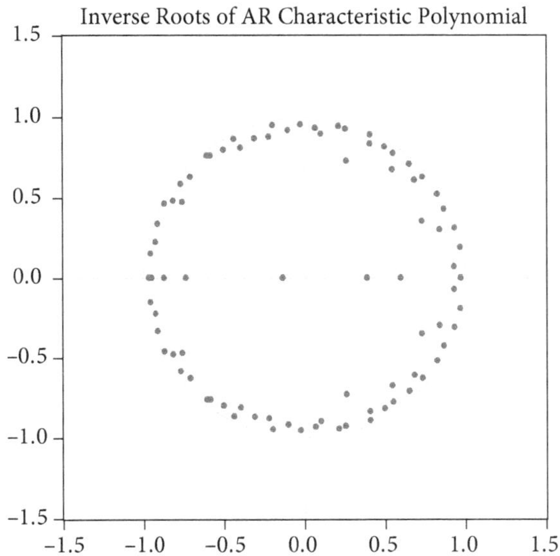

Fig. 5.2: Inverse roots for the VAR model

Tab. 5.2: Granger Causality Test Results

Dependent Variable: BTC			Dependent Variable: ETC		
Independent Variables	**Chi Square**	**Prob.**	**Independent Variables**	**Chi Square**	**Prob.**
CHF	23.1976	0.0261*	BTC	7.6557	0.8114
ETC	13.5821	0.3282	CHF	12.6890	0.3920
EUR	31.8649	0.0015*	EUR	13.5062	0.3333
GBP	24.3800	0.0180*	GBP	12.8869	0.3773
JPY	6.4373	0.8925	JPY	12.3608	0.4172
TRY	7.6143	0.8145	TRY	14.5165	0.2689

Note: * imply significance at the 5 %

differ depending on the alternative ordering of the variables (Bozkurt, 2007: 98; Bozdağlıoğlu and Özpınar, 2011: 51). In this regard, the variables were ordered taking into account the impact levels of the variables according to the Granger causality analysis (from the most affected to the least affected) and the predictions of the economy theory. Fig. 5.3 shows the results of Impulse Response Analysis.

Fig. 5.3 shows the reactions of ETC and BTC cryptocurrencies to a shock resulting from one standard deviation. The shock caused by one standard deviation in the GBP has a positive impact on ETC for ten periods. The impact of CHF on ETC is distinctly negative until the sixth period, whereas the impact gradually decreases in both positive and negative directions after that period. The reaction of ETC to a shock caused by one standard deviation in TRY fluctuates both negatively and positively. The reaction of ETC to a shock caused by one standard deviation in JPY is stable until the seventh period, and it changes both negatively and positively afterwards. The reaction of ETC to a shock caused by one standard deviation in EUR is positive until the sixth period, it approaches the balance value until the ninth period and is positive at the end of this period. On the other hand, the results of the impulse response analysis related to BTC show that the reaction of BTC to a shock caused by one standard deviation in GBP is positive between the second and eighth periods and negative in the first and last periods. The reaction of BTC to a shock caused by one standard deviation in CHF is negative until the sixth period, positive after this period, and gradually gets closer to the balance value. It can be said that TRY and JPY do not have a big effect on BTC. The reaction of BTC to a shock caused by one standard deviation in both exchange rates is very close to the balance value during the analyzed period. BTC is usually negatively affected by a shock in TRY, while it is affected positively by a shock in JPY and this impact disappears gradually. The reaction of BTC to a shock caused by one standard deviation in EUR is positive until the fifth period and negative after this period.

The Variance Decomposition Analysis that shows the percentages of changes in variables resulting from the variables themselves and other variables also provides information about the levels of the causality relationships among variables. The sources of prediction error variance of variables are analyzed using the Variance Decomposition Analysis. Tab. 5.3 shows how much of the changes caused by the ETC and BTC variance result from the variance of exchange rates.

According to the results regarding the ETC variable, it is possible to state that ETC itself accounts for most of the prediction error variance in the ETC variable in the first period (approximately 97 percent) while the GBP variable accounts for only 3 percent. At the end of ten periods, ETC itself accounts for approximately 43 percent of the prediction error variance in the ETC variable while CHF, GBP, TRY, EUR, JPY, and BTC account for 18 percent, 13 percent , 12 percent, 6 percent, 5 percent, and 4 percent, respectively. According to the Variance Decomposition Analysis results of the BTC variable, BTC itself accounts for 58 percent, i.e., more than half of the prediction error variance in the first period, while JPY accounts for 25 percent and the other exchange rates account

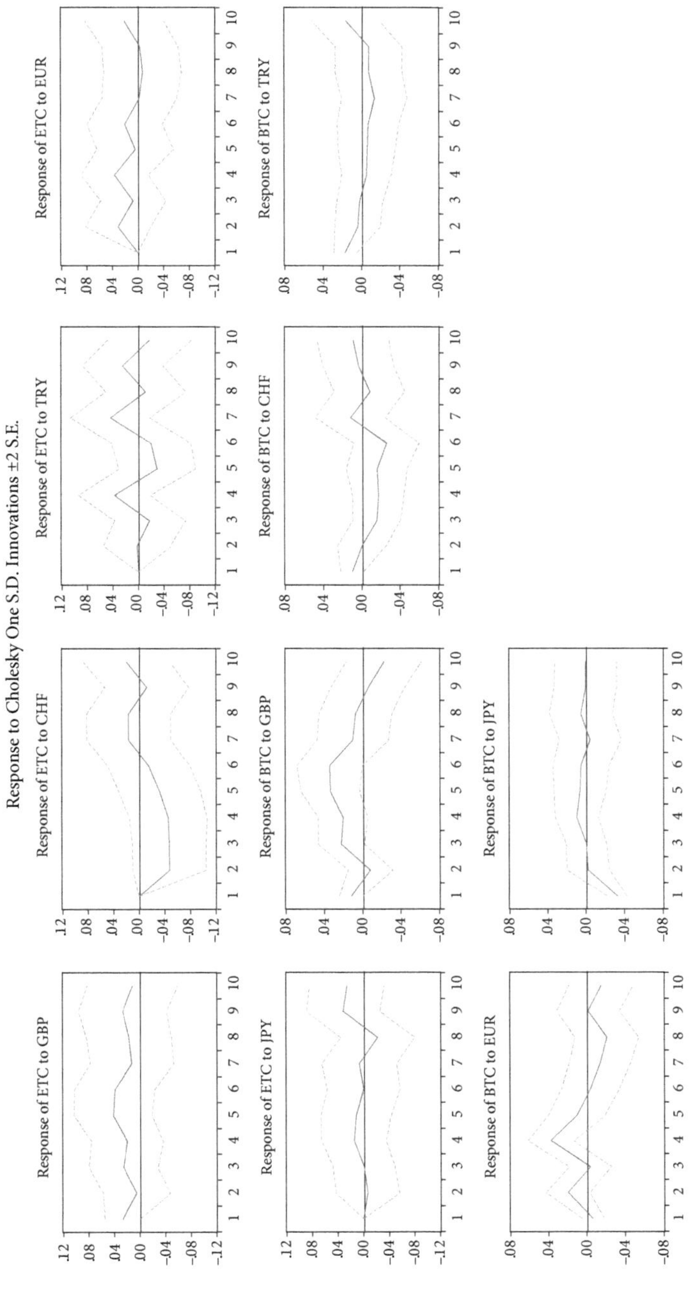

Fig. 5.3: Impulse response functions

Tab. 5.3: Variance Decomposition Analysis Results

Variance Decomposition Results for ETC Variable								
Period	**S.E.**	**GBP**	**ETC**	**CHF**	**TRY**	**EUR**	**JPY**	**BTC**
1	0.145	3.485	96.512	0.000	0.000	0.000	0.000	0.000
2	0.158	3.059	81.778	9.159	0.013	3.789	0.182	2.022
3	0.170	4.921	72.783	15.753	1.134	3.471	0.160	1.778
4	0.186	5.221	61.162	19.264	4.998	6.709	0.770	1.876
5	0.197	9.111	54.148	19.683	6.684	5.967	1.029	3.378
6	0.204	12.211	50.753	18.941	7.211	6.546	0.962	3.377
7	0.210	11.853	48.093	18.477	11.169	6.189	1.003	3.216
8	0.213	12.147	46.762	18.524	11.172	6.145	2.122	3.130
9	0.220	12.910	44.279	17.758	11.720	5.808	4.032	3.493
10	0.224	12.643	42.543	17.784	11.848	6.483	5.157	3.542
Variance Decomposition Results for BTC Variable								
Period	**S.E.**	**GBP**	**ETC**	**CHF**	**TRY**	**EUR**	**JPY**	**BTC**
1	0.064	3.580	2.246	2.463	7.073	1.099	25.305	58.235
2	0.069	4.434	2.804	2.118	6.408	9.071	21.869	53.295
3	0.075	12.504	3.587	6.159	5.513	7.984	18.603	45.650
4	0.090	13.828	5.339	7.973	4.178	23.011	13.993	31.678
5	0.100	22.449	7.871	8.933	3.722	19.674	11.683	25.666
6	0.110	28.385	7.061	13.006	3.496	16.453	9.910	21.689
7	0.115	26.706	10.170	12.944	4.603	16.431	9.208	19.938
8	0.118	25.727	9.688	12.795	4.791	18.801	8.917	19.280
9	0.120	25.157	11.515	12.471	5.064	18.223	8.636	18.933
10	0.125	26.605	10.964	12.068	6.412	18.364	7.993	17.594

for the rest. JPY is not the cause for BTC according to the Granger causality test results, but we may have reached this conclusion as BTC is a cryptocurrency that emerged in Japan. At the end of ten periods, it is seen that the variable with the greatest impact on BTC is GBP (27 percent) which is followed by EUR (18 percent), BTC (18 percent), and CHF (12 percent). In fact, the results of the causality test (the GBP, EUR, and CHF variables are the cause for BTC) support this result.

Conclusion

The system of cryptocurrencies that are not subject to any central authority is based on cooperation among users. The facts that the trust in governments and the financial system has decreased at the macro level and the difficulty of finding a reliable third party during bilateral financial transactions at the micro level increase the interest in cryptocurrencies. Regardless of our point of view, the popularity and usage of cryptocurrencies are gradually increasing, and they are included in many academic and non-academic studies.

It is observed that the economic and financial importance of cryptocurrencies is gradually increasing. For this purpose, a time series analysis was conducted using weekly data related to the period between 2015 and 2017 in order to analyze the relationship of Bitcoin and Ethereum cryptocurrencies with exchange rates. The Granger causality test, Impulse Response Analysis, and Variance Decomposition Analysis were executed during the empirical part. The analysis results revealed a unidirectional causality relationship according to the Granger causality test. The Swiss Franc, Euro, and Pound Sterling are causes of Bitcoin. However, none of the cross exchange rates are causes of Ethereum. According to the Impulse Response Functions, a shock caused by one standard deviation in Pound Sterling has a positive impact on Ethereum and Bitcoin. Ethereum and Bitcoin have a negative trend until the sixth period against a shock caused by one standard deviation in Swiss Franc, and this trend changes both negative and positive afterwards. The fluctuating impact of Turkish Lira on Ethereum continues for ten periods. The reaction of Bitcoin to Turkish Lira is very close to the balance value. The impact of Euro on Bitcoin and Ethereum is positive until the fifth and sixth periods, respectively, and it loses its impact on Ethereum, and its impact on Bitcoin becomes negative afterwards. The impact of a shock on Japanese Yen caused by one standard deviation is very close to the balance value for ten periods. This impact increases and becomes positive for Ethereum, while it disappears in case of Bitcoin. The results of the Variance Decomposition Analysis show that Ethereum itself accounts for approximately 97 percent of the prediction error variance of Ethereum in the first period while Pound Sterling accounts for 3 percent. Results related to the Bitcoin variable indicate that Bitcoin itself accounts for 58 percent of the prediction error variance in the first period while Japanese Yen accounts for 25 percent. Analyses results support each other. As a much larger data set will be available for cryptocurrencies in the future, researchers will be able to conduct more detailed and conclusive studies on this matter.

References

Aslantaş Ateş, B. (2016), "Kripto Para Birimleri, Bitcoin ve Muhasebesi," *Çankırı Karatekin University Journal of the Institute of Social Sciences*, *7*(1): 349–366.

Atik, M., Köse, Y., Yılmaz, B., and Sağlam, F. (2015), "Kripto Para: Bitcoin ve Döviz Kurları Üzerine Etkileri," *Bartın University Journal of Faculty of Economics and Administrative Sciences*, *6*(11): 247–261.

Baek, C. and Elbeck, M. (2014), "Bitcoins as an Investment or Speculative Vehicle? A First Look," *Applied Economics Letters*, *22*(1): 30–34.

Bilir, H. and Çay, Ş. (2016), "Elektronik Para ve Finansal Piyasalar Arasındaki İlişki," *Niğde University Journal of Faculty of Economics and Administrative Sciences*, *9*(2): 21–31.

Bouoiyour, J. and Selmi, R. (2014) "What Does Crypto-currency Look Like? Gaining Insight into Bitcoin Phenomenon," *MPRA Paper*, No. 58133: 1–35.

Bozdağlıoğlu, E.Y. and Özpınar, Ö. (2011), "Türkiye'ye Gelen Doğrudan Yabancı Yatırımların Türkiye'nin İhracat Performansına Etkilerinin VAR Yöntemi ile Tahmin Edilmesi," *9 September Unıversity Journal of the Institute of Social Sciences*, *13*(3): 39–63.

Bozkurt, H. (2007), *Time Series Analysis*, Bursa: Ekin Publisher.

Cheung, A., Roca, E., and Su, J.J. (2015), "Crypto-Currency Bubbles: An Application of the Phillips–Shi–Yu (2013) Methodology on Mt. Gox Bitcoin Prices," *Applied Economics*, *47*(23): 2348–2358.

Dirican, C. and Canoz, İ. (2017), "Bitcoin Fiyatları ile Dünyadaki Başlıca Borsa Endeksleri Arasındaki Eşbütünleşme İlişkisi: ARDL Modeli Yaklaşımı ile Analiz," *Journal of Economics, Finance and Accounting*, *4*(4): 377–392.

Dulupçu, M.A., Yiyit, M., and Genç, A.G. (2017), "Dijital Ekonominin Yükselen Yüzü: Bitcoin'in Değeri ile Bilinirliği Arasındaki İlişkinin Analizi," *Süleyman Demirel University Journal of Faculty of Economics and Administrative Sciences*, *22*, Kayfor15: 2241–2258.

Dyhrberg, A.H. (2015), "Hedging Capabilities of Bitcoin. Is it the Virtual Gold?," *UCD Centre for Economic Research Working Paper Series*; WP2015/21.

Eross, A., McGroarty, F., Urquhart, A., and Wolfe, S. (2017), "The Intraday Dynamics of Bitcoin," Research Gate, 15th INFINITI Conference on International Finance, Valencia-Spain.

Eswara, M. (2017), "Cryptocurrency Gyration and Bitcoin Volatility," *International Journal of Business and Administration Research Review*, *3*(18): 187–195.

Georgoula, I., Pournarakis, D., Bilanakos, C., Sotiropoulos, D.N., and Giaglis, G.M. (2015), "Using Time-Series and Sentiment Analysis to Detect the Determinants of Bitcoin Prices," https://papers.ssrn.com/sol3/papers.cfm?abstract_id=2607167 (28.05.2018).

Glaser, F., Zimmermann, K., Haferkorn, M., Weber, M.C., and Siering, M. (2014), "Bitcoin-asset or Currency? Revealing Users' Hidden Intentions," Twenty Second European Conference on Information Systems, Tel Aviv.

Hepkorucu, A. and Genç,S. (2017), "İnvestigation of Bitcoin as Financial Asset and an Application on Unit Root Structure," *Osmaniye Korkut Ata University Journal of Faculty of Economics and Administrative Sciences*, *1*(2): 47–58.

Koçoğlu, Ş., Çevik, Y.E., and Tanrıöven, C. (2016), "Effectiveness of Bitcoin Markets, Liquidity and Volatility," *Journal of Business Research*, *8*(2): 77–97.

Kristoufek, L. (2015), "What Are the Main Drivers of the Bitcoin Price? Evidence from Wavelet Coherence Analysis," *PloS ONE*, *10*(4): 1–15.

Malhotra, A. and ve Maloo, M. (2014), "BITCOIN-Is It a Bubble? Evidence from Unit Root Tests," https://papers.ssrn.com/sol3/papers.cfm?abstract_id=2476378 (28.05.2018).

Rosinach, M.A. and Raventos, H. (2012), "Bitcoin Data Analysis," High License Thesis, HEC, Paris.

Sovbetov, Y. (2018), "Factors Influencing Cryptocurrency Prices: Evidence from Bitcoin, Ethereum, Dasd, Litcoin and Monero," *Journal of Economics and Financial Analysis*, *2*(2): 1–27.

Sönmez, A. (2014), "Virtual Money Bitcoin," *The Turkish Online Journal of Design, Art and Communication (TOJDAC)*, *4*(3): 1–14.

Vockathaler, B. (2015), "The Bitcoin Boom: An in Depth Analysis of The Price of Bitcoins," https://ruor.uottawa.ca/bitstream/10393/32888/1/Vockathaler_Brian_2015_researchpaper.pdf (28.05.2018).

Yermack, D. (2013), "Is Bitcoin a Real Currency?," National Bureau of Economic Research Working Paper, No. 19747: 1–14.

http://www.tepav.org.tr/tr/blog/s/6195/Bitcoin_in+toplam+piyasa+degeri+160+milyar+dolari+asti.

https://koinbulteni.com/odemeleri-bitcoinle-kabul-eden-8-buyuk-firma-4991.html.

https://bitcoinlerim.com/en-iyi-bitcoin-borsalari/.

https://tr.investing.com

https://www.ceifx.com/news/400/Top-10-Most-Traded-Currencies-in-the-World

Özlem Akın and S. Mehmet Özsoy

6 Global Trends in Liquidity Creation: The Role of the Off-Balance Sheet

Abstract: Banks create liquidity by transforming liquid liabilities into illiquid assets and this is one of their main functions. Yet excessive liquidity creation, especially via off-balance sheet activities, might have contributed to the 2008–2009 financial crisis. In this chapter, we analyze the dynamics of liquidity creation in Turkey and the United States, and the contribution of off-balance sheet activities therein.

Keywords: Liquidity Creation, Off-Balance Sheet, Financial Crisis, Banks

1 Introduction

In the 21st century off-balance items became important items for banks to provide liquidity which in turn played a major role in 2008–2009 financial crisis. With the rise of off-balance sheet items such as derivatives and loan commitments, understanding bank's off-balance sheet structure has been one of the major risk management concerns, especially after 2008.

We investigate liquidity creation in Turkish banking system and compare it with the global trends. Following Berger and Bouwman (2009), we calculate aggregate liquidity creation for the time period between 2002 and 2017. Using quarterly detailed regulatory data set, liquidity created on- and off-balance sheets are computed separately. Comparing these two liquidity creation measures, we document the role played by off-balance sheet items and how it changed over time. We also compare the trends in Turkish and US banking systems in terms of liquidity creation and the role played by off-balance sheet activities.

We find that liquidity created via balance sheets in both Turkish and US banking systems has an upward trend over time. However, the trend is much steeper in the Turkish case. This fast pace of liquidity creation in Turkish banking system is very likely to be related to the increased efficiency of Turkish banks, as well as the strong growth performance of Turkish economy.

When we analyze the role played by the off-balance sheet activities in liquidity creation, we observe that US banks create more liquidity from their off-balance sheets than they do on their balance sheets. We further analyze small banks separately as we want to compare the trends in the United States to the ones in Turkey, and the Turkish banks are more comparable to the small-size US banks.

We find that in the United States the role of off-balance sheet is less important for smaller banks. When the Turkish and the US cases are analyzed together, it seems to be the case that the liquidity created in off-balance sheets decreased in Turkish banks and the small-size US banks, while it increased for the large US banks between 2002 and 2008. However, after the 2008–2009 financial crisis, while the role of off-balance sheet activities in creating liquidity diminishes for all sizes of US banks, it increases for Turkish banks until 2013.

We further investigate the contribution to the liquidity creation from the asset and liability sides separately and how it changed over time. Overall, we can say that both for Turkey and the United States the liquidity created via balance sheets is mostly driven by the liability side. We also look for the details of off-balance sheet activities to understand sharp drop of liquidity created in Turkish banks' off-balance sheets after 2013. We observe that loan commitments of Turkish banks take a dramatic deep dive in 2013, while at the same time the use of derivatives begins a trend of a steady increase.

The chapter proceeds as follows. The second section reviews the literature and third section describes our data sources and variables. The fourth section presents the empirical findings. Finally, Conclusion and Policy Implications discusses the policy implications of the results and concludes the paper.

2 Literature Review

The first study that has investigated bank liquidity creation is Deep and Schaefer (2004). The authors analyzed bank liquidity creation for 200 US banks during 1997 – 2001. To measure liquidity creation, they used only liquid items from assets and liabilities side, and they found that banks were creating low level of liquidity. In a follow-up study, Berger and Bouwman (2009) emphasized the importance of a comprehensive liquidity creation measure. The authors constructed an extensive measure that considers all asset and liability items on-balance sheet and off-balance sheet items. They showed that liquidity creation was increasing over time for US banks during 1993–2003. Furthermore, they found that large banks, retail banks, and recently merged banks created the most liquidity.

Berger and Bouwman (2013) analyzed the effects of US monetary policy on bank liquidity creation. They examined the period of 1984–2008 and compared the normal times with crisis times. Additionally, they also investigated whether liquidity creation changes depending on bank size. They found that tight monetary policy rules affect liquidity creation in small banks, but the effect is not strong in crisis times. Moreover, they documented that total liquidity creation increases before the financial crises. This result indicates that total liquidity creation might be used for predicting financial crisis.

Berger et al. (2016) explore the effect of regulatory interventions and capital injections on liquidity creation. Using a sample of German savings banks, the authors find that government interventions led to a decrease in liquidity creation.

Pana et al. (2010) analyzed how bank mergers affect liquidity creation. They conducted their analysis with US banks for the time period of 1997–2004, and found that bank mergers resulted in a higher level of liquidity creation as a result of increase in capital.

The comprehensive liquidity measure proposed by Berger and Bouwman (2009) has also been used in studies that are analyzing liquidity creation in other developed countries, as well as emerging countries. Hacekthal et al. (2010) explored the potential determinants of liquidity creation using a sample of German savings banks. They checked the effects of both macroeconomic factors (monetary policy and unemployment rate) and bank-specific factors such as bank size and its financial performance. Their results showed that the tightening of monetary policy leads to a decrease in liquidity creation. On the other hand, bank-specific factors seem to have no effect on liquidity creation. Fungácová et al. (2013) tested a different aspect of liquidity creation and analyzed the role of liquidity creation of banks on bank failures for a sample of Russian banks. They documented that excessive liquidity creation increased the probability of bank failure.

Another stream of research analyzes specifically the impact of capital on liquidity creation. Theoretical studies in the 2000s discuss the effect of bank capital on liquidity creation. These theories have two opposite views on the relationship between bank capital and liquidity creation. The hypothesis of the first group of studies is called "financial fragility-crowding out." This group of studies predict that increase in bank capital will lead to drop in the capacity of liquidity creation (Diamond and Rajan, 2000, 2001; Gorton and Winton, 2000). On the other hand, the studies that support the view of "risk absorption" argue that as bank capital ratio increases the capacity of liquidity creation will increase. This result is actually intersection of two different groups of work. A group of studies suggest that creating more liquidity will cause increase in the risk exposure of bank (Allen and Santomero, 2001; Allen and Gale, 2004). However, another group of studies indicates that capital will absorb the risk and increase bank's tolerance to risks (Bhattacharya and Thakor, 1993; Repullo, 2004; Von Thadden, 2004; Coval and Thakor, 2005). Given the findings of these two groups of studies, it is expected that the higher capital ratio will lead to higher liquidity creation. Berger and Bouwman (2009) was the first empirical study that tested the validity of these two opposite theoretical approaches by testing the relationship between bank's liquidity creation and capital ratio. Their results indicate that this relationship is positive in large banks and negative in small banks. Horvath et al. (2014) explored the relationship between capital and liquidity creation using Berger and Bouwman (2009) measure for Czech banks and found that the banks with lower capital ratio create more liquidity. Lei and Song (2013) reached the same conclusion using data from China. Umar et al. (2017) conducted similar analysis for India and found negative relationship between bank capital and on-balance sheet liquidity creation, but bank capital does not affect off-balance sheet liquidity creation.

To the best of our knowledge this chapter is the first to analyze liquidity creation of banks operating in Turkey using both asset and liabilities side and on- and off-balance sheet items. Alper et al. (2012) defined liquidity as the difference between liquid assets and liquid liabilities. Similar to Deep and Schaefer (2004), they took into account items from both assets and liabilities side. But different from Berger and Bouwman (2009) they did not include loans and any semi-liquid items (both from asset and liability sides) in their analysis. Other studies that analyzed liquidity creation in Turkey measured liquidity as the share of liquid assets in total assets and had not used any items from liabilities side (Akıncı et al., 2013; Ozsuca and Akbostanci, 2012).

The studies that analyze the liquidity creation of banks operating in Turkey are not only using different measure of liquidity but also asking different questions. Alper et al. (2012) analyzed thirteen banks for the period of 2001–2011 and showed that the liquidity position of banks and the aggregate liquidity created in the economy affected bank lending. Akıncı et al. (2013) used regulatory data set for twenty-five banks and investigated how monetary policy affected Turkish banking lending. Their results showed that monetary policy affects bank lending and this effect changes depending on bank's liquidity and capital. Ozsuca and Akbostancı (2012) similarly analyzed the effect of monetary policy on lending behavior of banks and found that the response of banks differed depending on their capital and liquidity ratios.

The growing pattern of off-balance sheet activities has attracted attention of both regulators and academicians. The importance of off-balance sheet has risen even more after the recent crisis as off-balance sheet activities of banking sector are blamed as one of the main reasons of crisis. It has been argued that the standard capital adequacy and liquidity ratios that did not consider the riskiness of off-balance sheet activities have been misleading (Barrell and Davis, 2008).

Globally, there is a growing pattern in off-balance sheet activities. Acharya and Richardson (2009) reported growing pattern of the securitization-generated income in many OECD countries, especially after 2003. Altunbas et al. (2009) provided evidence on the increasing securitization in European banks.

There is an extensive literature on the factors that influence specifically the banks' usage of derivatives. Although there has been an increasing usage of derivatives overall, at bank level there is a lot of heterogeneity. The factors that influence the usage of derivatives could be grouped as bank-specific and macroeconomic. The literature documents the effects of several bank-specific characteristics such as bank size, credit rating, the number of branches, profitability, and interest rate risk exposure on derivative usage of banks. There are also studies investigating the effects of macroeconomic factors such as interest rates, growth, and inflation on the derivative usage.

Simons (1995) analyzed US banks and found that bank size and derivative usage had a negative relationship. On the other hand, Hundman (1998) documented that larger banks used more derivatives by analyzing US commercial banks with assets of more than $500 million. Hundman (1998) found that banks with higher capital-to-assets ratio utilized more from derivatives. In a more recent study by Hassan and Khasawneh (2009), the authors documented that bank size and derivatives usage had a positive relationship, whereas banks with low credibility utilized less from derivatives. They were unable to document any significant relationship between macroeconomic factors such as GDP, inflation, interest rates and balance of payments, and derivatives usage[1].

Altan and Parlakkaya (2004) reported that in Turkish banking sector the share of off-balance sheet items increased significantly especially after the crisis of 1994, but these transactions did not positively affect the performance of the banks due to their ineffective use.

Anbar and Alper (2011) investigated the effects of bank-specific and macroeconomic factors on derivative usage of banks operating in Turkey. They analyzed the banks that were listed on Istanbul stock exchange for the period 1999–2010 and found that the banks with higher return on equity and higher net interest margin and smaller banks used derivatives more intensely. They also documented a significant relationship between derivative usage and interest rates, but they were unable to find any statistically significant relationship with other macroeconomic variables such as economic growth and inflation.

1 There are also studies analyzing banks usage of specific type of derivatives. See, for example, Carter and Sinkey (1998), Gunther and Siems (2002), and Charumathi (2009) for interest rate derivatives usage, and Adkins et al. (2007) for the usage of foreign exchange derivatives.

3 Data

Our sample consists of fifty-one commercial (regular and Islamic) banks operating in Turkey for the time period 2002–2017. We obtained quarterly detailed regulatory data set from the Banks Association of Turkey. Our analysis uses unconsolidated bank balance sheets and income statements[2]. Finally, our sample contains 2831 bank-quarter observations. We used the inflation data obtained from the Central Bank's webpage to convert nominal values into real.

Our main variable of interest is the aggregate liquidity created in Turkish banking system. We first compute bank level liquidity created following Berger and Bouwman (2009) and then aggregate it at quarter level. Liquidity created from on-balance sheet activities and from off-balance sheet activities are computed separately. We follow a three-step procedure: (1) Each item in on- and off-balance sheet will be classified as "liquid," "semi-liquid," and "illiquid" (2) The value of each item will be multiplied by the weight that Berger and Bouwman (2009) assigned, and (3) finally the items classified will be summed under the categories defined in previous steps. Now, we explain the steps of computing liquidity creation measure in detail.

At first step, Berger and Bouwman (2009) classified each item on and off-balance sheet as "liquid," "semi-liquid," or "Illiquid." In asset side cash and similar items are classified as liquid assets and premises and investments are classified as illiquid assets. Loans are classified based on their category[3]. For instance, consumer loans, credit cards, and loans to depository institutions are considered as semi-liquid, and the rest of the loans are classified as illiquid. On the liabilities side, we classicd. Finally, off-balance sheet items of loan commitments and letter of credits are classified as "Illiquid," whereas derivatives will be classified as "Liquid" due to their easy sell and buy.

At second step, we assign the weights of Berger and Bouwman (2009) to each item based on its category. We multiply all items that are classified as liquid by ½, semi-liquid items will be multiplied by 0, and finally the items classified as illiquid will be multiplied by -1/2.

2 Consolidated and unconsolidated statements are reported starting by December 2002.

3 Berger and Bouwman (2009) classified loans in more detail as sub-categories of loans show significant differences in terms of liquidity. They specifically classify loans based on category (such as business loans, real estate loans, etc.) and based on maturity (less than one year, more than one year…). As we do not have details at maturity level, we classify them based on their type.

At third and final step, we sum the value of items multiplied by corresponding weights at bank-quarter level.

In the end for both Turkey and the United States, we aggregate bank level liquidity at quarter level and obtain two aggregate liquidity creation measures: (i) liquidity created from on-balance sheet (non-fat) and (ii) liquidity created from off-balance sheet (fat). We compare these two measures to understand the role of on- and off-balance sheet activities in liquidity creation over time.

In further steps, we decompose on- and off-balance sheet items to identify the source of changes in liquidity creation. We first analyze the contribution to the liquidity creation from the asset and liability side separately and how it changed over time, and then we examine the components of off-balance sheet.

4 Results

This section presents the empirical findings. We first compare fat measure with non-fat measure over time for United States in Fig. 6.1. We observe that they have similar behavior over time although fat measure is much larger. On average fat measure is more than twice of non-fat measure of liquidity creation. That means US banks create more liquidity from their off-balance sheet than they do on their balance sheet. More importantly, this is not a recent trend. In Fig. 6.2, we see that as of the first quarter of 1984 the ratio of fat to non-fat was 1,7 and at the end of the sample, fourth quarter of 2016, it is 1,86. However, there has been significant time variation in this ratio. The liquidity created of off-balance sheet activities were rising pre-2008 and the ratio of fat-to-non-fat reached its peak value of 2,9 around the 2008–2009 financial crisis. Since the financial crisis was a decade ago, the role of off-balance sheet activities in providing liquidity has decreased and come to the level in 1980s and 1990s.

The patterns depicted in Fig. 6.1 and 6.2 include all US banks. When only small banks are included, the patterns are similar: there is an upward trend in liquidity creation with a negative impact of 2008–2009 financial crisis. However, the role of off-balance sheet is less important for smaller banks. We can observe this by comparing Fig. 6.2 and 6.3. For instance, as of 2016, small-size US banks create only 18 percent more liquidity with the help of off-balance sheet items. This contribution, when all banks are included, is 86 percent.

As it is noted by Berger and Bouwman (2009) as well, most of the liquidity creation in the US banking system comes from the largest size banks. This is also apparent from the comparison of Fig. 6.1 and 6.4. The small banks create roughly 10 percent of the all liquidity created by the US banking system. We highlight these comparisons between the small US banks and the whole banking system

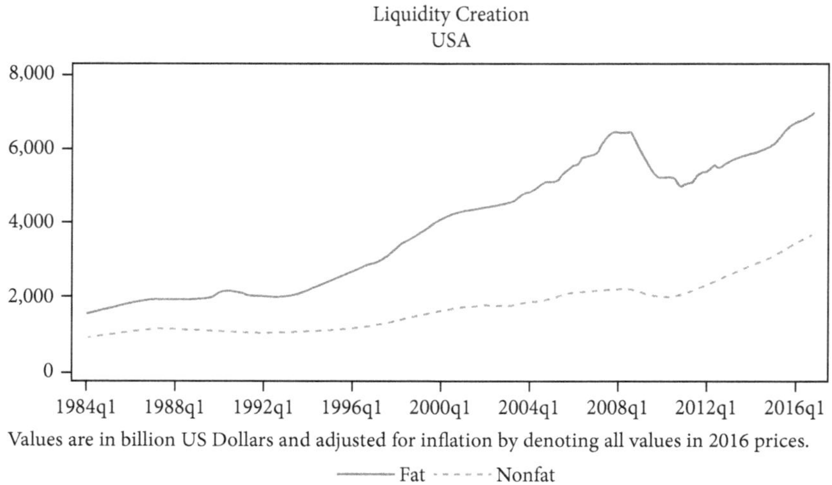

Fig. 6.1: Fat and Non-Fat measures of liquidity creation in US

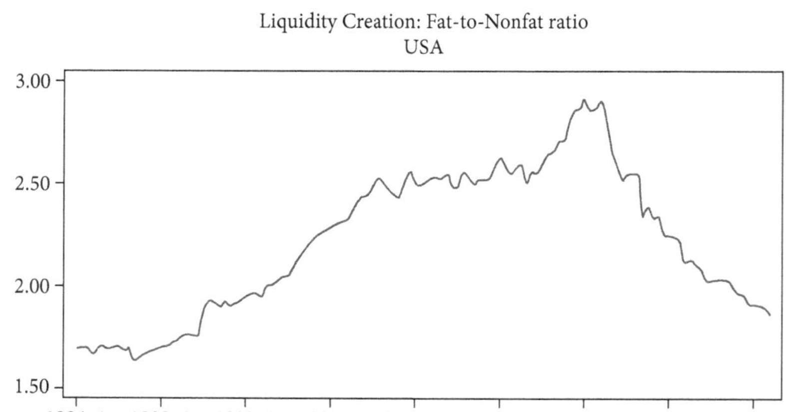

Fig. 6.2: The ratio of liquidity creation measures in US

because in the United States there are a handful of very large banks that create most of the liquidity. This is especially important for our purposes, since we want to compare the trends in the United States to the ones in Turkey and the Turkish banks are more comparable to the small-size US banks.

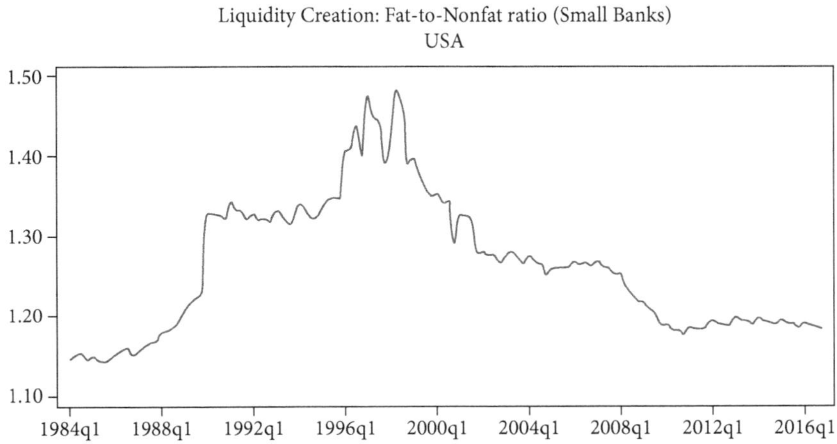

Fig. 6.3: The ratio of liquidity creation measures in US for small banks

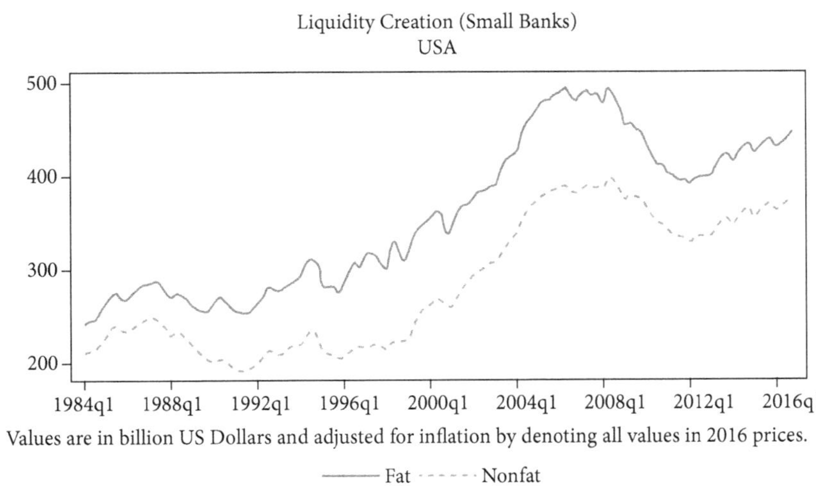

Fig. 6.4: Fat and Nonfat measures of liquidity creation in US for small banks

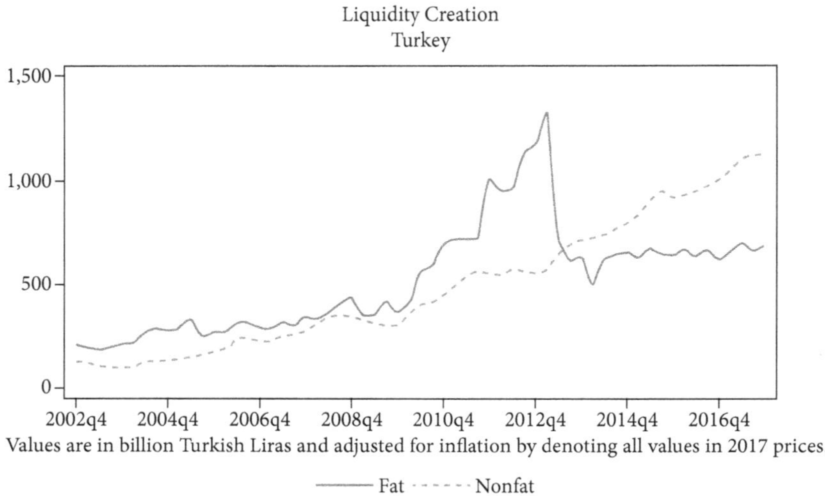

Fig. 6.5: Fat and Non-Fat measures of liquidity creation in Turkey

The liquidity creation in Turkish banking system has some similarities and differences compared to the one in the US banking system. First, similar to the trends in the US case, the liquidity created via on- and off-balance sheets of Turkish banks –Fat – has an upward trend since 2002[4]. Moreover, compared to the United States, the trend is much steeper in Turkish case (Fig. 6.5). From the last quarter of 2002 to the last quarter of 2017 the Fat measure increased more than 700 percent, while the increase in the US case is only around 100 percent, and even lower if we consider only the small US banks. This fast pace of liquidity creation in Turkish banking system is very likely to be related to the increased efficiency of Turkish banks, as well as the strong growth performance of Turkish economy.

The rate of increase in liquidity creation over time is not the only difference between the Turkish and the US banking systems: The role played by the off-balance sheet activities differ significantly. From 2002 to 2008 the ratio of fat to non-fat increased in the United States, while it decreased in Turkey (see Fig. 6.5 and 6.6). The case of United States can be understood when the reckless risk-taking behavior of banks in the period prior to the 2008–2009 financial crisis,

4 We should note that this trend is not due to inflation as all the values are real terms, denominated in 2016 prices.

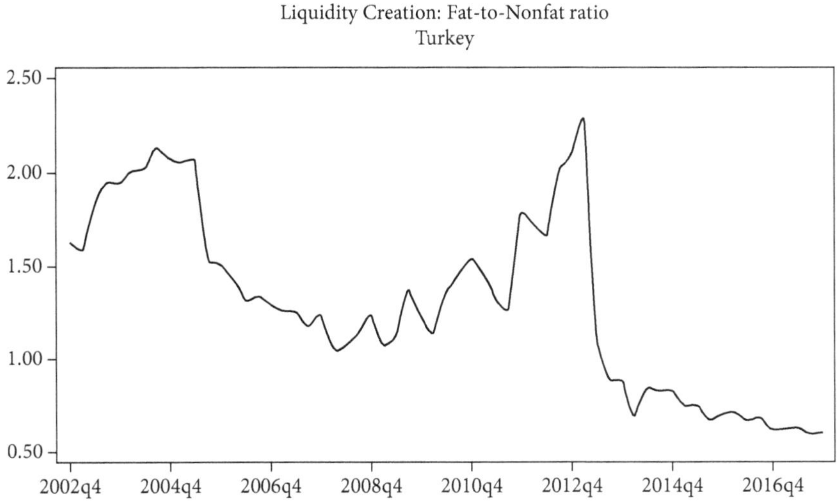

Fig. 6.6: The ratio of liquidity creation measures in Turkey

especially using derivative contracts, is taken into consideration. Importantly, we should note that this rise in the importance of off-balance sheet liquidity creation is driven by large banks. As we can see in Fig. 6.3, similar to the Turkish banks, from 2002 to 2008 the ratio of fat-to-non-fat decreased for small US banks. When the Turkish and the US cases are analyzed together, it seems to be the case that the liquidity created in off-balance sheets decreased in Turkish banks and the small-size US banks, while it increased for the large US banks. This again confirms the similarity between the Turkish banks and small-size US banks. Having said that, the similarity between the Turkish banks and the small-size US banks disappears in the aftermath of the financial crisis. After the 2008–2009 financial crisis, while the role of off-balance sheet activities in creating liquidity diminishes for all sizes of US banks, it increases for Turkish banks until 2013. In other words, in the period from 2008 to 2013, the ratio of fat-to-non-fat rose and reached its peak in Turkey, while it decreased in the United States. Starting in 2013, Turkish banks' off-balance sheet activities became liquidity destructive rather than contributing to the liquidity creation. In the following subsections, we look for the details of off-balance sheet activities to understand sharp drop of liquidity created in Turkish banks' off-balance sheets.

The main mechanism that banks create liquidity is to transform liquid liabilities into illiquid assets. For instance, one major liability item for banks –deposits – can

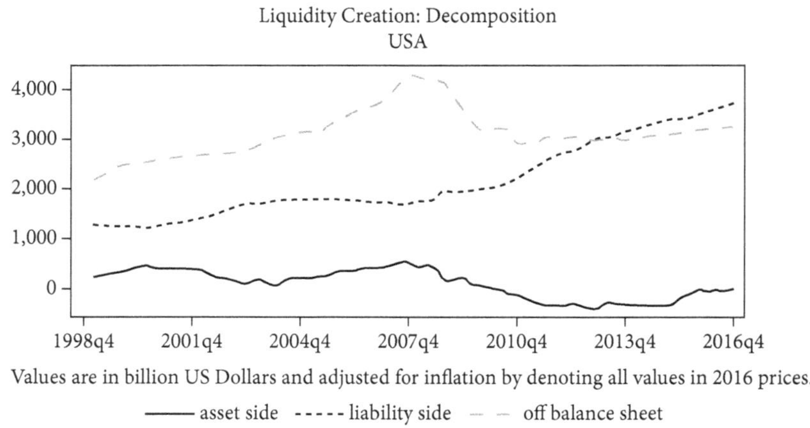

Fig. 6.7: Decomposition of liquidity creation in US

easily be withdrawn and thus highly liquid liabilities. Banks extend loans to companies using these deposits. Yet the loans are illiquid, banks cannot collect them back at any time. When banks invest into liquid assets such as treasury bills, they do not really create any liquidity; they transform liquidity by converting liquid deposits to liquid assets. Thus, the liquidity creation is a two-step process, one is on the liability side and the other is on the asset side of balance sheets. We next study the contribution to the liquidity creation from the asset and liability side separately and how it changed over time.

In Fig. 6.7 and 6.8 when we only look at the liquidity created in asset and liability sides separately, we see some similar patterns between the Turkish and the US liquidity creation mechanisms. First, the liability side plays a more important role in the sense that a bigger chunk of liquidity creation is due to liquid liabilities than illiquid assets. Second, the liquidity creation on the asset side is negative in some periods. Negative liquidity creation on the asset side means that banks holds more liquid assets than illiquid assets. This is the case for US banks in the period after 2009 and for the Turkish banks in the period before 2011. Overall, we can say that both for Turkey and the United States the non-fat measure of liquidity creation is mostly driven by the liability side. When we consider only the small-size US bank, the conclusion does not change (Fig. 6.9). We next analyze the role of off-balance sheet activities in creating liquidity.

The comparison we studied earlier –between fat and non-fat measures – provides a preliminary evidence regarding the role of off-balance sheet activities.

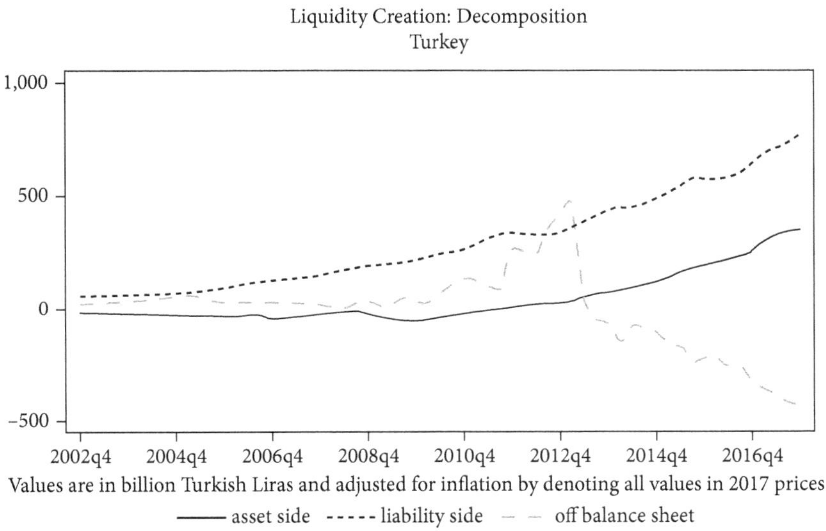

Fig. 6.8: Decomposition of liquidity creation in Turkey

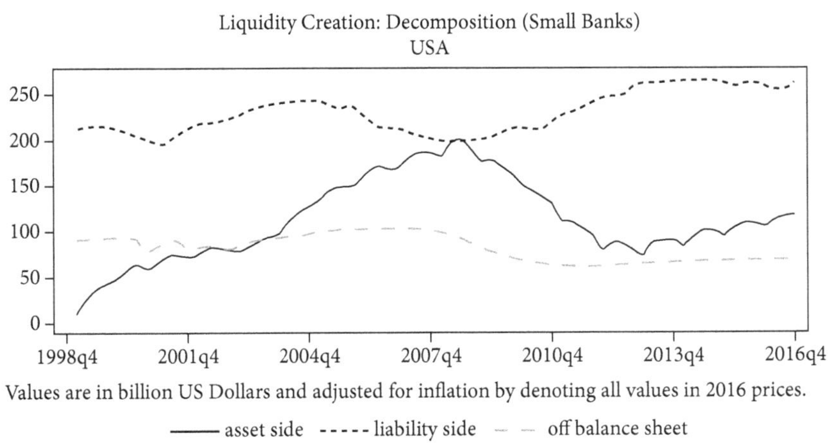

Fig. 6.9: Decomposition of liquidity creation for small banks in US

We observe in Fig. 6.2 and 6.6 that the relative role of off-balance sheet liquidity creation decreased in the United States after 2008 and in Turkey after 2012. We infer this finding by comparing fat and non-fat measures of liquidity creation, for the only difference between them is the off-balance sheet liquidity creation.

Fig. 6.7 and 6.8 confirm our inference by plotting directly the liquidity created on off-balance sheets of banks. In the United States, there seems to be a temporary increase in liquidity creation via off-balance sheet items prior to the 2008–2009 financial crisis and in the aftermath of the crisis liquidity created on off-balance sheets turns to pre-crisis levels. The case of Turkey seems more interesting. Starting 2009, the liquidity created on the off-balance sheets increases rapidly and reaches 500 billion Turkish Liras by 2013 (in 2017 prices). What follows is also interesting: in a couple of quarters after reaching its peak, the liquidity creation via off-balance sheet activities turn negative and stays negative for the rest of the sample. Put differently, Turkish banks have been destroying liquidity with the use of off-balance sheet items since the third quarter of 2013. However, we should not jump to any conclusion because the steps taken via off-balance sheet items can be complementary to steps taken in the asset or liability side. Banks can potentially be using these off-balance sheet items to support liquidity creation on the balance sheet, with a side effect of some liquidity destruction. We should also note that excessive liquidity creation can be considered as a risk factor, and thus banks might have cut their risk taking starting 2013[5]. To drill further down, we next look into the components of the off-balance sheet and which items led to this drastic change in the value of the off-balance-sheet.

In Fig. 6.10 we observe that loan commitments of Turkish banks take a dramatic deep dive in 2013, while at the same time the use of derivatives begins a trend of a steady increase. In Fig. 6.11 we further decompose the derivatives according to the purpose of derivative use. What is visible in Fig. 6.11 is that although banks' use of derivatives for trading purposes were on the rise pre-2013 the pace increased afterwards. The increase in derivatives for hedging purposes is very limited and thus falls short of explaining the increase in bank's derivative use.

Conclusion and Policy Implications

In this chapter, we analyze in detail the aggregate liquidity creation in Turkish banking system. Similar to its counterpart in the United States, the aggregate liquidity created by Turkish banks shows interesting dynamics: it usually rises

5 The taper tantrum of 2013, which began with the Federal Reserve Chairman Ben Bernanke's announcement of gradually ending the bond purchasing program, led bond yields to raise and massive fund flows from emerging markets to developed economies. Decreasing the liquidity creation might be an optimal strategy that Turkish banks adapted to deal with heightened global uncertainty driven by the taper tantrum

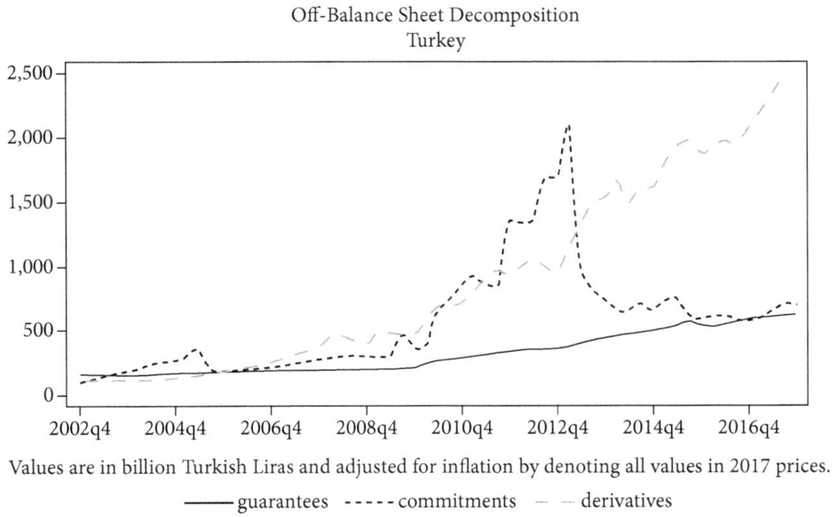

Fig. 6.10: Decomposition of off-balance sheet items in Turkey

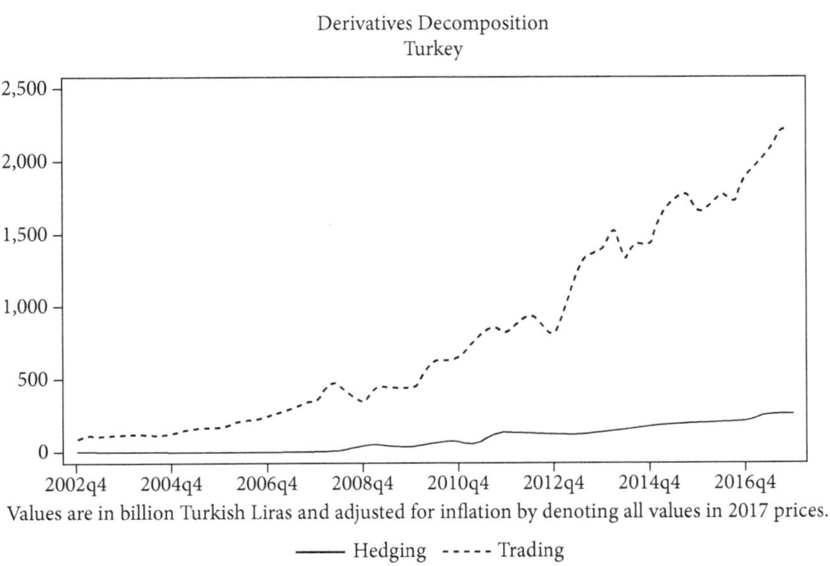

Fig. 6.11: Decomposition of derivatives in Turkey

prior to the financially distressed periods and decreases during financial crises. The increasing aggregate liquidity creation found prior to the financial crises, as in Berger and Bouwman (2010), indicates that perhaps the aggregate liquidity creation in a banking system should also be included among systemic risk indicators to be monitored[6].

The level of the aggregate liquidity creation is not the only aspect of it that changes with financial cycles: the composition of liquidity created changes as well. The role of off-balance sheet activities in creating liquidity diminished for the US banks with the 2008–2009 financial crisis. The decrease in the role of off-balance sheet items for Turkish banks starts few years later, around 2013. We also observe a divergence in the way the Turkish banks utilize their off-balance sheets after 2013. While they provided much less loan commitments, they rapidly expanded their use of derivatives, mostly for trading purposes. Together with how the liquidity creation via off-balance sheets changed over time, this finding indicates the necessity to have a nuanced view regarding the role and regulation of banks' off-balance sheet activities. Banks can create liquidity via their off-balance sheets, can support on-balance sheet liquidity creation with their off-balance sheets, or they can destroy liquidity on their off-balance sheets. Why they choose to utilize their off-balance sheets differently at different times is interesting and to be studied.

References

Acharya, V.V., & Richardson, M. (2009). "Causes of the Financial Crisis." *Critical Review*, *21*(2–3), 195–210.

Adkins, L.C., Carter, D.A., & Simpson, W. G. (2007). "Managerial Incentives and the Use of Foreign-Exchange Derivatives by Banks." *Journal of Financial Research*, *30*(3), 399–413.

Akinci, D.A., Matousek, R., Radić, N., & Stewart, C. (2013). "Monetary Policy and the Banking Sector in Turkey." *Journal of International Financial Markets, Institutions and Money*, *27*, 269–285.

Allen, F. & Gale, D. (2004). "Financial Fragility, Liquidity, and Asset Prices." *Journal of the European Economic Association*, *2*(6), 1015–1048.

Allen, F. & Santomero, A.M. (2001). "What Do Financial Intermediaries Do?" *Journal of Banking & Finance*, *25*(2), 271–294.

6 Fungácová et al. (2013) show that excessive liquidity creation at bank-level for Russian banks increases the probability of bank failure, which supports excessive liquidity creation as a risk factor.

Alper, K., Hulagu, T., & Keles, G. (2012). "An Empirical Study on Liquidity and Bank Lending." *Central Bank of the Republic of Turkey Working Paper*, 12/4, 1–18.

Altan, M. & Parlakkaya, R. (2004). "Bilanço Dışı İşlemlerin Banka Performansına Etkisi: Türk Bankacılık Sektörü Örneği." *Economics, Business and Finance*, *19*(219), 107–122.

Altunbas, Y., Gambacorta, L., & Marques-Ibanez, D. (2009). "Securitisation and the Bank Lending Channel." *European Economic Review*, *53*(8), 996–1009.

Anbar, A. & Alper, D. (2011). "Bankaların Türev Ürün Kullanım Yoğunluğunu Etkileyen Faktörlerin Belirlenmesi." *Journal of Financing and Accounting* (50), 77–94.

Barrell, R. & Davis, E.P. (2008). "The Evolution of the financial Crisis of 2007—8." *National Institute Economic Review*, *206*(1), 5–14.

Berger, A.N. & Bouwman, C.H. (2009). "Bank Liquidity Creation." *Review of Financial Studies*, *22*(9), 3779–3837.

Berger, A.N. & Bouwman, C.H. (2013). "How Does Capital Affect Bank Performance During financial Crises?" *Journal of Financial Economics*, *109*(1), 146–176.

Berger, A.N., Bouwman, C. H., Kick, T., & Schaeck, K. (2016). "Bank Liquidity Creation Following Regulatory Interventions and Capital Support." *Journal of Financial Intermediation*, *26*, 115–141.

Bhattacharya, S., & Thakor, A. V. (1993). Contemporary Banking Theory. *Journal of Financial Intermediation*, *3*(1), 2–50.

Carter, D.A. & Sinkey, J.F. (1998). "The Use of Interest Rate Derivatives by End-Users: The Case of Large Community Banks." *Journal of Financial Services Research*, *14*(1), 17–34.

Charumathi, B. (2009). "On the Determinants of Interest Rate Swap Usage by Indian Banks." In *Proceedings of the World Congress on Engineering*, 2, 1–3.

Coval, J.D. & Thakor, A.V. (2005). "Financial Intermediation as a Beliefs-Bridge between Optimists and Pessimists." *Journal of Financial Economics*, *75*(3), 535–569.

Deep, A. & Schaefer, G.K. (2004). Are Banks Liquidity Transformers?. KSG Working Paper No. RWP04-022. Available at SSRN: https://ssrn.com/abstract=556289 or http://dx.doi.org/10.2139/ssrn.556289

Diamond, D.W. & Rajan, R.G. (2000). "A Theory of Bank Capital." *The Journal of Finance*, *55*(6), 2431–2465.

Diamond, D.W. & Rajan, R.G. (2001). "Banks and Liquidity." *The American Economic Review*, *91*(2), 422–425.

Fungácová, Z., Ariss, R.T., & Weill, L. (2013). "Does Excessive Liquidity Creation Trigger Bank Failures?." *BOFIT Discussion Papers, 2013*(2), 4.

Gorton, G. & Winton, A. (2000). "Liquidity Provision and the Social Cost of Bank Capital." Working Paper.

Gunther, J.W. & Siems, T.F. (2002). "The Likelihood and Extent of Banks' Involvement with Interest Rate Derivatives as End Users." *Research in Finance, 19*, 125–142.

Hackethal, A., Rauch, C., Steffen, S., & Trell, M. (2010). "Determinants of Bank Liquidity Creation." Working Paper.

Hassan, M. & Khasawneh, A. (2009). "The Determinants of Derivatives Activities in US Commercial Banks." Networks *Financial* Institute. Indiana State University. Working Paper.

Horváth, R., Seidler, J., & Weill, L. (2014). "Bank Capital and Liquidity Creation: Granger-Causality Evidence." *Journal of Financial Services Research*, *45*(3), 341–361.

Hundman, K. (1998). "An Analysis of the Determinants of Financial Use by Commercial Banks." *Illinois Wesleyan University*.

Lei, A. C., & Song, Z. (2013). Liquidity Creation and Bank Capital Structure in China. *Global Finance Journal*, *24*(3), 188–202.

Ozsuca, E.A. & Akbostanci, E. (2012). "An Empirical Analysis of the Bank Lending Channel in Turkey." *Middle East Technical University ERC Working Papers in Economics*, *12*(05), 1–33.

Pana, E., Park, J., & Query, T. (2010). "The Impact of Bank Mergers on Liquidity Creation." *Journal of Risk Management in Financial Institutions*, *4*(1), 74–96.

Repullo, R. (2004). "Capital Requirements, Market Power, and Risk-Taking in Banking." *Journal of Financial Intermediation*, *13*(2), 156–182.

Umar, M., Sun, G., & Majeed, M.A. (2017). "Bank Capital and Liquidity Creation: Evidence of Relation from India." *Journal of Asia Business Studies*, *11*(2), 152–166.

Von Thadden, E.L. (2004). "Asymmetric Information, Bank Lending and Implicit Contracts: The Winner's Curse." *Finance Research Letters*, *1*(1), 11–23.

Çiğdem Kurt Cihangir and Seçil Öztürk

7 Green Banking in Turkey

Abstract: Situations like climate change, ecosystem degradation, poverty, etc., have increased the importance of financing resources for green investments. In this chapter, instruments offered by the banking sector to finance green investments in Turkey are evaluated. Moreover, the role and effectiveness of the Turkish banking system in achieving sustainable development are determined.

Keywords: Green Finance, Ecosysytem Degradation, Climate Change, Banking System

1 Introduction

In today's world, policies oriented toward economic growth increase the income and welfare of people on the one hand, while upsetting the ecological balance and leading to climate change on the other. *Climate change* is defined by the United Nations (UN) Framework Convention on Climate Change in a way to cover human impact as "a change of climate which is attributed directly or indirectly to human activity that alters the composition of the global atmosphere and which is in addition to natural climate variability observed over comparable time periods" (DPT, 2000: 1).

It is accepted in scientific circles that the main cause of climate change is the increase in greenhouse gas emissions. The use of fossil fuels (coal, oil, natural gas) to meet increasing energy needs in the process of industrialization, together with the inefficient use of agricultural areas, deforestation, etc., is the most important indicator that this universal problem is of human origin (IPCC, 2013). The UN estimates that the world economy will spend an additional 36–135 billion US dollars annually by 2030 to address environmental sustainability issues, including climate change (Alexander, 2016: 9).

Every day around the world, 41 million trees are cut down, more than 100,000 flights are flown, 1.2 billion vehicles are driven, and 10.5 million tons of coal, 9.5 billion cubic meters of natural gas, and 95 million barrels of oil are burned. As a result, 95 million cubic meters of carbon dioxide are released into the atmosphere every day. Humans cause climate to change 170 times faster than natural forces. The UN Environment Program 2011 report emphasizes that the New Green Deal has three key objectives on a global scale. These are (UNEP, 2011: 17–18):

- To revive the world economy, prevent losses of jobs, create employment opportunities, and protect vulnerable groups;
- To form the economy based on a sustainable and inclusive growth model, to contribute to the eradication of absolute poverty;
- To reduce carbon dependency and to slow down ecosystem degradation.

As the concept of sustainability is predicated on economic, environmental, and social factors, it encompasses the whole society and even the universe, and it contributes to the management of the following risk factors. For example, "extreme (anomalous) weather events" have been ranking first in the classification of global risks over the past two years. It is observed that the economic factors have decreased in importance and the risks arising from climate change have become increasingly important since 2013. Tab. 7.1 shows the top five risk factors threatening the world and their effects. For example, "extreme (anomalous) weather events" have been ranking first in the classification of global risks over the past two years.

While the financial system has a direct and indirect impact on various aspects of sustainable development, it is also affected by environmental degradation (Delphi Int. and Ecologic GMBH, 1997; Peiyuan and Yongda, 2010; Helleiner, 2011; Weber, 2014; Alexander, 2016: 9). Aşıcı (2012) stated that negative ecological impacts, and even the crisis, are caused by excessive consumption, increasing income, and falling prices, and this is directly related to the international financial architecture. Accordingly, in an economy where liberal policies are adopted, the financial sector will grow faster than the real sector and the hot money coming to the country will trigger consumption by increasing the value of the national currency. The asset bubbles (especially assets like houses, stocks, etc.) formed by increasing demand will burst after a while, resulting in negative economic and ecological consequences.

Banking sector is one of the most important sub-sectors of the financial system, and the sector holds over US$ 135 trillion in global assets. In a broad sense, banks are organizations that perform the financial intermediation function in an economy. They have an important role, especially in the capital markets. Banks are the source of credit and investment capital for the economy that can be used to mitigate the adverse effects of environmental sustainability risks while ensuring sustainable economic development (Alexander, 2016: 9). As of the end of 2017, the banking sector constitutes 82 percent of the total size of assets of the financial system. In the first half of 2018, the total assets of the banking sector in Turkey was 3,671,537 million TRY, whereas the GDP was 792,690 million TRY.

Tab. 7.1: Global Risks and Their Effects. Source: World Economic Forum 2018, Global Risks Reports

Top 5 Global Risks in Terms of Likelihood						
	2013	**2014**	**2015**	**2016**	**2017**	**2018**
1st	Severe income disparity	Income disparity	Interstate conflict with regional consequences	Large-scale involuntary migration	Extreme weather events	Extreme weather events
2nd	Chronic fiscal imbalances	Extreme weather Events	Extreme weather Events	Extreme weather events	Large-scale involuntary migration	Natural disasters
3rd	Rising greenhouse gas emissions	Unemployment And underemployment	Failure of national governance	Failure of climate change mitigation and adaptation	Major natural disasters	Cyber attacks
4th	Water supply crises	Climate change	State collapse or crisis	Interstate conflict with regional consequences	Large-scale terrorist attacks	Data fraud or theft
5th	Mismanagement of population aging	Cyber attacks	High structural unemployment or underemployment	Major natural catastrophes	Massive incident of data fraud/theft	Failure of climate change mitigation and adaptation

(*continued on next page*)

Tab. 7.1: (continued)

Top 5 Global Risks in Terms of Impact						
	2013	**2014**	**2015**	**2016**	**2017**	**2018**
1st	Major systemic financial failure	Fiscal crises	Water crises	Failure of climate change mitigation and adaptation	Weapons of mass destruction	Weapons of mass destruction
2nd	Water supply crises	Climate change	Rapid and massive spread of infectious diseases	Weapons of mass destruction	Extreme weather events	Extreme weather events
3rd	Chronic fiscal imbalances	Water crises	Weapons of mass destruction	Water crises	Water crises	Natural disasters
4th	Diffusion of weapons of mass destruction	Unemployment and underemployment	Interstate conflict with regional consequences	Large-scale involuntary migration	Major natural disasters	Failure of climate change mitigation and adaptation
5th	Failure of climate change mitigation and adaptation	Critical information infrastructure breakdown	Failure of climate change mitigation and adaptation	Severe energy price shock	Failure of climate change mitigation and adaptation	Water crises

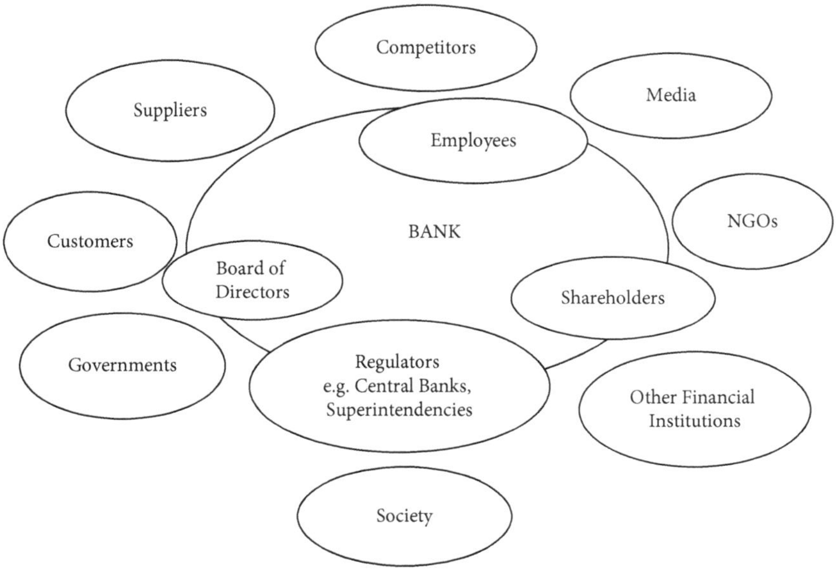

Fig. 7.1: *Bank-related parties (stakeholders) Source: Jeucken, 2001*

Therefore, we can say that the banking sector in Turkey has a significant role in achieving sustainable economic growth and development.

Acting as intermediaries in the financial system and facilitating the channeling of funds, these financial institutions affect all units in the economy and society (see, Fig. 7.1). Not only the financial properties of an investment or a project, but also the non-financial properties will affect the decisions of the parties either on investment or finding funds.

The practices of the World Business Council for Sustainable Development established in 1995 regarding the promotion of social responsibility, the launch of the Equator Principles in 2003, the official entry into force of the Kyoto Protocol in 2005, and the announcement of the UN Sustainable Development Goals (SDGs) in 2015 introduced various international standards and objectives. All these processes increased expectations regarding the role of companies and the intermediaries that provide them with funds in sustainable development. This also led to the transformation of reporting in a way to include the activities performed to achieve these objectives and their consequences. Along with this transformation, corporate reporting began to incorporate sustainability reports, corporate social responsibility reports, and corporate governance principles compliance reports, in addition to the financial reports. Eventually, the concept of integrated reporting was introduced.

This chapter aims to explain the green economy, sustainable finance and green banking concepts, to identify the risks posed by climate change to banks, the most effective financial intermediaries for achieving sustainable finance, and to examine Turkey from the perspective of green banking. To this end, we first addressed the concepts of green economy and sustainable finance, and then identified the risks posed by climate change to the banking sector. Finally, we examined the green banking practices in Turkey.

2 Green Economy and Sustainable Finance

The term *sustainability* emerged after the 1970s, when the environmental and social problems caused by the economic growth and development achieved through industrialization were addressed. As part of addressing global environmental issues, the UN launched the United Nations Environment Program (UNEP) at the Conference on the Human Environment in 1972 (www.mfa.gov.tr), and the concept of sustainable development was first used by UNEP in the World Conservation Strategy in 1980 (Bozlağan, 2005: 1018). In 1982, the UN General Assembly adopted the World Charter for Nature. The World Charter for Nature drew attention to the relationship between nature and man and the importance of ecosystem (Wood, 1985). In 1987, sustainable development was defined as "development that meets the needs of the present without compromising the ability of future generations to meet their own needs" in the Brundtland Report (Our Common Future) of the UN World Commission on Environment and Development (WCED) (UN World Commission on Environment and Development, 1991). The Brundtland Report drew attention to the relationship between development and environment. The report addressed such global issues as population and human resources, food security, ecosystems, energy, industry, and urbanization and led policy makers to cooperate in resolving economic, environmental and social problems. At the UN Conference on Environment and Development (UNCED) held in Rio in 1992, Agenda 21 and the Rio Declaration containing twenty-seven principles on the objectives for sustainable development in the Brundtland Commission were adopted. Thus, the issues highlighted by the Brundtland Report were addressed within an international institutional framework. Agenda 21 is an action plan for sustainable development, which covers four main topic areas: social and economic dimensions; conservation and management of resources; the role of major groups in the implementation of sustainable development agenda; and the means of implementation which includes

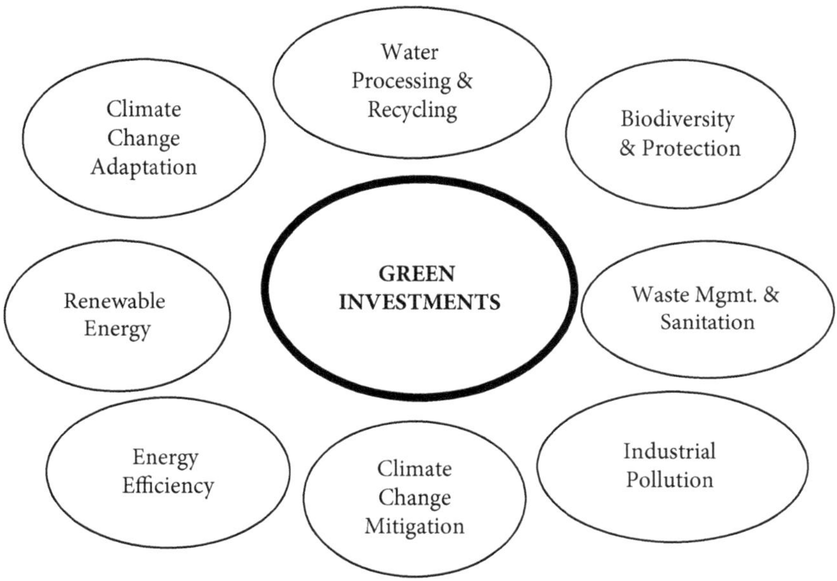

Fig. 7.2: Green investment types. *Source: Peralta, 2016*

technology transfer, finance, science, education, and public knowledge (UNEP, 2007: 6–8).

The issue of green economy was discussed at the UN Conference on Sustainable Development (Rio + 20) held in Rio de Janeiro on June 20–22, 2012. Green economy was defined by UNEP as a system results in improved human well-being and social equity, while significantly reducing environmental risks and ecological scarcities (UNEP, 2010). The aim of the green economy transition is to protect and improve the environmental and social structure together with economic growth and increased investments. Thus, it is aimed to reduce or even eliminate the environmental problems known as negative externalities (Özçağ and Hotunluoğlu, 2015: 314).

Green economy refers to a low-carbon, resource efficient, and socially inclusive economic order, where income and employment are driven by public and private investments that reduce carbon emissions and pollution, enhance energy and resource efficiency, and prevent the loss of biodiversity and ecosystem services. While increasing economic growth and investment, environmental and social criteria must be included in public and private investment conditions in order to increase environmental quality and social inclusion simultaneously.

Besides, when measuring the key indicators of economic performance (such as growth of GDP), pollution, resource depletion, ecosystem deterioration, and distribution of natural capital losses should be taken into account (UNEP, 2011: 16). Private sector investments in low-emission technologies should be encouraged.

At the World Economic Forum held in Davos (2018), business and political leaders agreed that overheating due to climate change is the biggest threat facing the world. At the same Forum, the World Bank's Director for Climate Change stated that the risks arising from climate change which had become increasingly worrisome for companies and governments also brought some opportunities. There is a 23 trillion USD investment opportunity for developing countries in order to realize their promises within the scope of the Paris Agreement. The biggest opportunity created by the introduction of low carbon economy for banks is to provide financing for renewable energy, energy efficiency technologies, and technologies for reducing greenhouse gas absorption. In addition, making transactions or providing consultancy in the transaction markets and weather derivative markets or providing microcredits may also be considered as an opportunity (Alper and Anbar, 2008).

Green project incorporates the concepts such as investment, renewable energy, energy efficiency, pollution prevention and control, sustainable management of natural resources, biodiversity conservation, clean transportation, and sustainable water management (Jun et al., 2016: 13). From this point of view, the financing of investments that contribute to the sustainable environmental development can be defined as *green finance*. As seen in Fig. 7.2, projects or investments contributing to decreasing air, water, and soil pollution; reducing greenhouse gas emissions; increasing energy efficiency during the use of natural resources; mitigating climate change, etc., may be considered within the scope of green investment.

Bahl (2012) defined *green banking* as a type of banking that enables the implementation of techniques which helps reducing internal carbon footprint and external carbon emissions in a selected area. Loans, which are one of the basic financial instruments for the banking sector, are considered as green loans if they are provided by taking account of the above-mentioned environmental and social sensitivity and the specified principles. As seen in Fig. 7.3, after the provision of green loans by banks, monitoring of the investment-project and review of the compliance with the principles still continues.

Green banks develop and finance clean energy projects with the financial instruments/products they offer, and they enable private capital to benefit from public capital through their intermediary function. In this way, they encourage investments/projects that are necessary for economic development. Banks in

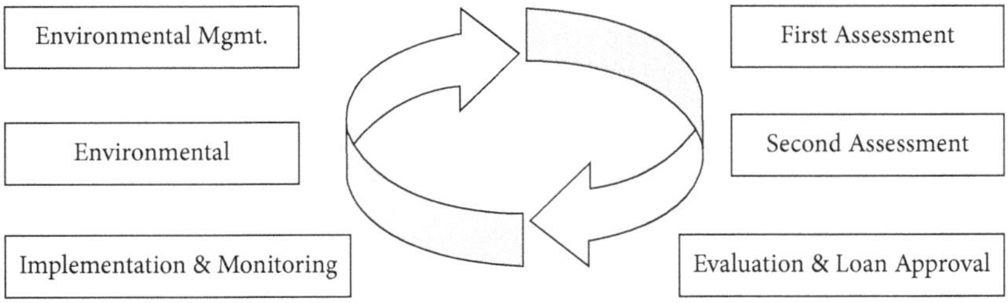

Fig. 7.3: Green loan cycle. *Source: Peralta, 2016*

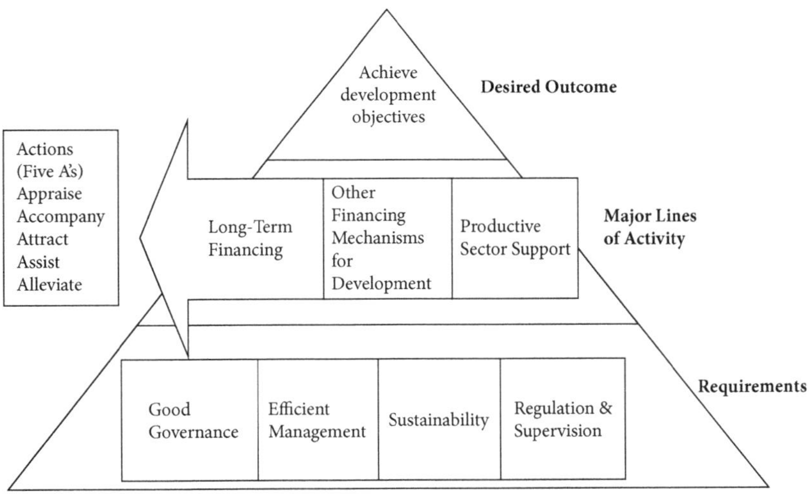

Fig. 7.4: A pyramid of national development banking activity. *Source: United Nations, (2005: 11)*

practice are classified as deposit (trade) banks and development and investment banks. The main function of deposit banks is to collect deposits and create deposit money. Development and investment banks have no authority to collect deposits, and they have functions such as specialization in investment loans, providing loans for projects, long-term financing, etc. Fig. 7.4 shows systematically that investment banks can achieve sustainable development and inclusive growth by providing funds for investments and projects.

National development banks contribute to sustainable growth with their actions known as Five A's (United Nations, 2005: 11):

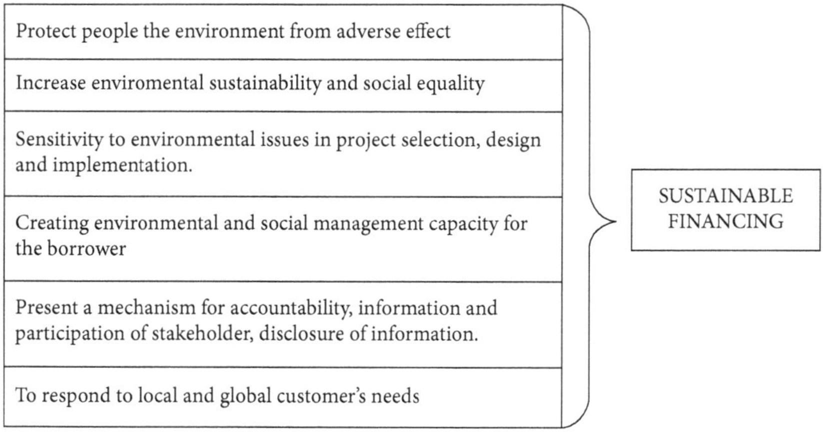

Fig. 7.5: Objectives of environmental and social protection measures. *Source: Kiss, 2011*

- Appraising—Appraising the economic and social development impacts of projects looking for financing;
- Accompanying—Accompanying investors over the long run through long-term loans.
- Attracting —Attracting investors by playing a role of catalyst for financing operations.
- Assisting —Assisting sectors that are essential to growth through technical assistance.
- Alleviating—Alleviating the negative impact of financial crises by offering loans even during downturns and by pooling efforts with regional financing institutions.

Sustainable finance is defined as increasing the number of companies aiming to be a good "corporate citizen" and implementing the economic, environmental, social principles, together with those who finance them (Kiss, 2011). First, projects or investments that comply with environmental and social principles are determined and then they are financed. Fig. 7.5 shows the objectives of environmental and social risk management on the basis of sustainability for financing organizations.

Jeucken (2001: 71) defined *sustainable banking* as the banks' act of adapting the key objectives and philosophy of sustainable development and adjusting their activities to these principles. He argued that the process of achieving sustainability by banks takes place in four phases: defensive, preventative, offensive, and sustainable banking. The phase of defensive banking: a bank's only goal is to increase its growth and profitability without making any contribution to sustainable development. Banks that take up cost savings by considering sustainability during the phase of preventative banking perform all of their activities (internal and external) by considering sustainability during the phase of offensive banking.

According to the G20 Green Finance Study Group (2016), green finance involves the effective management of environmental risks. Sustainable banking can be achieved by incorporating two fundamental structures into the corporate process. These are (Kurt, 2009: 82):

- Integration of environmental, social responsibility, and corporate governance issues into the banking operations; adoption and implementation of them by all employees; performing banking activities with minimal impact on the environment; supporting sustainable business processes approach through social responsibility projects; and
- Making environmental and social responsibility a corporate philosophy; adoption of corporate governance; incorporating it into the main business lines and reflecting it on corporate culture, policy, and strategy.

3 Risks of Climate Change to the Banking Sector

Banks are exposed to certain risks as a result of green banking activities. Some of these risks directly affect them, while some other affect indirectly.

Physical Risk is the impact of the situations that may arise due to climate change on banks' own assets. *Activity Risk* is the possibility that extreme (anomalous) weather events may cause disruption and/or interruption of the activities of banks (due to reasons such as power outages, rupture of the lines of communication, Internet disconnection) (Alper and Anbar, 2008).

Reputational Risk is the risk arising from financing non-environmentally sensitive investments and is of greater importance than material risks. If the owner of a financed investment and project does not take the necessary environmental precautions, the bank financing this investment is exposed to reputational risk, which is very difficult to define and measure indirectly. *Operational Risk* is the risk of loss arising from inadequate or unsuccessful assessment of the effects of climate change. Operational risk consists of errors in human processes and decisions, system errors caused by software-hardware, errors in the process or workflow, and malicious use of the services provided. Therefore, it is a type of risk valid for all activities of a bank. *Legal Risk* is the possibility that the legal regulations related to climate change may increase the liabilities of the banks or affect the markets negatively.

Credit Risk is the possibility that the persons or companies borrowing loans and funds from banks may fail/not be able to fulfill their obligations due to the additional costs arising from climate change and/or related legal regulations. Credit risk especially increases for loans provided to sectors such as transportation, energy, construction, and tourism, which are more affected by climate change. The credit risk which indirectly affects the bank is vulnerable to the reputation and brand of the company that uses the funds, as well as the fluctuation in its revenues. Together with the legal arrangements, increased environmental awareness in the society and increased effectiveness of the non-governmental organizations are also risk factors that will reflect on the credit risks banks are exposed to, since they will require businesses to regulate their activities according to such awareness.

Market Risk is the risk arising from uncertainty of input and/or output prices due to climate change. This type of risk arises from increases in input prices or decreases in output prices. Among the taxes collected within the scope of green economy, motor vehicles tax, value added tax, excise tax, and tax-like fees imposed on greenhouse gas emissions are some of the market risk factors. For example, an increase in electricity prices due to the limitation on greenhouse gas emission might adversely affect the credit quality of businesses operating in sectors where the cost of electricity has a significant share in total input costs (Ecosecurities, 2006: 64). Banks providing loans to businesses that are subject to high market risk due to climate change are also indirectly exposed to market risk.

Environmental and Social Risk is the type of risk arising from the factors that threaten occupational health and safety when the social perspective, which is complementary to environmental issues, is taken into consideration. These risks can be listed as follows (Kurt, 2009):

- The company may suspend making investment and/or manufacturing due to environmental and social impacts; interruption in the investment process due to environmental problems that arise during the investment period;
- A high number of occupational accidents due to the insufficiency or lack of measures taken during the investment and/or operation period;
- The negative public opinion on the planned investment; failure to receiving opinions of local people while making the investment decision, and the existence of contradictory grounds;
- The facility that fulfills the requirements during the investment period starts to harm the environment after the commissioning (releasing wastewater to the natural environment without treatment or releasing hazardous and toxic wastes improperly and inattentively to the environment and even contradicting with the legal authorities with regard to these matters);

- Commencing a financed project before meeting the legal environmental requirements (unfinished Environmental Impact Assessment; making the local people suffer, etc.);
- Causing harm to the environment (i.e., vegetation, biodiversity, surface and underground resources) through investment.

The impacts of climate change and the related environmental liabilities on the banking sector vary depending on the sector provided with credit and the credit period. Extension of the credit period increases the risks and this is reflected in the costs. If the loan has a maturity of more than five years, risks arising from climate change will increase both directly (such as reputational risk, technology risk, legal risk) and indirectly (credit and market risk). For loans with a maturity of less than five years, banks will be affected to a lesser extent since it will be possible to manage these risks and to adjust to them. Similarly, if the sector provided with a loan is affected more than the regulations and practices related to climate change, the related risks that affect the banks will increase. For example, construction, energy, or transportation sectors are the sectors most affected by climate change; therefore, providing loans to these sectors also increase the credit risk of banks.

Fig. 7.6 shows how the risks arising from climate change are reflected in the operating system of a trade bank (deposit bank). Among the risk factors arising from climate change, reputational risk, legal risk, and credit risk are the ones mostly emphasized. Given the fact that transforming deposits into loans is a performance indicator, legal risk and reputational risk for the sake of collecting more deposits directly affect the bank's climate-related risk. The credit risk, i.e., default risk, may arise when the collected deposits are made available to those who request funds as loans.

4 Green Banking Activities in Turkey

As of 2017, the banking sector constitutes 82 percent of the total size of assets of the financial system which amount to 3987 billion TL. We may say that banks are the most important part of the financial system in Turkey. As of June 2018, there are fifty-two banks in Turkey. Of these, thirty-four are deposit banks, thirteen are development and investment banks, and five are participation banks (TBB). In Turkey, banks have an important role in terms of sustainable finance.

Combatting Climate Change and the finance Sector was the main theme of the 5th Forum on Sustainable Development held on September 29, 2017. Such voluntary organizations show that the Turkish business and financial sector has increased awareness of sustainability. Within the scope of "sustainable

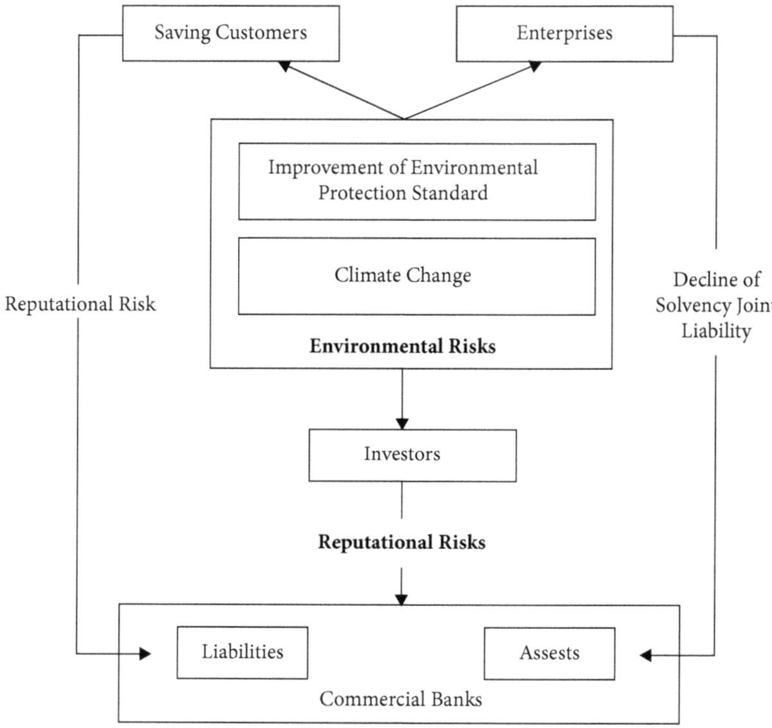

Fig. 7.6: Risks for trade banks caused by environmental costs. *Source: ICBC, 2016: 10*

development" banking, these organizations carry out such activities as financing energy efficiency, taking into account environmental and social impacts during lending processes, financial inclusion, financing sustainable agriculture, supporting women entrepreneurship, etc. (SKD, 2017).

Seven banks operating in Turkey[1] signed the UN Global Compact and accepted to make environmental and social risk assessment a part of the loan assessment process and include it in our relevant policies while financing projects worth of US$ 50 million and above.

Turkey Sustainable Energy financing Facility (TurSEFF) is a program created to provide funds for Sustainable Energy and Resource Efficiency investments

1 Akbank, Garanti Bankası, ING Bank, Türkiye İş Bankası, Yapı Kredi Bankası, and Türkiye Sinai ve Kalkınma Bankası.

that will be made by the public and private sector. The project was developed by the European Bank for Reconstruction and Development (EBRD). It has been supported by the EU since 2010. In total, the amount of carbon dioxide emissions reduced annually equals the amount of carbon dioxide emitted by approximately 840,000 cars per year. In Turkey, the total energy savings achieved is almost equal to the amount of electricity consumed by 3.4 million people every year. In July 2018, TurSEFF provided a total of EUR 554 million for 1014 projects through a leasing company and two trade banks contracted. The credit limit for financing these investments/projects is determined by the European Bank for Reconstruction and Development and loans are provided through common local banks. Therefore, the common bank's own criteria and credit rating process are valid during the lending process.

The Industrial and Development Bank of Turkey has been the first bank to prepare an integrated report of the finance sector with the 2016 Integrated Report which was prepared in line with the 2016 activity results. It has also been the first Turkish bank to issue green bonds and subordinated bonds in international markets. It aims to finance investments and projects that produce solutions to climate change with the funds obtained from issuing bonds. With the aim of transition to low-carbon economy, the bank is financing for projects especially in the fields of renewable energy, resource efficiency, combating climate change, and equal opportunities. The Industrial Development Bank of Turkey (TSKB) provided funds to more than 210 clean energy projects as of July 2018, thus reducing Turkey's annual carbon dioxide emissions by 13 million tons. Investment loans with the theme of sustainability account for approximately 60 percent of the total loan portfolio. TSKB also set a new theme for lending to ensure equal opportunities which is one of the objectives of sustainable development. Accordingly, support has been provided to investments made by companies that offer women friendly working environments. Supported by the Turkish Educational Foundation (TEV), this project has been transformed into a social responsibility project with the help of the project titled "From Education to Production." The loan with total amount of USD 10 million borrowed by Zorlu Energy from the Garanti Bank in July 2018 to meet its operational capital needs was Turkey's first "Green Loan" agreement. Within the scope of this loan, sustainability performance of Zorlu Energy in the environmental, social, and governance areas will be scored on a yearly basis by an international sustainability rating agency, i.e., Vigeo-Eiris. According to the sustainability score attained, the pricing of the margin will be adjusted accordingly each year.

Investments with an aim to ensure sustainable development in Turkey are financed with funds by the finance institutions such as the World Bank, the European Investment Bank, Council of Europe Development Bank, the Reconstruction Credit Institute - KfW, French Development Agency, the European Bank for Reconstruction and Development, and the Japanese Development Bank. Private institutions and semi-private public institutions operating in Turkey such as private banks, the Development Bank of Turkey, the Industrial Development Bank of Turkey, Turk Eximbank, the Turkish Sustainable Energy Financing Facility, the Small and Medium Enterprises Development Organization (KOSGEB), and the Ministry of Tourism act as intermediaries and undertake a risk in granting such loans to investment projects.

The value created by companies and their contribution to the society and the environment along with their financial performances are also important for the stakeholders in order to identify their sustainability risk. The Sustainable Development Association developed a method to implement the Reporting Matters method implemented by the World Business Council for Sustainable Development (WBCSD) since 2013 in Turkey. With the method, sustainability reports are assessed on three criteria: principles (principles of good reporting); content (attention paid to the report content); and experience (experience of those reading the report; accessibility; and comprehensibility). According to the Reporting Matters 2017 assessment of Turkey, reporting is most common in the financial sector (www.skdturkiye.org). In Turkey, there are various banks incorporating sustainability policies in their corporate reports.

Conclusions

Human-induced climate change is not a national or regional problem, but a problem of all. All individual or institutional contributions are valuable for a world to live in and to be passed on to future generations. Banks may be said to be the most effective financial intermediaries in promoting sustainable finance. The multiplier effect of banks is very large; therefore, they have the power to affect every sector. Every step on the road to sustainable development will be successful only when adopted as a business model, not just as a volunteering principle. Especially while providing loans, thinking long-term, developing and implementing a business plan, and reporting the results constitute the basis for green banking activities.

We may say that the banking sector in Turkey is adapting to international changes and innovations. Despite Turkey's late involvement in the cooperation mechanisms and the implementation of international principles established for the management of risks arising from climate change such as low-carbon economy, clean energy, and so forth, the country closed the gap in terms of product range offered. Green banking products provided by deposit banks and investment-development banks are different. Green mortgage loans, green vehicle loans, and green credit cards are the products offered by deposit banks. While investment banks are issuing green bonds, on the other hand they provide financing for environment-friendly natural capital investments. As a result, the Turkish banking sector as a whole develops financing opportunities for financing investments and projects that will support economic development on the basis of sustainability.

References

Alexander, K. (2016), Greening Banking Policy, G20 Green Finance Study Group (GFSG) http://unepinquiry.org (25.07.2018).

Alper, A. & Anbar, A. (2008), "İklim Değişikliğinin Finansal Hizmet Sektörüne Etkileri,", *Electronik Journal of Social Sciences*, 7(23):223–253.

Aşıcı, A.A. (2012), "Sürdürülebilir Yaşam İçin Bir Dönüşüm Önerisi: Yeşil Yeni Düzen," Aşıcı, A.A. ve Şahin, Ü. (eds.), Yeşil Ekonomi içinde (105–132).

Bahl, S. (2012), "Green Bankıng—The New Strategıc Imperatıve," *Asian Journal of Research in Business Economics and Management*, 2(2):176–185.

Birleşmiş Milletler Dünya Çevre ve Kalkınma Komisyonu (1991), Ortak Geleceğimiz, Belkıs Çırakçı (çev.), Ankara: Turkey Foundation of Environmental İssues Edition.

Birleşmiş Milletler Çevre Programı (2018), http://www.mfa.gov.tr (08.08.2018).

Bozlağan, R. (2005), "Sürdürülebilir Gelişme Düşüncesinin Tarihsel Arka Planı," *Social Politics Conference Journal*, 50:1011–1028.

Delphi International Ltd, Ecologic GMBH (1997), The Role of Financial Institutions in Achieving Sustainable Development. http://ec.europa.eu (11.08.2018).

DPT (2000), "İklim Değişikliği Özel Ihtisas Komisyonu Raporu (Ankara: Sekizinci Beş Yıllık Kalkınma Planı (2001–2005)," SPO Edition: 2532.

Ecosecurities(2006), Global Climate Change: Risk to Bank Loans. http://www.unepfi.org/fileadmin/documents/global_climate_change_risk.pdf (10.08.2018).

G20 Green finance Study Group (2016), http://unepinquiry.org (05.08.2018).

Helleiner, E. (2011), "Introduction: The Greening of Global Financial Markets?," *Global Environmental Politics*, 11(2):51–53.

Hükümetlerarası İklim Değişikliği Paneli (IPCC) (2013), http://www.ipcc.ch (05.08.2018).

ICBC (2016), "Impact of Environmental Effects on Credit Risk of Commercial Banks," (Industrial and Commercial Bank of China) http://www.greenfinance.org.cn (01.08.2018).

Jeucken, M. (2001), *Sustainable Finance and Banking: The Financial Sector and the Future of the Planet* London: Earthscan Publication LTD.

Jun, M., Christopher, K., Sean, K., & Nicholas, P. (2016), "Green Bonds: Country Experiences, Barrıers and Options," *G20 Green Finance Study Group Report*, http://unepinquiry.org (07.08.2018).

Kiss, A. (2011), "Dünya Bankası Çevresel ve Sosyal Koruma Önlemleri Politikaları," Finansal Aracılara ve Uygulayıcı Kuruluşlara Yönelik Eğitim Çalıştayı. https://slideplayer.biz.tr/slide/2805835/ (05.08.2018).

Kurt, H. (2009), "Finansal Kurumlar için Çevre ve Sürdürülebilir Bankacılık," Bankacılar, 70:70–81.

Özçağ, M. & Hotunluoğlu, H. (2015), "Kalkınma Anlayışında Yeni Bir Boyut: Yeşil Ekonomi," Celal Bayar University, *Journal of Social Sciences*, 13(2):303–324.

Peiyuan, G. & Yongda, Y. (2010), "Sustainable Finance in China: The Progress and the Future." http://opim.wharton.upenn.edu/gc/philadelphia/abstract/Guo.pdf (E.T.07.08.2018).

Peralta, B.O., (2016), "Asian Development Bank Introduction to Green finance & Credit Cycle," Association of Development financing Institutions in Asia and the Pacific Green Energy Finance Workshop ACEF.

Sürdürülebilir Kalkınma Derneği (2017), http://www.skdturkiye.org/files/yayin/skd_turkiye_repo rtingmatters.pdf (28.07.2018).

TBB, Association of Banks of Turkey. https://www.tbb.org.tr (02.08.2018).

Turkey Sustainable Energy Financing Program, http://www.turseff.org (11.08.2018).

United Nations (2005) "Rethinking the Role of National Banks," United Nations Department of Economic and Social Affairs, Financing for Development Office, Ad Hoc Expert Group Meeting "Rethinking the Role of National Development Banks." http://www.un.org/ (10.08.2018).

UNEP (2007), "Global Environment Outlook, Environment for Development (GEO-4)," Nairobi, Kenya.

UNEP (2010), "Green Economy Developing Countries Success Stories," Geneva.

UNEP (2011), "Towards A Green Economy: Pathways to Sustainable Development and Poverty Eradication— A Synthesis for Policy Makers," France.

Weber, O. (2014), "The Financial Sector's Impact on Sustainable Development," *Journal of Sustainable Finance & Investment*, *4*(1): 1–8.

Wood, H.W. (1985), "The United Nations World Charter for Nature: The Developing Nations Initiative to Establish Protections for the Environment," *Ecology Law Quarterly*, *4*(12): 977–996.

World Economic Forum (2018), "Global Risks Reports." http://www3.weforum.org/docs/WEF_GRR18_Report.pdf (10.08.2018).

Özer Yılmaz

8 The Relationship Marketing Approach to Creating Competitive Advantage in the Banking Sector[1]

Abstract: Under the fierce competition environment in the banking sector, banks have to make difference in order to gain new customers and provide customer retention. One of the fundamental strategies on the point of creating difference is relationship marketing activities. In this chapter, general framework of relationship marketing activities is reviewed and the strategical importance from the viewpoint of banks is discussed.

Keywords: Relationship Marketing, Transactional Marketing, Banking Sector, Competition

1 Introduction

The relationship marketing approach that emerged in 1980s has become more popular in many sectors, especially the service sector, due to the increased competition. We can say that the banking sector is one of the sectors in need of relationship marketing activities in Turkey.

There were twenty-nine deposit banks with private and public capital and five foreign-capital banks with branches in Turkey in July 2018. If we count private financial institutions, the number of financial institutions competing for deposits approaches forty (TBB, 2018-a). These banks aim to optimize their profitability with their 10,393 branches and 188,564 employees (TBB, 2018-b).

Banks need to create differences in order to gain customers and retain the available customers in the intense competition within the sector. At this point, banks aim to attract customer demands by offering financial advantages as in many goods and services. However, the financial advantages that can be offered to customers can be limited due to regulations made by auditing and regulatory institutions related to the banking sector, and this makes it harder to achieve desired results. At this point, it is a necessity for banks to resort to relationship marketing activities that prioritize social and structural relationships with customers during their differentiation efforts.

1 This chapter is reproduced from the doctoral dissertation written in 2014.

Thanks to relationship marketing, banks that establish relationships with customers, protect and improve these relationships, will make their available customers highly satisfied in the short term. Highly satisfied customers will both make more frequent and high amount transactions with the bank and enable the bank to reach new customers without any costs by giving a positive reference about the bank in the medium and long terms. This will make a significant contribution to achievement of the desired profitability level by the bank.

This chapter firstly analyzes the relationship marketing approach, and then discusses the bonding strategies banks can use within the scope of relationship marketing. Some of the studies on the efficiency of the relationship marketing activities in the banking sector are analyzed, and information is provided about their results in the last part.

2 The Relationship Marketing Concept and Its Differences from Transactional Marketing

Relationship marketing that originated from industrial marketing and service marketing dates back to the early years of the medieval age. Merchants at that time knew the importance of maintaining relationships with customers. However, the beginning of industrialization and the resulting increase in mass production caused businesses to grow, decreased the relationship between buyers and sellers, and transformed customers from being a strong party to a relationship to being a market statistic most of the time due to the demand surplus in the market (Bühler and Nufer, 2010: 18–19). But this mentality started to be questioned after the second half of the 1900s. Companies entered an intensive competition environment due to globalization, and they started to think that long-term customer relations enabled more profitable sales than short-term gains. This created the need for a new marketing approach based on relationships instead of the traditional marketing approach.

The popularity of the relationship marketing approach based on the "symbiotic marketing" concept developed by Adler in 1966 in line with this need (Kim, Han, and Lee, 2001) increased mostly because of the increased raw material costs resulting from stagflation[2] caused by the energy crisis that took place in the late 1970s, the rapid development of service marketing, and adoption of the supplier selection logic aimed at decreasing the number of suppliers in order to increase the quality level with lower costs (Sheth, 2002: 590).

2 Stagflation: A macroeconomic situation in which economic recession and inflation take place at the same time.

There are many definitions of the relationship marketing approach that started to be analyzed frequently in the marketing literature as of the 1980s and 1990s (Malhorta, Uslay, and Bayraktar, 2016: 11). One of the outstanding definitions was made by Berry and Parasuraman (1991). The authors defined *relationship marketing* as "establishing and maintaining relationships with customers." Morgan and Hunt (1994) defined relationship marketing as all marketing activities aimed at establishing, maintaining, and improving a successful exchange of relationships. Gummesson (1994) defined relationship marketing as activities that ensure the continuity of the business profitability by maintaining a mutual relationship between the business and the customers. Harker (1999) analyzed many different definitions of relationship marketing and developed a more comprehensive definition based on these definitions. According to the author, relationship marketing refers to all activities related to the processes of creating, developing, and maintaining a common commitment, interactive and profitable change with a business partner.

Although the literature contains various studies making different definitions of relationship marketing (e.g., Sheth and Parvatiyar, 1995; Grönroos, 1996, etc.), all definitions have a common ground. According to this common ground, relationship marketing is a marketing approach that develops permanent relationships with customers and focuses on increasing business profitability, thanks to available customers. Therefore, relationship marketing is regarded as a development that is highly different from transactional marketing that was the dominant marketing approach in the past and aims to reach a certain amount of sales (Tomer, 1998: 1). Furthermore, since the purpose of transactional marketing is to maximize transactions, the customer's purchase history is not given importance and establishing connections between the customer's behaviors in different situations is not important. In the case of relationship marketing, the situation is reversed, and the long-term relationship becomes important (Güven, 2007: 31–32).

Another important difference between relationship marketing and transactional marketing is related to the production mentality. Activities mostly rely on the marketing mix (4P) and non-personalized relations in transactional marketing (Grönroos, 1996: 8) and therefore the mass production mentality is adopted. However, there is an interactive approach that integrates the point of view of the seller and the buyer in the relationship marketing (Jüttner and Wehrili, 1994: 59), and therefore it is not wrong to say that the production mentality of mass individualization has been adopted.

As a result, transactional marketing has not attached importance to relationships and establishing relationship, and it has been seen as an independent organism that always maneuvers to achieve the best conditions. Businesses have not hesitated to pass from one supplier or distributor to another in case of an advantage, and they have spent most of their energy to gain new customers assuming that they could normally retain their available customers. Relationship marketing entered the marketing science as an innovative marketing approach that cooperates, accepts the importance of various parties (suppliers, employees, distributors, dealers, etc.), and is based more on listening and learning than talking (Kotler, 2011: 54). Today this has become an approach that is adopted and used in almost all service sectors such as banking, tourism, and transportation.

3 Goals of Relationship Marketing

There are many goals of relationship marketing that helps businesses to establish and improve relationships with customers and other partners (Wang, 2007: 203) and aims to ensure profitability of the parties as a result of this relationship (Kanagal, 2009: 3). All these goals have an ultimate goal in the long term: increasing sales (Takala and Uusidalo, 1996: 46). On the other hand, within the scope of this main objective, it is possible to gather other goals of relationship marketing under the following headings (Ballntyne, 2000, 274–275; Berry, 2002: 60; Selvi, 2007, 34; İlban, Doğdubay, and Gürsoy, 2009: 123):

- **Retaining customers and gaining new ones:** One of the main objectives of relationship marketing is to retain customers. Thanks to relationship marketing, businesses aim to develop good relations with available customers, thus benefiting from the tendencies of the more loyal customers who buy and pay more (Steffes, 2005: 67). Businesses that increase their marketing efficiency and productivity thanks to retained customers can create more value for both themselves and their customers (Rao and Abagaz, 2017: 98).
- **Ensuring customer satisfaction:** Another important objective of relationship marketing is customer satisfaction. Satisfaction refers to the feeling of getting more benefits than expected. Satisfaction is considered to be a determining factor of both relationship quality and perceived service quality. As satisfaction of customer needs is at the heart of a relationship, customers who are satisfied with the services offered by a business will have good relations with this business (Selvi, 2007: 39), and these customers will probably choose the same business with high service quality as they want the same satisfaction in case of a future need. In addition, the customers will be very likely to recommend this business to other people (Keith, Lee, and Lee, 2004: 15).

- **Establishing partnerships:** Relationship marketing includes a partnership between the producer and customer that is made with a commitment to do business with each other. As a result of this partnership, the parties do not turn to alternative competitive presentations in order to make short-term profits. Focusing on relationships that create value, this approach has played an integrative role in creating an interaction between the parties with close economic, emotional, and structural ties (Tomer, 1998: 208). This partnership paves the way for the parties to become dependent on each other and to cooperate with each other without conflict rather than being independent while making decisions (choices) (Sheth and Parvatiyar, 1995: 399–400).
- **Increasing profitability—reducing costs:** Businesses can achieve higher profitability, better communication, and a more efficient business plan thanks to highly satisfied customers (Priluck, 2003: 37). When a business can take its relationship with customers to long term, it can increase its revenue as a result of the increase in customer satisfaction (*Profit from Cross Sales*). Based on this assumption, it can be thought that the increasing customer confidence in the company will increase the frequency and intensity of the purchases. Another positive impact of the relationship established with customers is the positive word of mouth communication by the satisfied customer (*Reference Effect*). People who are not customers of the business will evaluate it by taking this message into account (Bühler and Nufer, 2010: 25–26).
- **Developing long-term customer relations by determining customer demands:** It is a necessity for businesses to learn customer demands and needs in various ways and to ensure customer satisfaction and loyalty by offering goods and services in line with customer expectations based on such information. This necessity compels businesses to implement different strategies than their rivals, adopt a customer-rival oriented culture, and establish a dynamic learning process (Öztürk, 2009: 25).

Businesses that can determine the needs of their target group in a short period of time, thanks to relationships formed with relationship marketing, will have an important competitive advantage in satisfying the needs in the best possible way.

4 Bonds and Bonding Strategies in Relationship Marketing

Bonds are the main concept representing the size of the relationship between the buyer and the seller in relationship marketing. Basically, bonds are output obstacles that connect the customers to the business and cause them to maintain the relationship (Lima and Fernandes, 2015: 328). There are three main types of bonds in relationship marketing. The first one is financial bond using tactics such as price discounts or rewards for frequent purchases that will lead customers towards forming relationships in the short term (Lee et al., 2015: 831). At this stage, the product cost is reduced for the customer, and the customer is financially rewarded for maintaining the relationship as opposed to the rivals (Nathve and Nukherjee, 2012: 169). Social bonds constitute the second stage of relationship bonds. At this stage, businesses try to make clients loyal by offering them personalized goods or services (Huang et al., 2014: 186). It is aimed to form personal bonds such as sincerity, personal recognition, friendship, and harmony, etc., with customers (Lima and Fernandes, 2015: 328). Structural bonds that constitute the final stage of relational bonds aim to create a structure where the business can share information and processes with customers (Hossain, Kibria, and Farhana, 2017: 366). At this stage, the business starts to provide its customers with benefits that cannot be easily offered by other businesses (Nath and Nukherjee, 2012: 169), thus decreasing the possibility of the customers abandoning the business.

As mentioned above, businesses carrying out relationship marketing activities need to establish financial, social, and structural bonds in order to gain customers. As establishing this bond accurately will make it easier for the business to retain its customers, it will create a competitive advantage. The strategies a business can use to form a strong relationship with its customers are divided into two categories: core strategies and supporting strategies.

4.1 Core Relationship Marketing Strategies

It is highly important for a business to develop the right strategies during the planning stage in order to form relationship bonds. As Tomer (1998, 209–210) suggests, in order to strategically maintain relationship marketing

1) There must be comprehensive communication between the customer and the sales person of the business,
2) It must be possible to share the culture and values of the business, and
3) Financial integration must be ensured between the parties.

There are several possible relationship marketing strategies that can be included in the marketing plan to be developed in order to meet these conditions. These are (Berry, 2002: 62):

1) Core Service Strategy: The basic service strategy that is the key strategy of relationship marketing includes a basic service design and marketing to establish customer relations. An ideal core service will reinforce the company's ability to sell additional services and gain new customers over time due to its versatility and ability to meet needs (Berry, 2002, 62–63).

2) Relationship Customization: The business encourages its customers to remain as the customers of the same supplier instead of turning to other suppliers thanks to the relationship customization strategy that includes offering products adapted to known qualities of certain customers. The number of possibilities for adapting the relationship will increase significantly especially when individual service skills and skills related to the electronic data process are combined. Furthermore, this strategy is an important strategy for improving relationships, and it helps the business offer different services than rival businesses (Selvi, 2007: 159).
3) Service Augmentation: Basically, increasing services refers to production of extra innovative services by businesses in order to be different from others (rivals) (Terzioğlu, 2008: 73). Businesses need to develop new additional services that cannot be found easily at their rivals and can be important for customers.
4) Relationship Pricing: Berry and Yadov explained the relationship pricing concept as a life philosophy toward development of long-term and profitable customer relations by a business (Reported in Arguslidis and Indounis, 2010: 461). Relationship pricing can be defined as offering the best prices for best customers (Terzioğlu, 2008: 73). Price discounts offered to customers in a relationship with the business can be offered in the form of faster services and individualized additional services. If a business benefits customers through special treatment in various ways, this will increase the loyalty and commitment of customers. Benefits obtained from special treatment can be expected to affect customer satisfaction (Selvi, 2007: 161).
5) Internal Marketing: *Internal marketing* refers to organizing company activities in a way that ensures satisfaction of internal and external customers, employing and retaining talented personnel in order to achieve the ultimate company mission, and satisfying external customers by using all employees of the company, internal communication, and other motivating factors (Dündar and Fırlar, 2006: 132).

These strategies can be used in combinations and it is even possible to use all five strategies simultaneously at service businesses. These strategies must be used as a whole, not independently.

4.2 Supportive Relationship Marketing Strategy

Tinsley (2002) suggests that businesses must benefit from the other supportive marketing strategies given in Tab. 8.1 in order to implement relationship marketing activities and increase productivity in their activities.

Tab. 8.1: Other Strategies That Can Help Relationship Marketing Strategies. **Reference:** Tinsley (2002), 71

Supporting Marketing Strategies	
Market Segmentation	Service differentiation
Customer Valuation	Customer Satisfaction
Database Marketing	Internet Usage
Enhancing Strategies	
Market Strategies	Marketing Strategies
Supply Chain Management	Offering Value to Customer
Market Focused Organization	Personalization
Market Orientation	Long Term Relationship
Total Quality Management	Product Innovation
Customer Relations Management	Product Line Pricing
	Pricing by Product Life Cycle

The author suggests that businesses must make use of supportive and augmentative marketing strategies, so that relationship marketing activities can be carried out.

5 Studies on Relationship Marketing in the Banking Sector

The increased impact of the banking sectors on the world economy as of 1980s and the intense competition in these sectors caused the need for relationship marketing activities to increase as well. In this context, the number of studies on using relationship marketing activities in the banking sector has increased since the 1990s.

Abratt and Russell (1999) investigated whether relationship marketing activities affected bank preferences in the study they conducted on retail bank customers in South Africa. They used a survey consisting of fifty-three criteria in the study. One hundred and eighteen suitable surveys were obtained from the application on 600 people, and the analyses continued with those surveys. The analyses revealed that the most important criterion for retail bank preferences of consumers was price. The study also showed that trust, service quality, and the possibilities offered by banks during crisis periods had a moderating impact on the correlation between prices and bank preferences. In line with these results, relationship marketing activities were found out to be an important criterion for retail bank preferences of customers.

Ndubisi (2007) conducted a study to determine the correlation between relationship marketing strategies and customer loyalty and used trust, commitment, communication, and conflict management as the sub-dimensions of relationship marketing. The study was conducted on 220 people selected among customers of fifteen different banks in Malaysia. The multiple regression analysis developed to test the research hypothesis revealed that all variables related to relationship marketing helped explain customer loyalty.

Alrubaiee and Al-Nazer (2010) studied the impact of relationship marketing orientation on customer loyalty and analyzed the impacts of demographic qualities (gender, education, income) on the relationship between relationship market orientation and customer loyalty. The survey used in the study included sub-dimensions of relationship market orientation such as bonding, trust, communication, satisfaction, and commitment, and the data was collected from 400 bank customers in Amman, Jordan.

The analyses showed that the four sub-dimensions of relationship market orientation (bonding, trust, communication, and satisfaction) had a significant impact on customer loyalty. The bonding dimension was found out to be the dominant impact (standardized beta coefficient: 0.422). On the other hand, it was found out that commitment did not have a significant impact on customer loyalty.

Wan Omar and Mohd Ali (2010) studied the interaction between the relationship marketing activities and customer loyalty in the Islamic banking system in Malaysia. Their main claim was that there was a significant and positive correlation between relationship marketing and customer loyalty.

They analyzed relationship marketing under three sub-dimensions: trust, commitment, and communication skills. The data used in the study was collected through surveys made face to face with 500 customers of three Islamic banks in Pulau Pinang, Kedah, and Perlis states of Malaysia. The multiple regression analysis conducted on the research data showed that relationship marketing that was measured through three sub-dimensions (commitment, trust, and communication skills) had significant impacts on brand loyalty.

Lee, Chu, and Chao (2011) conducted a study on Internet banking customers in order to determine the relationship among service quality, relationship quality, and customer loyalty. The research data was obtained from Internet banking customers in Taiwan through surveys. Some of the data was obtained from surveys filled in via the Internet, and the rest was obtained from surveys made by the researchers with people around them and those at bank branches. A total of 444 people were reached in the study. The correlation analysis conducted during the study showed that there was a positive and significant correlation between relationship quality, service quality, and customer loyalty, and both relationship quality and service quality affected customer loyalty positively.

Ünal and Demir (2017) conducted a survey on 100 bank customers in order to determine the extent to which the relationship marketing activities in the Turkish banking sector were regarded as important by the customers and found out that offering steady and good prices and long-term customer representative applications were relationship marketing activities to which the customers attached utmost importance.

Wachyudi (2018) studied the impacts of relationship marketing activities on the loyalty of bank customers. The author conducted laboratory experiments on eight groups at the end of a preliminary preparation process and analyzed the results with regression analysis. The analysis results showed that relationship marketing activities affected bank loyalties of customers significantly to a great extent. Furthermore, another important result of the study was that switching costs of customers had a moderating effect on the correlation between relationship marketing and customer loyalty.

Ogbechi, Okafor, and Orukotan (2018) analyzed the impacts of relationship marketing activities carried out at banks on customer retention and loyalty. The study was conducted in Lagos State, Nigeria, through the survey technique and the data was collected from 800 bank customers. The study results showed that Customer satisfaction, Customer Trust, Commitment, Reliability, Assurance, and Responsiveness had statistically significant and positive impacts on retention and loyalty of bank customers.

Conclusion

The banking sector is one of the sectors where intense competition takes place all around the world. Banks offer similar services, and they cannot distinguish themselves from their rivals at many points due to relevant regulations. Therefore, customers get similar benefits from basic banking products at all banks. This makes banks carry out marketing activities aimed at retaining their available customers. One of the differentiation strategies used by banks to make available customers more profitable and loyal is relationship marketing.

When used accurately, relationship marketing will create significant competitive advantages for banks while achieving long-term customer loyalty and gaining new customers. That is because people do not like risk and certainty, and they prioritize not losing over winning (Kahneman and Tversky, 1979). According to this theory, customers who work with a bank using relationship marketing activities accurately and become satisfied as a result of this transaction will be free of uncertainty, and their risk perception will be reduced. As a natural result of this, customers will intend to maintain their relationship with the same bank and make purchases again as they want to avoid switching costs, and they care about the relationship they have established with the bank. Furthermore, they will make positive word-of-mouth advertising to people around them about the bank, thus helping the bank gain new customers without incurring any costs. On the other hand, firstly the current attitudes and behaviors of available customers must be determined, and suitable relationship bond strategies must be used so that relationship marketing can be applied accurately. Also core and supportive relationship marketing strategies that are necessary to maintain relationship marketing strategically must be planned and implemented accurately.

Errors made while planning and implementing relationship marketing activities will both cause available customers to be lost and create negative word-of-mouth about the bank. As it is more difficult and costlier to regain a lost customer than gaining new customers in most cases, this negative situation can cause the bank to lose prestige and profits to a great extent.

References

Abratt, R. & Russell, J. (1999). "Relationship Marketing in Private Banking in South Africa." *International Journal of Bank Marketing, 17*(1), 5–19.

Alrubaiee, L. & Al-Nazer, N. (2010). "Investigate the Impact of Relationship Marketing Orientation on Customer Loyalty: The Customer's Perspective." *International Journal of Marketing Studies, 2*(1), 155–174.

Argouslidis, P.C. & Indounas, K. (2010). "Exploring the Role of Relationship Pricing in Industrial Export Settings: Empirical Evidence from the UK." *Industrial Marketing Management, 39*(3), 460–472.

Ballantyne, D. (2000). "Internal Relationship Marketing: A Strategy for Knowledge Renewal," *International Journal of Bank Marketing, 18* (6), 274–286.

Berry, L. & Parasuraman, A. (1991). *Marketing Services: Competing through Quality*, Simon and Schuster, New York.

Berry, L.L. (2002). "Relationship Marketing of Services—Perspectives from 1983 and 2000," *Journal of Relationship Marketing, 1* (1), 59–77.

Bühler A. & Nufer G. (2010). *Relationship Marketing in Sports*, Butterworth Heineman ve Elsevier Ltd, ISBN: 978-0-7506-8495-8.

Dündar, İ.P. & Fırlar, F.B. (2006). "İçsel Pazarlama ve Toplam Kalite yönetimi: Türkiye'deki Ulusal Basın İşletmelerinin Değerlendirilmesine Yönelik Bir Araştırma." *BİLİG Journal*, 37, 131–153.

Grönroos, C. (1996). "Relationship Marketing: Strategic and Tactical İmplications," *Management Decision, 34*(3), 5–14.

Gummesson, E. (1994). “Making Relationship Marketing Operational,” *International Journal of Service Industry Management, 5*(5), 5–20.

Güven, Ö.Z. (2007). İlişkisel Pazarlama Ekseninde Otel İşletmelerinde Müşteri Bağlılığının Öncel ve Sonuçlarının Belirlenmesine Yönelik Bir Model Geliştirilmesi, Dumlupınar Unıversity, Social Sciences Institute, Department of Business Administration, Doctoral Thesis, Kütahya.

Harker, M.J. (1999). “Relationship Marketing Defined? An Examination of Current Relationship Marketing Definitions,” *Marketing Intelligence & Planning, 17*(1), 13–20.

Hossain, M.Z., Kibria, H., & Farhana, S. (2017). “Do Customer Loyalty Programs Really Work in Airlines Business?—A Study on Air Berlin.” *Journal of Service Science and Management, 10*(04), 360-375.

Huang, C., Fang, S., Huang, S., Chang, S., & Fang, S. (2014). “The Impact of Relational Bonds on Brand Loyalty: The Mediating Effect of Brand Relationship Quality,” *Managing Service Quality, 24*(2), 184–204.

İlban, M.O., Doğdubay, M., & Gürsoy H. (2009). “Otel İşletmelerinde İlişkisel Pazarlama Üzerine Karşılaştırmalı Bir Araştırma,” *Eskişehir Osmangazi University, Journal of Social Sciences, Cilt: 10*, 2, 117–144.

Jüttner, U. & Wehrli, H.P. (1994). “Relationship Marketing from a Value System Perspective,” *International Journal of Service Industry Management, 5*(5), 54–73.

Kahneman, D. & Tversky, A. (1979). “Prospect Theory: An Analysis of Decision under Risk,” *Econometrica, 47*(2) (Mar., 1979), 263–292.

Kanagal, N. (2009). “Role of Relationship Marketing in Competitive Marketing Strategy,” *Journal of Management and Marketing Research. 2*, ISSN: 1941–3408 Online.

Keith, J.E., Lee, D-J., & Lee, R.G. (2004). “The Effect of Relational Exchange between the Service Provider and the Customer on the Customer’s Perception of Value,” *Journal of Relationship Marketing, 3*(1), 3–33.

Kim, W.G., Han, J.S., & Lee, E. (2001). “Effects of Relationship Marketing on Repeat Purchase And Word-Of-Mouth.” *Journal of Hospitality and Tourism Research, 25*, 272–288.

Kotler, P. (2011). “Marketing Insights from A to Z,” çev: Aslı Kalem Bakkal, *Onuncu Baskı, Kapital Medya Hizmetleri A.Ş, İstanbul.*

Lee, G-Y., Chu, P-Y., & Chou, Y. (2011). “Service Quality, Relationship Quality, and Customer Loyalty in Taiwanese Internet Banks.” *Social Behavior and Personality, 39*(8), 1127–1140.

Lee, Y.K., Kim, S., Kim, M., Lee, J., & Lim, K. (2015). “Relational Bonding Strategies in the Franchise Industry: The Moderating Role of Duration of the Relationship,” *Journal of Business & Industrial Marketing, 30*(7), 830–841.

Lima, M. & Fernandes, T. (2015, February). "Relationship Bonds and Customer Loyalty: A Study across Different Service Contexts." In *International Conference on Exploring Services Science* (pp. 326–339). Springer, Cham.

Malhotra, N., Uslay, C., & Bayraktar, A. (2016). *Relationship Marketing Re-Imagined: Marketing's Inevitable Shift from Exchanges to Value Co-Creating Relationships*. Business Expert Press, New York.

Morgan R.M. & Hunt, S.D. (1994). "The Commitment-Trust Theory of Relationship Marketing," *Journal of Marketing*, *58*(3) (Jul., 1994), 20–38.

Nath, P. & Mukherjee, A. (2012)."Complementary Effects of Relational Bonds in Information Asymmetry Contexts," *Journal of Services Marketing*, *26*(3), 168–180.

Ndubisi, N.O. (2007). "Relationship Marketing and Customer Loyalty," *Marketing Intelligence & Planning*, *25*(1), 98–106.

Ogbechi, A.D, Okafor, L.I., and Orukotan, C.I. (2018). Effect of Relationship Marketing on Customer Retention and Loyalty in the Money Deposit Bank Industry. African Research Review (AFRREV), *12*(2), 23–34 http://dx.doi.org/10.4314/afrrev.v12i2.3.

Öztürk,İ. (2009). "Konaklama İşletmelerinde İç ve Dış Müşteri Tatmininin İlişkisel Pazarlama Bağlamında İncelenmesi: Zincir Otel İşletmesi ÖrneğI," Sakarya University, *Journal of Social Sciences,* Department of Tourism Management, Master's Thesis, Sakarya.

Priluck, R. (2003). "Relationship Marketing Can Mitigate Product and Service Failures," *Journal of Services Marketing*, *17*(1), 37 – 52.

Rao, G.S. & Abegaz, G.T. (2017). "The Role of Relationship Marketing on Customer Retention: The Case of Abay Bank in Dessie Region in Ethiopia." *International Journal of Advanced Research in Management and Social Sciences*, *6*(3), 97–111.

Selvi. M.S. (2007-a). *İlişkisel Pazarlama: Stratejiler ve Teknikler*, Ankara: Detay Publications.

Sheth, N.J. & Parvatiyar, A. (1995). "Relationship Marketing in Consumer Markets: Antecedents and Consequences," *Journal of Academy of Marketing Science*, *23*(4), 255–271.

Sheth, J.N. (2002). "The Future of Relationship Marketing," *Journal of Services Marketing 16*(7), 590–592.

Steffes, E.M. (2005). "Establishing the Link between Relationshıp Marketing, Customer Profitability and Customer Lifetime," The University of Texas at Dallas, Doctoral Thesis, UMI Number: 3176140.

Takala,T., & Uusitalo,O. (1996). "An Alternative View of Relationship Marketing: A Framework for Ethical Analysis", *European Journal of Marketing*, *30*(2), 45–60.

TBB (The Banks Association of Turkey) (2018-b). Banka Çalışan ve Şube Sayılar https://www.tbb.org.tr/Content/Upload/istatistikiraporlar/ekler/989/Banka_Calisan_ve_Sube_Sayilari-Haziran_2018.pdf.

TBB (The Banks Association of Turkey) (2018-a). Banka, Sektör Bilgileri (https://www.tbb.org.tr/tr/bankacilik/banka-ve-sektor-bilgileri/banka-bilgileri/banka-ve-sube-sayilari/70).

Terzioğlu, B. (2008). *Değişen Pazarlama Anlayışı Açısından Müşteri Sadakati Yaratmada İlişkisel Pazarlama ve Bir Uygulama*, Marmara Üniversitesi, Social Science Institute, Department of Business Administration, İstanbul.

Tinsley, D.B. (2002). "Relationship Marketing's Strategic Array." *Business Horizons*. Jan-Feb 2002, 70–76.

Tomer, J.F. (1998). "Beyond Transaction Markets, toward Relationship Marketing in the Human Firm: A Socio-Economic Model," *Journal of Socio-Economics, 10535357, 1998, 27*(2), 207–228.

Ünal, S. & Demir. M. (2017), Banka ve Müşteri Arasında Uzun Soluklu İlişkide İlişkisel Pazarlama Faktörü, International Congress on Afro - Eurasian Research II – Kongre Bildirileri Kitabı, ISBN: 978-605-67620-1-7 ss.238–245.

Wachyudi, N. (2018). "A Study of the Relationship Marketing Effect in Banks: The case of an Emerging Market." *Journal of Governance & Regulation*, *7*(1), 26–39. http://doi.org/10.22495/jgr_v7_i1_p2.

Wan Omar, M. & Mohd Ali, M.N. (2010), "Brand Loyalty and Relationship Marketing in Islamic Banking System." *Canadian Social Science Journal*, *6*(1), 25–32.

Wang, R. (2007). "Relationship, Loyalty, and Marketing-A Correlation Study of Taiwan Hotel Customers' Perspectives," Faculty of the Graduate College of the Oklahoma State University, Doctoral Thesis, UMI Number: 3291448.

Nimet Varlık

9 Macroeconomic Factors Affecting Non-Performing Loans in the Turkish Banking Sector

Abstract: The study investigates the macroeconomic factors increasing non-performing loans (NPLs) in Turkey for the period 2001M12-2018M03 by employing the Autoregressive Distributed Lag (ARDL) model. Model findings show that all selected macroeconomic variables which are real effective exchange rate, consumer price index, industrial production index, unemployment rate, interest rate, and M2 money supply have significant effects on NPLs.

Keywords: Non-Performing Loans, Macroeconomic Factors, Banking Sector, ARDL Model

1 Introduction

Insolvency is one of the significant problems in balance sheets of banks resulting from the deterioration of asset quality (Dimitrios, Helen, and Mike, 2016). When we look at the history of banking crises, we see that a vast majority of total assets owned by banks and non-bank financial institutions that had insolvency problems consisted of loans that were managed poorly or provided incorrectly (Fofack, 2005; Khemraj and Pasha, 2009; Saba, Kouser, and Azeem, 2012; Tomak, 2013; Makri, Tsagkanos, and Bellas, 2014). As a matter of fact, we know that the size of non-performing loans (NPL) increased right before the banking crises in East Asian and sub-Saharan African countries (Reinhart and Rogoff, 2011; Louzis, Vouldis, and Metaxas, 2011), and the economic crisis in 2008 was triggered by mortgage loans that lapsed into default.

There are no international standards to define non-performing loans. In general, non-performing loans are defined as total debts accumulated when the debtor does not make the planned payments for at least ninety days (Rinaldi and Sanchis-Arellano, 2006; Rajeev and Mahesh, 2010; Saba et al., 2012). In a broader sense, non-performing loans are loans whose principal and interest payments lapse into default when the repayment agreement made with a written commitment between the bank and the debtor is violated (Sipahi, 2003). In Turkey, loans whose partial or complete repayments exceed ninety days are defined as non-performing loans in the Banking Law No 5411 (BDDK, 2005). According to Article 5 of the "Regulation on Procedures and Principles

Regarding Determination of Loans and Other Receivables by Banks and the Relevant Reserves to be Allocated" published in the Official Gazette No 26333 dated November 1, 2006, a loan is deemed a non-performing loan if its repayment exceeds ninety days partially or completely. Furthermore, such loans are called problematic loans.

The share of non-performing loans among the total amount of loans is highly important for some economic and financial indicators. Increases in the amount of non-performing loans can affect private investments negatively and cause deposit liabilities of banks to increase, loans provided for the private sector to be limited due to a decrease in the bank capital, and private consumption to decrease (Fofact, 2005). Saba et al. (2012) show increases in NPLs as the main reason for the decrease in bank profits. They suggest that high interest rates, unsuccessful loan policies of banks, and weak payment capacities of debtors are the factors triggering such increases. Some macroeconomic and financial indicators affecting NPLs are important in addition to these economic and financial problems caused by NPLs. GDP, unemployment rate, interest rates on consumer loans, inflation rate, public sector budget balance, nominal or real effective exchange rate, money supply, and industrial production index are the most frequently used indicators (Fofack, 2005; Khemraj and Pasha, 2009; Adebola, Yusoff, and Dahalan, 2011; Louzis et al., 2011; Nkusu, 2011; Klein, 2013; Messai and Jouini, 2013; Makri et al., 2014; Skarica, 2014; Vatansever and Hepsen, 2015). Factors related to the banking sector are mostly caused by the weakness of the supervision system of banks, high loan risk, and bad management system (Rajeev and Mahesh, 2010; Abid, Ouertani, and Zouari-Ghorbel, 2014; Dimitrios et al., 2016). On the other hand, empirical studies on NPLs show that there is no standard approach related to factors affecting NPLs and conditions specific to countries play an important role.

This chapter focuses on macroeconomic variables rather than factors related to the banking system while analyzing non-performing loans. The aim is to exclusively evaluate the impacts of macroeconomic factors on non-performing loans. The findings show that the macroeconomic environment in a country has a significant impact on NPL increases.

This chapter consists of five sections including the conclusion part. The second section following the introduction discusses the general outlook of the banking sector and analyzes the development of NPLs. The macroeconomic determinants of NPLs are explained in the third section that includes the economics literature. The fourth section consists of data definition, econometric model, and empirical findings. The chapter ends with the Conclusion.

2 The Development of Non-Performing Loans in the Turkish Banking System

The banking system in Turkey covers a very large part of the financial system as in many developing countries and plays a leading role in economic growth. The non-performing loans are important in the banking system considering that non-performing loans deteriorate the liquidity structure of banks (Chikoko, 2013; Yüksel, 2016) and weaken the capacity to provide loans by affecting management of assets and liabilities negatively (Tomak, 2013; Selimler, 2015).

The financial crises that took place in Turkey in November 2000 and February 2001 showed that the banking sector had a fragile nature in general. The weak liquidity structures and low asset qualities of banks reveal the fragile nature of the sector. The shares of non-performing loans within the total amount of loans were 11.6 percent and 23.2 percent in the balance sheets of the banking sector prepared in 2000 and 2001, respectively.

The weakness of the bank balance sheets revealed the necessity of a supervision system and importance of complying with the international financial standards. In this regard, the supervision system related to the banking system was strengthened in the Turkish banking sector after 2001. Precautionary measures taken for allocation of required reserves within the framework of efficient loan management and regulations such as making bank balance sheets more transparent had a positive effect on bank balance sheets. As a result, although the amount of non-performing loans increased during the Global financial Crisis in 2008, this increase was not as big as the previous periods. Fig. 9.1 shows the changes in non-performing loans in Turkey by years.

The economic recession caused by the global financial crisis in 2008 affected the asset quality of the banking sector in Turkey and the non-performance ratio of loans that was 3.7 percent at the end of 2008 increased to 5.3 percent at the end of 2009 (BDDK, 2008). The increase in loans provided by banks declined to some extent in 2010 due to the global crisis, while the non-performance ratio of loans decreased in the same period. The negative effect of the expansion in loan volumes has been reflected in non-performing loans since 2015.

3 Macroeconomic Determinants of NPLs

Studies analyzing determinants of non-performing loans classify variables affecting non-performing loans as macroeconomic determinants and bank-specific determinants. Country-specific macroeconomic variables are used in studies that mostly focus on macroeconomic determinants (Fofack, 2005; Rinaldi

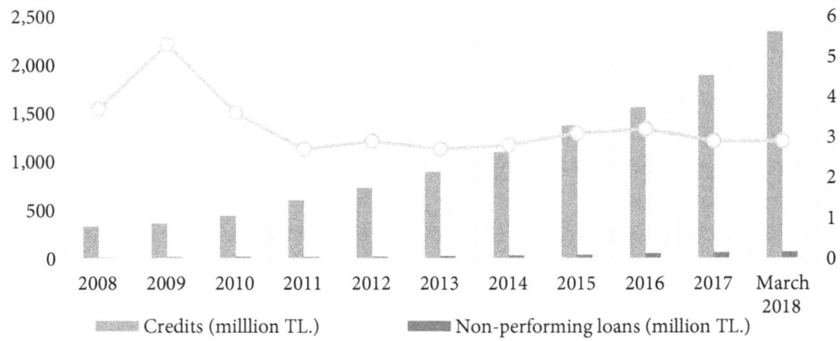

Fig. 9.1: Development of non-performing loans. *Source: Compiled from the reports published by BDDK about the overview of the Turkish banking sector*

and Sanchis-Arellano, 2006; Pilinkus, 2010; Adebola et al., 2011; Bofondi and Ropele, 2011; Nkusu, 2011; Reinhart and Rogoff, 2011; Castro, 2013; Klein, 2013; Skarica, 2014). On the other hand, studies using bank-specific determinants analyze variables related to loan growth, bank profitability, and bank sizes (Louzis et al., 2011; Saba et al., 2012; Chikoko, 2013; Messai and Jouini, 2013; Makri et al., 2014; Dimitrios et al., 2016).

Increases in the real effective exchange rate indicate that the national currency has appreciated and the prices of domestically produced goods and services have increased considerably. As pointed out by Fofack (2005), Khemraj and Pasha (2009), Reinhart and Rogoff (2011), and Nkusu (2011), competitive powers of export companies decrease and their solvency is affected negatively due to increases in real effective exchange rates. Therefore, increases in real effective exchange rates can cause the amount of non-performing loans to increase.

Castro (2013) states that increase in inflation decrease the real values of non-performing loans, as well as erode the real income of the debtor, thus increasing the credit risk. The studies conducted by Klein (2013) on the Eurozone and Skarica (2014) on the Central and East European countries determined a positive relationship between non-performing loans and inflation increase. On the other hand, Nkusu (2011) suggests that inflation affects the solvency of the debtor from different channels and its impacts on non-performing loans can be either negative or positive. High inflation rates can make the loan facility more advantageous by decreasing the real value of the non-performing loans. However, high inflation rates can affect solvency of debtors negatively by decreasing the real income in an economy with strict wages.

Studies analyzing the relationships between non-performing loans and macroeconomic variables reveal an inverse relationship between non-performing loans and growth rates of countries (Salas and Saurina, 2002; Das and Ghosh, 2007; Chaibi and Ftiti, 2015). The economic system is more stable (Bhattarai, 2016; Yüksel, 2016) and debtors have better solvency (Thiagarajan, Ayyappan, and Ramachandran; 2011) in countries with high growth rate. As a result, the ratio of non-performing loans in bank balance sheets of such countries is relatively lower. In addition, as loan quality drops and companies get loans with higher interest margins (Mileris, 2012) during period of economic recession, a negative correlation is expected between growth rate and non-performing loans.

Unemployment rate reflects uncertainty of future incomes. As high unemployment rates bring about lower income levels, solvencies of companies and households decrease and problems emerge while repaying loans (Rinaldi and Sanchis-Arellano, 2006; Bhattarai, 2014; Makri et al., 2014). Therefore, it is expected that increases in unemployment rates will increase the amount of non-performing loans. Furthermore, as Rinaldi and Sanchis-Arellano (2006) point out, debts are affected considerably when real loan interests increase and therefore the amount of non-performing loans increases when real interest rates increase. For this reason, interest rates have a positive impact on non-performing loans (Bofondi and Ropele, 2011; Messai and Jouini, 2013).

Changes in money supply reflect household and bank behaviors and affect bank profitability to a great extent (Mileris, 2012). As Fofack (2005) states, when the money supply expands in a country, the amount of loans provided for the real sector increases and the share of non-performing loans within the total amount of loans increases, too.

4 Data, the Model and Empirical Evidence

The research model is based on the hypothesis assuming that increases in the amount of non-performing loans in the Turkish banking sector depend on macroeconomic factors. For this purpose, we determined six independent macroeconomic variables that are considered to affect non-performing loans. These are: real effective exchange rate (REER), consumer price index (CPI), industrial production index (IP), unemployment rate (UR), interest rates on consumer loans (INT), and M2 broad money supply. The share of non-performing loans (NPLs) in the total amount of loans was included in the model as the dependent variable. This study covers the period from December 2001 to March 2018 and the data used in the study was obtained from the Electronic Data Delivery Service of the Central Bank of Turkey.

It draws attention that most of the macroeconomic time series include unit roots. The spurious regression problem must be avoided as the series include unit roots and are not stationary. There are various methods developing solutions for this problem. One of them is the method developed by Engle and Granger (1987). In this method, differences of all series containing unit roots are taken in the same order and their I(1) stationarity is ensured and the cointegration between the variables can be investigated. However, in the method that was firstly developed by Johansen (1988) and then improved by Johansen and Juselius (1990), all series must not be in the same order, and they need to be stationary when their first differences are taken. Pesaran and Pesaran (1997) claim that such cointegration tests are not reliable and reveal inconsistent results. The Autoregressive Distributed Lag (ARDL) bound test developed by Pesaran, Shin, and Smith (1999, 2001) eliminates this problem. The ARDL bound test makes it possible to investigate the presence of a cointegration between series regardless of their stationarity levels. The bound test can be applied if one or more series are I(0) and/or I(1), other than I(2). On the other hand, Pesaran et al. (2001) found out that long and short-term parameters of the model could be estimated simultaneously.

Unit root tests were conducted before the model estimation in this study in order to test the stationarity of the variables. As the series to be used in the model had different orders of stationarity, the cointegration between them was tested with the ARDL bound test approach. The estimation of long-term relationship between variables consists of two steps in this approach. In the first step, the presence of a long-term relationship between the variables used in the model is tested. After the presence of a long-term relationship is tested, the second step in which the short and long-term parameters of the model are estimated starts.

Dickey and Fuller (1979), Augmented Dickey and Fuller (ADF) (1981), Phillips and Perron (PP) (1988), Kwiatkowski, Phillips, Schmidt, and Shin (KPSS) (1992), and Ng-Perron (NP) (2001) are the tests that are frequently used to test stationarity levels of series. Tab. 9.1 shows the results of unit root tests obtained through this method.

The results of the unit root tests show that *lnNPLs*, *lnREER,* and *lnIP* variables contain unit roots and therefore they are not stationary in any order. However, when the first differences of these series are taken and the unit root tests are conducted again, they become stationary and all series contained by the model become integrated in the first order.

The model related to the ARDL bound test that will be used to analyze the cointegration between the variables is as follows (Pesaran et al., 2001);

Tab. 9.1 Results of Stationarity Tests

Variables	*Stationarity Tests and Results*				Explanations
	ADF	PP	KPSS	NP	
lnNPLs	I(1)	I(1)	I(1)	I(1)	Used in a logarithmic style.
lnREER	I(1)	I(1)	I(1)	I(1)	Used in a logarithmic style.
lnCPI	I(0)	I(0)	I(0)	I(0)	Used in a logarithmic style. Seasonally adjusted.
lnIP	I(1)	I(0)	I(1)	I(1)	Used in a logarithmic style. Seasonally adjusted.
lnUR	I(0)	I(0)	I(0)	I(0)	Used in a logarithmic style. Seasonally adjusted.
lnINT	I(0)	I(0)	I(0)	I(0)	Used in a logarithmic style.
lnM2	I(0)	I(0)	I(0)	I(0)	Used in a logarithmic style.

Explanation (1): *The maximum lag length was taken as 12 in the ADF unit root test and the lag length was determined as the SIC criterion. The default (Battlett Kernel) estimation method and Newey-West Bandwith (automatic selection) criteria were used in the PP, KPSS, and NP unit root tests.*

Explanation (2): Logarithms of all the variables used in the model were taken and their aesthetic values were determined. *In addition, nCPI, lnIP and lnUR variables were seasonally adjusted in accordance with the TRAMO/SEATS method.*

$$\begin{aligned}\Delta lnNPLs_t &= \alpha_0 + \sum_{i=1}^{p} \alpha_{1i} \Delta lnNPLs_{t-i} + \sum_{i=1}^{p} \alpha_{2i} \Delta lnREER_{t-i} + \sum_{i=1}^{p} \Delta lnCPI_{t-i} \\ &+ \sum_{i=1}^{p} \alpha_{4i} \Delta lnIP_{t-i} + \sum_{i=1}^{p} \alpha_{5i} \Delta lnUR_{t-i} + \sum_{i=1}^{p} \alpha_{6i} \Delta lnINT_{t-i} + \sum_{i=1}^{p} \alpha_{7i} \Delta lnM2_{t-i} \\ &+ \beta_1 lnNPLs_{t-1} + \beta_2 lnREER_{t-1} + \beta_3 lnCPI_{t-1} + \beta_4 lnIP_{t-1} + \beta_5 lnUR_{t-1} \\ &+ \beta_6 lnINT_{t-1} + \beta_7 lnM2_{t-1} + \varepsilon_t\end{aligned} \tag{1}$$

In this equation, t, p, and ε represent the trend variation, lag count, and error term in the model, respectively. $a_1 \ldots\ldots a_7$ represents the short-term dynamics of the model while $\beta_1 \ldots\ldots \beta_7$ represents long-term findings.

Bound test is conducted and the *F* statistic is calculated while testing the presence of a long-term relationship between the variables in the ARDL model. If the null hypothesis of the cointegration between variables is $H_0 : \beta_1 = \beta_2 = \beta_3 = \beta_4 = \beta_5 = \beta_6 = \beta_7 = 0$, it is decided that there is no cointegration and the null hypothesis is rejected. Instead, an alternative hypothesis is created: $H_1 : \beta_{1..7} \neq 0$. The alternative hypothesis shows a cointegration between variables. The F statistic calculated in the bound test is compared with the lower

Tab. 9.2: Bound Test (F Statistic) Results

K	F Statistic	Critical Values (5 % Significance Level)	
		Lower limit	Upper limit
6	8,16	2,27	3,28

Explanation: *k is the number of independent variables in the model. The critical values are related to the 5 % error margin obtained from Table C1 created by Pesaran et al. (2001).*

and upper critical values $\left[I(0), I(1)\right]$given in the table in the study conducted by Pesaran et al. (2001). If the F statistic value is below the lower limit $I(0)$, the main hypothesis stating that there is no long-term relationship cannot be rejected. In other words, it is concluded that there is no cointegration between the variables. If the F statistic value is higher than the upper critical value $I(1)$, it is understood that there is a cointegration relationship. However, it is not known for sure whether there is a cointegration relationship when the statistic value is between these two critical values $\left[I(0) and\, I(1)\right]$.

As you can see in Tab. 9.2, a cointegration was determined between the variables used in the model as the F statistic calculated in this study was higher than the upper critical value.

According to the findings, the $I(0)$ veya $I(1)$ H_0 hypothesis was rejected without paying attention to whether the series were $I(0)$ or $I(1)$ and H_1alternative hypothesis suggesting a cointegration between the variables was accepted. In other words, it was concluded that there was a long-term cointegration between non-performing loans and macroeconomic variables.

After a long-term correlation is detected between the variables in the model, long-term and short-term parameters are calculated and interpreted based on the studies conducted by Pesaran et al. (2001). Accordingly, Equation 2 shows the ARDL model created to estimate the long-term relationship;

$$lnNPLs_t = \alpha_0 + \sum_{i=1}^{p}\alpha_{1i} lnNPLs_{t-i} + \sum_{i=1}^{p}\alpha_{2i} lnREER_{t-i} + \sum_{i=1}^{p}\alpha_{3i} lnCPI_{t-i} + \sum_{i=1}^{p}\alpha_{4i} lnIP_{t-i} + \sum_{i=1}^{p}\alpha_{5i} lnUR_{t-i} + \sum_{i=1}^{p}\alpha_{6i} lnINT_{t-i} + \sum_{i=1}^{p}\alpha_{7i} lnM2_{t-i} + \varepsilon_t \quad (2)$$

The Hannan-Quinn (HQ) criterion was used to determine the lag length while estimating long-term parameters. Suitable lag values were determined by adding

Tab. 9.3: Long-Term ARDL Model Estimations Based on the HQ Criterion

Variables	Coefficients	Std. Error	t-Statistic	Probability
lnNPLs(-1)	0.8979	0,0188	47,6159	0,0000
lnREER	-0.1688	0,0850	-1,9854	0,0488
lnREER(-1)	0.0624	0,1344	0,4647	0,6427
lnREER(-2)	0.1975	0,0891	2,2160	0,0281
lnCPI	-0.0015	0,0003	-3,9718	0,0001
lnIP	-0.0966	0,0486	-1,9850	0,0488
lnUR	0.4369	0,1104	3,9554	0,0001
lnUR(-1)	-0.3336	0,1150	-2,9013	0,0042
lnINT	-0.2428	0,2517	-0,9645	0,3362
lnINT(-1)	0.7636	0,3853	1,9815	0,0492
lnINT(-2)	-0.1675	0,4069	-0,4117	0,6811
lnINT(-3)	-0.2810	0,3822	-0,7352	0,4632
lnINT(-4)	0.9891	0,3666	2,6973	0,0077
lnINT(-5)	-1.1124	0,3626	-3,0674	0,0025
lnINT(-6)	0.0302	0,3557	0,0850	0,9323
lnINT(-7)	1.2019	0,3368	3,5683	0,0005
lnINT(-8)	-0.5819	0,2195	-2,6504	0,0088
lnM2	0.0152	0,1606	0,0951	0,9243
lnM2(-1)	0.6394	0,1961	3,2600	0,0014
lnM2(-2)	-0.3362	0,1908	-1,7618	0,0800
lnM2(-3)	-0.5451	0,1901	-2,8674	0,0047
lnM2(-4)	0.5133	0,1868	2,7477	0,0067
lnM2(-5)	-0.5768	0,1847	-3,1223	0,0021
lnM2(-6)	-0.0061	0,1850	-0,0330	0,9737
lnM2(-7)	0.4093	0,1405	2,9133	0,0041
C	-1.7759	0,5901	-3,0090	0,0030

$R^2 = 0.997,\ \overline{R^2} = 0.997,\quad \text{DW statistic} = 1.909,\ \text{F statistic} = 3056.3\ (0.000)$

the lag values of each variable to the model. The suitable lag lengths determined according to HQ in the study are 1, 2, 0, 0, 1, 8, and 7 for non-performing loans, real effective exchange rate, consumer price index, industrial production index, unemployment rate, interest rate, and money supply, respectively. Tab. 9.3 shows the long-term parameters related to the ARDL (1, 2, 0, 0, 1, 8, 7) model that was created accordingly.

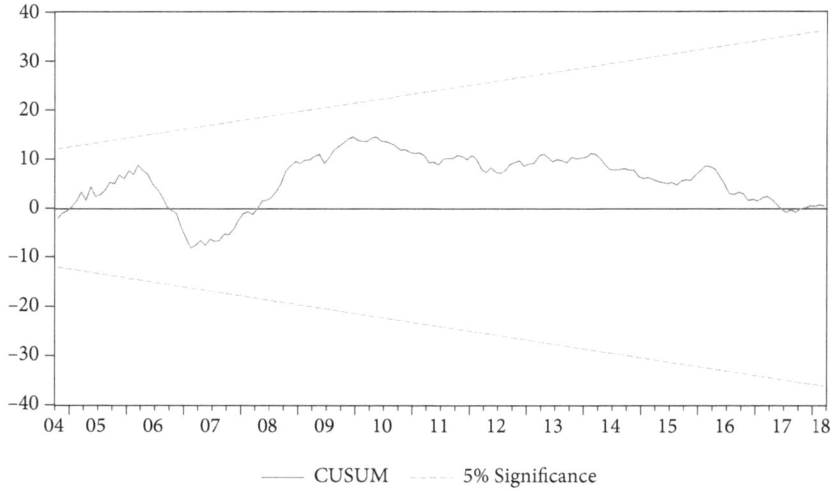

Fig. 9.2: CUSUM test

Tab. 9.4: ARDL Model Long-Term Coefficients

Variables	Long-Term Coefficients	Std. Error	t-Statistic	Probability
lnREER	0.8929	0,3627	2.4616**	(0.0149)
lnCPI	-0.0148	0,0046	-3.2316*	(0.0015)
lnIP	-0.9463	0,4966	-1.9055***	(0.0585)
lnUR	1.0116	0,2749	3.6797*	(0.0003)
lnINT	5.8682	1,2720	4.6131*	(0.0000)
lnM2	1.1075	0,4222	2.6230*	(0.0095)
C	-17.3951	7,0922	-2.4526**	(0.0152)

$R^2 = 0.628, \overline{R^2} = 0.588$, DW statistic = 1.909

Explanation: *, ** and *** represent 1 %, 5 % and 10 % significance levels respectively.

No autocorrelation, normality, and heteroscedasticity problems were detected in the estimated ARDL model. The results of the CUSUM test studying the stability of long-term parameters show that the residuals of the model are within the limits (Fig. 9.2). This result indicates that the model parameters are stable, and there are no structural breaks in the model.

Tab. 9.4 shows the long-term coefficient estimations. These estimation findings are long-term coefficient estimations obtained as a result of normalization based on the dependent variable.

All long-term coefficients are statistically significant according to the t-statistic and probability values in the table. If long-term coefficients are expressed as an equation:

$$\begin{aligned} lnNPLs = 0.892^{*}\, lnREER - 0.014^{*}\, lnCPI - 0.946^{*}\, lnIP + 1.011^{*}\, lnUR \\ + 5.86^{*}\, lnINT + 1.10^{*}\, lnM2 - 17.3^{*}\, C \end{aligned} \tag{3}$$

According to the equation, 1 percent increase in the real effective exchange rate increases non-performing loans by 0.8 percent and 1 percent increase in the consumer price index decreases non-performing loans by 0.01 percent. Nkusu (2011) found out that an increase in inflation increased the amount of non-performing loans, i.e., it decreased the real values of non-performing loans, thus increasing the debt service of the debtor. The finding that 1 percent increase in the industrial production index decreases non-performing loans by 0.94 percent indicates that economic growth affects non-performing loans negatively. One percent increase in unemployment rate increases non-performing loans by 1.01 percent. One percent increase in interests applied to consumer loans increases non-performing loans by 5.86 percent. One percent increase in M2 money supply increases non-performing loans by 1.10 percent.

An unrestricted error correction model (ECM) is created to analyze the short-term relationship between variables in the ARDL model developed by Pesaran et al. (2001). The model was adjusted as follows for the study:

$$\begin{aligned} \Delta lnNPLs_t = \alpha_0 + \sum_{i=1}^{p} \alpha_{1i} \Delta lnNPLs_{t-i} + \sum_{i=1}^{p} \alpha_{2i} \Delta \ln REER_{t-i} + \sum_{i=1}^{p} \alpha_{3i} \Delta \ln CPI_{t-i} \\ + \sum_{i=1}^{p} \alpha_{4i} \Delta lnIP_{t-i} + \sum_{i=1}^{p} \alpha_{5i} \Delta lnUR_{t-i} + \sum_{i=1}^{p} \alpha_{6i} \Delta lnINT_{t-i} + \sum_{i=1}^{p} \alpha_{7i} \Delta lnMT_{t-i} \\ + \gamma ECT_{t-1} + \varepsilon_t \end{aligned} \tag{4}$$

ECT_{t-1} is the error correction coefficient. It represents the lag of the error terms series obtained from the long-term relationship for one period. ECT_{t-1} coefficient shows how fast an imbalance that happens in the short term can be corrected in the long term. In addition, ECT_{t-1} indicates a long-term and stable relationship and cointegration between the dependent variable and independent variables.

Tab. 9.5: Short-Term ECM Estimation Results Based on the ARDL Model

Variables	Coefficients	Std. Error	t-Statistic	Probability
d(lnREER)	-0.1688	0,0771	-2,1880	0,0301
d(lnREER(-1))	-0.1975	0,0843	-2,3407	0,0205
d(lnUR)	0.4369	0,0988	4,4194	0,0000
d(lnINT)	-0.2428	0,2356	-1,0306	0,3042
d(lnINT(-1))	-0.0783	0,2509	-0,3121	0,7554
d(lnINT(-2))	-0.2458	0,2530	-0,9715	0,3327
d(lnINT(-3))	-0.5269	0,2246	-2,3451	0,0202
d(lnINT(-4))	0.4621	0,2267	2,0383	0,0431
d(lnINT(-5))	-0.6502	0,2168	-2,9988	0,0031
d(lnINT(-6))	-0.6199	0,2138	-2,8992	0,0043
d(lnINT(-7))	0.5819	0,2042	2,8490	0,0050
d(lnM2)	0.0152	0,1399	0,1091	0,9132
d(lnM2(-1))	0.5416	0,1328	4,0754	0,0001
d(lnM2(-2))	0.2053	0,1291	1,5904	0,1137
d(lnM2(-3))	-0.3397	0,1281	-2,6507	0,0088
d(lnM2(-4))	0.1736	0,1230	1,4108	0,1602
d(lnM2(-5))	-0.4032	0,1236	-3,2601	0,0014
d(lnM2(-6))	-0.4093	0,1235	-3,3137	0,0011
cointECT(-1)	-0.1020	0,0123	-8,2536	0,0000

$R^2 = 0.628, \overline{R^2} = 0.588$, DW statistic $= 1.90$

ECT_{t-1} coefficient must be negative and statistically significant so that the stability of the ECM model can be ensured. The γ coefficient shows how much an imbalance that happens in short term can be corrected in the long term.
Most of the coefficients are statistically significant according to the findings related to the ECM estimation. As you can see in Tab. 9.5, the ECT_{t-1} is negative as expected and significant at 1 percent. Accordingly, any short-term deviations in non-performing loans could approach the long-term equilibrium level. The fact that $ECT_{t-1}.ECT_{t-1}$ is -0.10 indicates that the equilibrium level could be approached with 10 percent speed of adjustment in case of imbalance in the short term.

Conclusion

Macroeconomic determinants of non-performing loans in the Turkish banking systems for the period from December 2001 to March 2018 were analyzed in this chapter. The share of the non-performing loans within the total amount of loans was used as a variable for the non-performing loans. The main findings of the study in which the ARDL bound test and ARDL error correction model were used are as follows: increases especially in non-performing loans are affected by macroeconomic conditions of the country in the long and short term. In other words, there is a long-term cointegration between non-performing loans and macroeconomic variables.

According to the results obtained from the model, the factors affecting increases in non-performing loans most are money supply, unemployment rate, and interest rates on consumer loans. As the volume of loans provided for companies and households will expand along with the money supply, an increase in the amount of non-performing loans is an expected finding. The fact that high unemployment rates decrease income levels and therefore weaken solvency increases the amount of non-performing loans. Furthermore, high interest rates in periods of economic recession affect non-performing loans negatively. This finding is supported by the fact that an increase in the industrial production index decreases the amount of non-performing loans. Increased solvency in periods of economic expansion increases loan quality and prevents non-performing loans from increasing. The impact of the real effective exchange rate on non-performing loans is positive as expected. Accordingly, appreciation of the national currency is expected to increase the amount of non-performing loans as it weakens the solvency of debtors. The findings obtained from the model indicate that the impact of the consumer price index on non-performing loans is considerably low.

The periods in which the amount of non-performing loans increased in the Turkish banking system can be divided into three categories: crisis periods (crises in November 2000 and February 2001, the global crisis in 2008), periods in which the loan volume expands (2015), and periods of macroeconomic recession (early 2000s). Considering the increases in the amount of non-performing loans during crisis periods, it is important to strengthen the effective banking supervision system and use a risk monitoring and early warning system. At this point, it is important to develop loan risk management at banks. Increases in the amount of non-performing loans during macroeconomic recessions show that it is important for policy makers to make efforts aimed at preventing excessive risks through macro prudential measures. Therefore, the findings of this study draw attention to the importance of strengthening and sustaining especially precautionary macroeconomic measures that will ensure financial stability.

References

Abid, L., Ouertani, M.N., & Zouari-Ghorbel, S. (2014). Macroeconomic and Bank-Specific Determinants of Household's Non-Performing Loans in Tunisia: A Dynamic Panel Data. *Procedia Economics and Finance, 13*, 58–68.

Adebola, S.S., Yusoff, W., & Dahalan, J. (2011). An ARDL Approach to the Determinants of Nonperforming Loans in Islamic Banking System in Malaysia. *Kuwait Chapter of Arabian Journal of Business and Management Review, 33*(830), 1-11.

BDDK (2005) "Banking Law No. 5411," https://www.bddk.org.tr/websitesi/turkce/mevzuat/bankacilik_kanunu/15405411_sayili_bankacilik_kanunu.pdf, (10.07.2018).

BDDK (2008). "Financial Markets Report," Number: 12, http://www.bddk.org.tr/WebSitesi/turkce/Raporlar/Finansal_Piyasalar_Raporlari/6320Finansal_Piyasalar_Raporu_Aralik_2008.pdf (10.07.2018).

Bhattarai, S. (2016). "Determinants of Non-Performing Loans: Perception of Nepali Bankers." *Economic Journal of Development Issues, 17*(1–2), 128–148.

Bofondi, M., & Ropele, T. (2011). Macroeconomic Determinants of Bad Loans: Evidence from Italian Banks.

Castro, V. (2013). "Macroeconomic Determinants of The Credit Risk in The Banking System: The Case of The GIPSI." *Economic Modelling, 31*, 672–683.

Chaibi, H., & Ftiti, Z. (2015). "Credit Risk Determinants: Evidence from a Cross-Country Study." *Research in international business and finance, 33*, 1–16.

Chikoko, L. (2013). "Zimbabwean Commercial Banks Liquidity Risk Determinants after Dollarisation".*Journal of Applied Finance & Banking, 3*(6), 97–114.

Das, A., & Ghosh, S. (2007). "Determinants of Credit Risk in Indian State-Owned Banks: An Empirical Investigation."*Economic Issues, 12*(2), 48–66.

Dickey, D.A., & Fuller, W.A. (1979). "Distribution of the Estimators for Autoregressive Time Series with a Unit Root," *Journal of the American Statistical Association, 74*:427–431.

Dickey, D.A., & Fuller, W.A. (1981). "Likelihood Ratio Tests for Autoregressive Time Series with a Unit Root." *Econometrica, 49*:1057–1072.

Dimitrios, A., Helen, L., & Mike, T. (2016). "Determinants of Non-Performing Loans: Evidence from Euro-Area Countries." *Finance Research Letters, 18*:116–119.

Engle, R.F., & Granger, C.W. (1987). "Co-Integration and Error Correction: Representation, Estimation, and Testing." *Econometrica: Journal of the Econometric Society*, 55(2), 251–276.

Fofack, H.L. (2005). *Nonperforming Loans in Sub-Saharan Africa: Causal Analysis and Macroeconomic Implications*. The World Bank. World Bank Policy Research Working Paper 3769, 1–36. https://doi.org/10.1596/1813-9450-3769

Johansen, S. (1988). "Statistical Analysis of Cointegration Vectors." *Journal of Economic Dynamics and Control, 12*(2–3), 231–254.

Johansen, S., & Juselius, K. (1990). "Maximum Likelihood Estimation and Inference on Cointegration—With Applications to the Demand For Money." *Oxford Bulletin of Economics and statistics, 52*(2), 169–210.

Khemraj, T., & Pasha, S. (2009). The Determinants of Non-Performing Loans: An Econometric Case Study of Guyana, MPRA Paper No. 53128, 1–26, https://mpra.ub.uni-muenchen.de/id/eprint/53128

Klein, N. (2013). *Non-performing loans in CESEE: Determinants and İmpact on Macroeconomic Performance*, IMF Working Paper, WP 13-72, 1–27, https://www.imf.org/external/pubs/ft/wp/2013/wp1372.pdf

Kwiatkowski, D., Phillips, P.C.B., Schmidt, P., & Shin, Y., (1992). "Testing the Null Hypothesis of Stationarity Against the Alternative of a Unit Root: How Sure Are We That Economic Time Series Have a Unit Root?" Journal of Econometrics, *54*(1):159–178.

Louzis, D.P., Vouldis, A.T., & Metaxas, V.L. (2012). "Macroeconomic and Bank-Specific Determinants of Non-Performing Loans in Greece: A Comparative Study of Mortgage, Business and Consumer Loan Portfolios." *Journal of Banking & Finance, 36*(4), 1012–1027.

Makri, V., Tsagkanos, A., & Bellas, A. (2014). "Determinants of Non-Performing Loans: The Case of Eurozone." *Panoeconomicus, 61*(2), 193–206.

Messai, A.S. & Jouini, F. (2013). Micro and Macro Determinants of Non-Performing Loans. *International Journal of Economics and Financial Issues, 3*(4), 852–860.

Mileris, R. (2012). "Macroeconomic Determinants of Loan Portfolio Credit Risk in Banks." *Engineering Economics, 23*(5), 496–504.

Ng, S. & Perron, P. (2001). "Lag Length Selection and the Construction of Unit Root Tests with Good Size and Power," *Econometrica, 69*(6): 1519–1554.

Nkusu, M.M. (2011). *Nonperforming Loans and Macrofinancial Vulnerabilities in Advanced Economies*, IMF Working Paper, WP 11/161,No. 11–161). International Monetary Fund, 1–25.

Pesaran, M.H. & Pesaran, B. (1997). *Working with Microfit 4.0: Interactive Econometric Analysis;[Windows Version]*. Oxford University Press, Oxford.

Pesaran, M.H., Shin, Y., & Smith, R.P. (1999). "Pooled Mean Group Estimation of Dynamic Heterogeneous Panels." *Journal of the American Statistical Association, 94*(446), 621–634.

Pesaran, M. H., Shin, Y., & Smith, R.J. (2001). "Bounds Testing Approaches to the Analysis of Level Relationships," *Journal of Applied Econometrics*, *16*(3):289–326.

Phillips, P.C.B. & ve Peron, P. (1988). "Testing for a Unit Root in Time Series Regression," *Biometrika 75*: 335–346.

Pilinkus, D. (2010). "Macroeconomic Indicators and Their Impact on Stock Market Performance in the Short and Long Run: The Case of the Baltic States. *Technological and Economic Development of Economy*, *16*(2), 291–304.

Rajeev, M., & Mahesh, H.P. (2010). *Banking sector reforms and NPA: A study of Indian commercial banks*. Institute for Social and Economic Change, WP 252, Bangalore. ISBN 978-81-7791-108-4. http://www.rjmarketings.com/themes/default/images/nparecovery.pdf

Reinhart, C.M., & Rogoff, K.S. (2011). "From Financial Crash to Debt Crisis." *American Economic Review*, *101*(5), 1676–1706.

Rinaldi, L., & Sanchis-Arellano, A. (2006). Household Debt Sustainability: What Explains Household Non-Performing Loans? An Empirical Analysis, ECB Working Paper, No. 570, European Central Bank (ECB), Frankfurt a. M.

Saba, I., Kouser, R., & Azeem, M. (2012). "Determinants of Non Performing Loans: Case of US Banking Sector." *The Romanian Economic Journal*, *44*(6), 125–136.

Salas, V., & Saurina, J. (2002). "Credit Risk in Two Institutional Regimes: Spanish Commercial and Savings Banks." *Journal of Financial Services Research*, *22*(3), 203–224.

Selimler, H. (2015). Sorunlu Kredilerin Analizi, Banka Finansal Tablo ve Oranlarına Etkisinin Değerlendirilmesi, Finansal Araştırmalar ve Çalışmalar Dergisi, 7 (12), 131–172, Doi: 10.14784/jfrs.74107

Sipahi, N. (2003). Problemli Kredilerin Yeniden Yapılandırılması Uluslar Arası Uygulamalar ve Türkiye Örneği. *TCMB Bankacılık ve Finansal Kuruluşlar Genel Müdürlüğü, Basılmamış Uzmanlık Yeterlilik Tezi, Ankara, www. tcmb. gov. tr/kutuphane/TURKCE/tezler/nihalsipahi.pdf, (12.07.2018).*

Škarica, B. (2014). Determinants of Non-Performing Loans in Central and Eastern European Countries." *Financial Theory and Practice*, *38*(1), 37–59.

Tomak, S. (2013). Determinants of Commercial Banks' Lending Behavior: Evidence from Turkey. *Asian Journal of Empirical Research*, *3*(8), 933–943.

Vatansever, M. & Hepsen, A. (2015), "Determining impacts on non-performing loan ratio in Turkey." *Journal of Applied finance and Banking*, *5*(1), 1.

Yüksel, S. (2016). "Bankaların Takipteki Krediler Oranını Belirleyen Faktörler: Türkiye İçin Bir Model Önerisi." *Journal of Bankers*, *98*, 41–56.

Tuba Derya Başkan

10 Analyzing the Relationship between the Valuation Method Used within the Scope of TFRS-9 Financial Instruments Profitability and Capital Structure of the Turkish Banking Sector

Abstract: The purpose of this chapter is to determine how the profitability and capital structure of Turkish banks using this appraisal method is affected. According to the results of the analysis, while there is a significant relationship between the capital structure and liquidity in the valuation methods of financial instruments, there is no meaningful result between capital structure and profitability.

Keywords: TFRS-9, Banking Sector, Profitability, Valuation Method

1 Introduction

Senior executives and owners of companies have taken advantage of situations susceptible to abuse due to some loopholes in the accounting legislation and the lack of a common accounting language in the world. This eventually caused a big crisis in the world and the main reason for this was determined to be accounting errors and fraud. Comprehensive efforts have been made both in Turkey and in the world for about twenty years in order to prevent it. Accounting standards have been established as a result of these efforts and arrangements that are in compliance with the Turkish legal legislation and the world accounting standards have been made.

Many countries apply the financial reporting standards that were published by the International Accounting Standards Board. A communique was published in 2003 to make sure that companies subject to the Capital Markets Board would prepare financial statements in accordance with the International Accounting Standards. Afterwards, the Public Oversight Authority (POA) was authorized to coordinate them, and it was made compulsory for public companies and international import and export companies in Turkey to use accounting standards. The "TAS-39: Financial Instruments-Recognition and Measurement" standard within the scope of the Turkish Accounting Standards is one of these accounting standards. Many factors such as financial instrument types, registration, clarification, valuation, etc., are important in terms of accounting records. This standard defines the scope, qualities, classification of financial instruments, as well as the additional information that must be given about them, and it specifies how valuation of such instruments will be shown in balance sheets. financial instruments are evaluated in detail when they are included in balance sheets for the first time and this valuation is followed by others in the following balance sheet periods (Örten, Kaval, Karapınar, 2013: 436).

Historical cost is the valuation method that is preferred most by companies for financial reporting. TAS Conceptual Framework states that historical cost can be measured with the total amount paid for the initial acquisition of the asset. The historical cost method is an effective method for providing reliable information, revealing the values of assets and liabilities at the time of acquisition and making decisions based on reports. However, it is an insufficient valuation method in terms of changes that can take place in values of assets and liabilities in the periods after acquisition (Kaya, 2016:144).

The fair value concept started to be used instead of the historical cost concept underlying financial reporting. Information obtained from business activity reports based on the historical cost principle can cause users to make wrong decisions. It guides standard users while determining asset values of companies. Adopting the fair value approach for accurate and reliable financial reporting following the big financial crises and accounting standards is considered to be more effective as it takes into account current and future values of assets and liabilities (Tokay, Deran, & Aktai, 2005:11–12).

The most significant difference between the fair value principle and historical value principle is that value changes that may happen in the future are taken into account. The fair value approach makes it possible to report unrealized profits and losses. In other words, profits and losses are included in the financial reporting process as soon as they are realized in the historical cost method while possible impacts of the company activities that may emerge in the future are included in the fair value method. The fair value method is more reliable because values of assets and liabilities can change very rapidly under current conditions. It became mandatory to use the "TFRS-13 Fair Value Measurement" standard at publicly held companies as of 31.12.2012 as the fair value measurement method has many advantages. Fair value is the amount agreed upon by informed and willing groups through mutual bargaining for exchange of an asset or payment of a debt (KGK, TFRS-13). Tangible and intangible fixed assets that are a part of a company's assets and liabilities, investment property, marketable securities, financial assets whose fair value differences are reflected in profits and losses, cash and securities, trade receivables and other receivables, provisions for termination indemnities are assets that are evaluated with fair values (Pamukçu, 2011:83). It is thought that financial reports based on this valuation method will satisfy needs of information users better and provide clearer results about businesses (Gücenme, 2007: 14).

The financial instruments included in this study are analyzed within the scope of TFRS-9 financial Instruments standard. This standard aims to determine the principles for presenting Financial instruments as liabilities and equities and clarifying them. This standard is applied in financial instruments of almost all businesses with some exceptions. These exceptions have been determined as follows (POA, TAS-32).

Shares in affiliates, subsidiaries, or joint ventures that are accounted within the scope of TFRS 10 Consolidated Financial Statements, TAS 27 Separate financial Statements, or TAS 28 Investments in Associates and Joint Ventures,

Employer rights and liabilities within the scope of pension benefit plans in which TAS 19 Employee Benefits standard is applied,

Financial Instruments that are a part of TFRS 4 as they include insurance contracts defined in TFRS 4 Insurance Contracts and whose participation is optional,

Financial instruments, contracts and liabilities in share-based payments to which TFRS 2 Share-Based Payments standard applies.

Although this standard is not a financial agreement, when parties make acquisitions in cash or with financial instruments through purchase and sale agreements, they will perform valuation according to this standard (Örten et al., 2013:433).

- When companies acquire financial instruments or liabilities for sale in the short term, they are deemed to be assets possessed with intent to sell. Furthermore, derivative products other than those having financial guarantee agreements or efficient hedging instruments are also included in this group.
- Financial instruments of companies that can be held until the maturity date.
- Marketable financial instruments of companies.
- Financial instruments in the form of credits and receivables that are not traded in an active market.

The following parts of the chapter analyze the relationship between usage of the fair value method by banks included in the study and profitability, capital structure, and liquidity.

2 Literature

Certain studies on the fair value method are analyzed in this part of the chapter. Topbaş (2009) conducted a study analyzing the impacts of the fair value method on financial systems of banks in a financial crisis environment. He examined the fair value method, revealed the developments at foreign banks and criticism about this method within the framework of the International Accounting Standards, evaluated the opportunities provided for the Turkish banking sector, and revealed the feasibility of this method. Another study on this method was conducted by Özkan and Terzi (2009). They analyzed the fair value measurement method in terms of international accounting standards and the American Accounting Standards, revealing the feasibility of the fair value method, as well as its impacts on assets.

As for studies analyzing the fair value measurement method in terms of accounting, Özdemir and Elitaş determined the differences emerging in accounting transactions of securities in the banking sector in accordance with the TAS-39 standard. For this purpose, they emphasized the importance of fair value accounting and revealed the accounting differences emerging in line with keeping securities in banks. They also tried to explain situations resulting when profit and loss differences to be reflected in equities are evaluated with the historical cost method. Ayçiçek (2011) examined the measurement methods of financial instruments, and measurement methods and accounting of bonds in a study on evaluation of financial instruments. He stated that the first accounting for the issued bonds would be performed with the fair value method in accordance with the standard; however, the part of the financial liabilities directly corresponding to transaction costs would be reported as expense, and they would not be included in the fair value. Kaya (2015) conducted a study on accounting of financial instruments in accordance with the Turkish Accounting Standards and financial Reporting Standards and concluded that financial instruments were not explained sufficiently and financial liabilities were not paid due attention. The study also examined whether the fair values of company assets were determined, whether they caused cash management and interest collection, and found out that the financial assets were evaluated and accounted in accordance with the relevant contracts.

In another study, İşseveroğlu (2014) analyzed valuation and reporting applications of companies trading in the BIST 100 index in accordance with the TAS-39 standard and reports about the increases and decreases in equity values of these companies. The study found out that 37 out of the 56 companies did not use the fair value measurement method and the remaining 19 companies used the fair value method between 2005 and 2012. It was determined that they did not add the valuation results to the capital, and they kept them in the valuation funds of equities. Bhat and Ryan (2015) analyzed damages caused by increases made by banks in accordance with the fair value method on financial instruments, and they determined with a market risk analysis that they increased returns of fair value increases and earnings. Halioui and Gharbi (2012) analyzed valuation of financial instruments with the fair value method and determined that it strengthened the banking sector. Furthermore, the findings revealed an adaption process between interbank problems caused by liquidity shortage in the market and accounting of financial instruments. There are other studies in the literature, but this study contains the relevant literature.

3 The Relationship between the Fair Value Method and Profitability, Capital Adequacy, and Liquidity Applications in the Turkish Banking Sector

3.1 Research Methodology

The logistic analysis method which is a multivariate statistical analysis technique also known as logit analysis was used in this study in order to determine how evaluating financial instruments of banks with the fair value method affects company profitability and capital structure. *Logistic analysis* is:

Qualitative classification of the dependent variable. A successful analysis method for models with a qualitative dependent variable (Baydemir, 2014:27).

This is a flexible method that requires fewer assumptions than similar statistical methods. This method does not have any requirements such as normal distribution of independent variables, presence of a linear correlation between them, and presence of equal variations between different categories.

It is easier to execute the model in the logistic model as the model is made linear.

Logistic regression does not have the problem of running into a negative possibility.

The logistic regression analysis method is a non-linear analysis and the key concept of logistic regression is "logit." Logit is the logarithm of the possibility ratio. The logistic regression model is written as follows.

$$\text{Logit}(p) = \log \frac{p}{p\text{-}1} = X^{1}\beta + u$$

where p and p-1 represent the fair value method and the case where the fair value is not used respectively. Xk, nX(k+1), $\boldsymbol{\beta}(\mathbf{k}+1)$, and u represent the independent variable, independent variable matrix, parameter vector, and error term, respectively (Ural, Gürarda, Önemli, 2015: 90).

In this method, the independent variable values are tried to be determined through possibilities by assigning two values to the dependent variable. The logistic analysis method is divided into groups according to the shape of the dependent variable. The first one is Simple (Binary) Logistic Regression Analysis in which the dependent variables have two categories, are divided into groups, and the groups are coded 0 and 1. This method was used in this study (Kocabaş, 2014:14).

Y= {businesses using the fair value method; 0= businesses not using the fair value method}.

The Yi dependent variable with two categories has been formulated as follows in a way that the best linear combination of independent (explanatory) variables is based on a non-linear function and i indicates the possibility that the financial instruments might belong to one of the two categories (Ayan, 2018:83).

$$Y = \frac{\mathbf{u}\beta 0 + \beta 1\mathbf{X}1 + \beta 2\mathbf{X}2 + \cdots + \boldsymbol{\beta}\mathbf{kXk}}{1 + \mathbf{u}\beta 0 + \beta 1\mathbf{X}1 + \beta 2\mathbf{X}2 + \cdots + \boldsymbol{\beta}\mathbf{kXk}}$$

The two-category Y dependent variable is based on a non-linear function of the best linear combination of dependent variables, which results in the following equation:

$$Y = u\ \beta_0 + \beta_1 X^1 1 + \beta_2 X^2 + \ldots + \beta_n\ X^n 1 + u$$

3.2 Research Hypotheses and Variables

This section tries to determine the impacts of evaluating financial instruments of banks with the fair value method on capital structures and profitability of companies. The relationship between the fair value method and profitability, capital structure, and liquidity of thirteen Turkish banks between 2002 and 2017 was examined using the simple logistic regression method. The hypotheses given in Tab. 10.1 were created for this purpose.

Some rations were used to test the hypotheses. These rations are stated in the table below (Akgüç, 2012). The data about these firms was obtained from their websites, Is Investment and the Public Disclosure Platform (KAP). The dependent variable was determined by assigning "1" to the companies using fair values and "0" to those not using fair values. The determined dependent variables are shown in Tab. 10.2.

The simple logistic regression model was formulated as follows after determining the variables

Tab. 10.1: Research Hypotheses

H1: There is a significant correlation between company profitability and valuation of financial instruments of banks using the fair value method.

H2: There is a significant correlation between capital structures of companies and valuation of financial instruments of banks using the fair value method.

H3: There is a significant correlation between liquidity of companies and valuation of financial instruments of banks using the fair value method.

Tab. 10.2: Research Variables

Res. Variables	Abbreviations	Calculations	Obtained from
Capital Structure1	Eqty/Tot. Asst.	Equity/Total Assets	KAP and Is Investment
Net Interest Margin	NII/Tot. Asst.	Net Interest Income/ Avr. Total Assets	KAP and Is Investment
Asset Structure and Qlt.	GDS/Tot.Asst.	Government Debt Securities/ Total Assets	KAP and Is Investment
Net Profit for the Period	PPrft.	Logarithm of Net Profit for the Period	KAP and Is Investment
Liquid assets 1	Lqd A 1	Cash assets and Receivables from the Central Bank, Banks, Other financial Institutions and Money Markets/Total Deposits	KAP and Is Investment

$$GUD_{it} = \beta_0 + \beta 1 \text{ÖzKyn/TopVar}_{it} + \beta_2 \text{NFG/TopVar}_{it} + \beta_3 \text{DBS / TopVar}_{it} + \beta_4 \ln \text{DNKâr}_{it} + \beta_5 \ln \text{LKT}_{it} + u_{i,}$$

4 Empirical Findings

The two-category dependent variable and five independent variables with different types and amounts of categories were subjected to a logistic regression analysis. For the model given above to be valid, the R^2 value must be between 0 and 1 and a probability level under 0.05 is sufficient (Çemrek and Burhan, 2014: 55).

Border values must be determined by conducting some tests regarding whether the model will be accepted. These detections that are called Goodness of Fit Statistics indicate the efficiency level of the model created to explain the

Tab. 10.3: Simple Logistic Analysis Results

Variables	Coefficient	Standard Error	t Statistic	Probability Value
Equity/Tot. Asst.	0,9246924	0,0226734	-3,19	0,001
Net Int. Inc./Tot. Asst.	4,544574	2,154715	3,19	0,001
Government Debt Securities/Tot. Asst.	09997731	0,0091582	-0,02	0,980
Log. Net Profit for the Period	1,037399	0,1081956	0,35	0,725
Log. Liquidity	1,482678	0,151199	3,86	0,000
Cons	0,0026846	0,0031719	-5,01	0,000
Corrected R^2	0,4790			
F Statistic Probability	(0.000)*			
Number of Observations	203			

Note: Significant at 1 %. (Dependent Variable: GUD)

dependent variable best. The Hosmer-Lemeshow test which is one of these measurements was also used in this study (Hosmer and Lemeshow, 2000: 156). This test shows the consistency of the logistic regression model within a whole. It is a powerful test when you work with small samples. The p value must be higher than 0.05, i.e., the result must not be significant while interpreting the results of this test. In other words, there must be no significant difference between the model and the values (Garson, 2008).

According to the Goodness of Fit results obtained from the Hosmer and Lemeshow test, the Probability value was 0.8531 and the model was found out to be feasible as it was higher than 0.05.

When we look at the Tab. 10.3, we see that the results of the analyses conducted in the banking sector showed that the corrected R^2 value of the model was 0.4790. According to these results, we can say that the independent and control variables in the model can account for 0.4790 percent of the dependent variable. The result of the F test that was conducted to determine whether the model was statistically significant revealed that the probability value showing the significance level of the statistic value was 0.000. Partial regression coefficients of the independent variables related to the quality of independent auditing revealed the following results:

- The coefficient, t, and probability values of the Equity/Total Assets variable measuring the capital structure were determined as 0.9246924, -3.19, and 0.001, respectively. According to this result, one unit increase in the Equity/

Total Assets variable increases the use of fair value by 0.9246924 units at 1 percent significance level. In other words, there is a significant and positive correlation between the capital structure and use of fair value in financial instruments.

- The coefficient, t, and probability values of the Net Interest Income/Total Assets variable were determined as 4.544574, -0.02, and 0.001, respectively. According to this result, one-unit increase in the Net Interest Income/Total Assets variable increases the use of fair value by 4.544574 units. In other words, there is a significant and positive correlation between Net Interest Income/Total Assets and use of fair value in financial instruments.
- The coefficient, t, and probability values of the Government Debt Securities/Total Assets variable were determined as 09997731, 3.19, and 0.980, respectively. According to this result, there is no significant and positive correlation between Government Debt Securities/Total Assets and the use of financial value in financial instruments at 1 percent, 5 percent, and 10 percent significance levels.
- The Net Profit for the Period coefficient value, t value, and probability value were determined as 1.037399, 0.35, and 0.725, respectively. The logarithm result of the net profit for the period was also subjected to analysis. According to this result, there is no significant and positive correlation between Net Profit for the Period and the use of financial value in financial instruments at 1 percent, 5 percent, and 10 percent significance levels.
- The coefficient, t, and probability values of the liquidity variable were determined as 1.482678, 3.86, and 0.000, respectively. According to this result, one unit increase in the Liquidity variable increases the use of fair value by 1.482678 units at 1 percent significance level. In other words, there is a significant and positive correlation between Liquidity and use of fair value in financial instruments.
- According to the model results, the first hypothesis that "There is a significant correlation between company profitability and valuation of financial instruments of banks using the fair value method" was rejected while the other hypotheses stating that "There is a significant correlation between capital structures of companies and valuation of financial instruments of banks using the fair value method" and "There is a significant correlation between liquidity of companies and valuation of financial instruments of banks using the fair value method" were accepted.

Tab. 10.4 shows the results obtained from the analysis conducted on the net profit of the company for the period with the fair value without using other variables.

Tab. 10.4: The Correlation between the Net Profit for the Period and GUD

Variables	Coefficient	t statistic	Probability Value
Net Profit for the Period	1,00	3,54	0,000
Corrected R2	0,2757		
F Statistic Probability	(0.000)*		
Number of Observations	203		
Hosmer-Lemeshow	0,9985		

According to the results, the coefficient, t, and probability values of the profit for the period variable were determined as 1.00, 3.54, and 0.000 respectively. According to this result, one-unit increase in the net profit for the period variable increases the use of fair value by 1.00 units at 1 percent significance level. In other words, there is a significant and positive correlation between the net profit for the period and use of fair value in financial instruments. According to the goodness of fit test result of the model, the efficiency level of the model was determined as 0.9985.

Conclusion

This chapter analyzed the fair value measurement method which is one of the evaluation methods within the scope of the TFRS-9 Financial Instruments standard, and tried to determine its relationship with liquidity, profitability, and capital adequacy in the Turkish banking sector.

According to the analysis conducted on public banks, a significant correlation was determined between the profitability and fair values of thirteen banks when the other variables were excluded. A positive and significant correlation was determined between the net periodic profits and fair values of the banks, and it was found out that a change in the net profit for the period affected the fair value by one fold. The fact that usage of fair value by companies increases as their net periodic profits increase indicates that it is important to perform a valuation on financial instruments of companies according to current conditions. On the other hand, as there were many other factors that could affect net profits (e.g., liability or capital ratios of companies), a correlation was determined between profitability and the fair value method when many factors such as whether companies had liquid assets, etc., were taken into account.

When we examine all variables together, variables such as equity/total assets, capital structure and debt ratios of companies, etc., measuring the capital structure are important both for company existence and in extraordinary circumstances. As evaluating financial instruments with the fair value method shows the current values of assets owned by companies, as well as affecting profit and loss statements, a correlation is assumed to exist between capital structure and the fair value method.

A positive and significant correlation with 0.001 probability value was determined between the Net Interest Income/Total Assets variable and the fair value method. Exchange profits or losses resulting from use of foreign exchange by banks affect interest incomes and expenses. In the event that banks have foreign exchange gaps, net interest margins are calculated very high when the national currency loses value. This result can be caused by the fact that this ratio could be more accurate when banks use the fair value method for their financial instruments. Determining bank assets with the fair value method makes it possible to perform a more accurate evaluation of profits and losses, affects deposit increases, and makes it necessary to evaluate the liquidity ratio within the framework of many factors such as the monetary policy of the Central Bank.

The study results revealed a correlation between capital structures and liquidity ratios of the companies and a significant correlation was found for profitability when the other factors were excluded. It could be possible to reach more general results in future studies by evaluating all assets and liabilities of banks with the fair value method.

References

Arsoy, P. A. (2012) "Muhasebe Standartlarında Ölçüm Süreci ve Ölçüm Esasları," *Journal of Balance*, *140*: 62–67.

Ayan, T.Y. & Değirmeni, N. (2018) "Firma Finansal Başarısızlık Öngörüsü İçin Bir Lojistik Regresyon Modeli," *International Journal of Economic and Administrative Review*, *18*. EYİ Private Number, 77–88.

Ayçiçek, F. (2011). TMS 39 Çerçevesinde Bir Finansal Araç Olarak Tahviller. Muhasebe ve Finansman Dergisi, (50), 59–76.

Baydemir, M.B. (2014) "Lojistik Regresyon Analizi Üzerine Bir İnceleme," Master's Thesis, İnönü University, Social Science Institute, Malatya.

Bhat, G. & Stephen, G.R. (2015) "The Impact of Risk Modeling on the Market Perception of Banks' Estimated Fair Value Gains And Losses for Financial Instruments," *Accounting Organizations Society*, *46*: 81–95.

Çemrek, F. & Burhan, E. (2014) "Petrol tüketiminin ekonomik büyüme üzerindeki etkisinin panel veri analizi ile incelenmesi: Avrupa Birliği Ülkeleri ve Türkiye örneği," *Journal of International Alanya Business Faculty*, *6*, 3: 47–58.

Garson, G.D. (2008) "Logistic regression," http://www2.chass.ncsu.edu/garson/PA765/logistic.htm.

Gücenme, Ü. (2007) *Türkiye Muhasebe Standartları ve Uygulamaları*, İstanbul: Türkmen Publishment.

Halioui, K. & L.Gharbi, (2012) "Does Fair Value for Financial Instruments Constitute a New Channel of Contagion?," *Global Business and Management Research: An International Journal, Vol: 4*, 1:60–75.

Hosmer, D.W. & Stanley, L. (2000) "Applied Logistic Regression," John Wiley and Sons, New York.

Kaya, G.A. (2015) "Türkiye Muhasebe-Finansal Raporlama Standartları'na Göre Finansal Araçların Muhasebeleştirilmesi," *Fırat University Journal of Social Science Institute*, Cilt: *25*, 1: 105–121.

Kaya, U. (2016) "Finansal Bilgi Kullanıcıları Açısından Gerçeğe Uygun Değer Muhasebesi," *World of Accounting and Auditing*, 1: 138–152.

Kocabaş, E. (2014) " Lojistik Regresyon Ve Bankacılık Verileri Üzerine Bir Uygulama," Master's Thesis, Yıldız Teknik University, Social Science Institute, İstanbul.

Örten, R., Kaval, H., & Karapınar, A. (2013). Türkiye Muhasebe-Finansal Raporlama Standartları (TMS-TFRS): Uygulama ve yorumları. Gazi Kitabevi, Ankara.

Özdemir, S. & Elitaş, C. (2011) "Bankacılık Sektöründe Menkul Değerlerin TMS 39 Standardına Uygun Olarak Muhasebeleştirilme İşlemlerinde Ortaya Çıkan Farkların Tespiti Üzerine Bir İnceleme," *Journal of Financial Solution*, 21: 27–47

Özkan, M., & Terzi, S. (2009). Gerçeğe uygun değer ölçümünün uluslararası muhasebe standartları ve Amerikan muhasebe standartları (SFAS) açısından incelenmesi. Mali Çözüm Dergisi, 92, 23–50.

Pamukçu, F. (2011) "Gerçeğe Uygun Değer Muhasebesi ve Finansal Tablolara Etkisi," *Journal of Financial Solution*, 79–95. http://archive.ismmmo.org.tr/docs/malicozum/103malicozum/5%20fatma%20pamukcu.pdf

Tokay, H., Deran, A., & Aktaş, R. (2005) "Uluslararası Muhasebe Ve Finansal Raporlama Standartlarında Gerçeğe Uygun Değer Yaklaşımı ve Muhasebe Uygulamalarına Etkisi," XXIV. Türkiye Muhasebe Eğitimi Sempozyumu-Muhasebe Ortamında Güncel Gelişmeler ve Muhasebe Eğitimine Etkileri.

Topbaş, N. (2009) "Finansal Kriz Ortamında Bankaların Muhasebe Sistemlerinde Gerçeğe Uygun Değerleme Yönteminin Etkileri," *Journal of Bankers*, *68*:56–64.

Ural, K., Gürarda, Ş., & Önemli, M.B. (2015) "Lojistik Regresyon Modeli İle Finansal Başarısızlık Tahminlemesi: Borsa İstanbul'da Faaliyet Gösteren Gıda, İçki ve Tütün Şirketlerinde Uygulama," *Journal of Accounting and Financing*, *67*: 85–100.

Gülçin Gürel Günal and Ertuğrul Deliktaş

11 The Market Structure of the Turkish Banking Sector That Changed with the Crisis in 2001: Merger and Acquisition Effect

Abstract: This chapter compares and analyzes the market structure of the Turkish banking sector before and after 2001 with structural and non-structural approaches within the frame of industrial organization theories. It differs from other studies considering not only the balance sheet values of banks but also the other important determinants of the market structure such as the mergers, capital ownership of banks, and technology.

Keywords: Turkish Banking Sector, Market Structure, Merger and Acquisition, Industrial Organization Theories

1 Introduction

The globalization process that started in commerce and developed rapidly in the fields of production, politics, and finance experienced the biggest and fastest transformation with financial globalization movements after 1980. A financial market has emerged where controls are lifted, interests and exchange rates are determined by the market mechanism, and national currencies are convertible due to financial globalization. All these developments have increased financial movements rapidly. In addition, financial markets have become one of the most important markets with the help of big technological advancements since 1990 (Hanson and Ramachandran, 2005). Accordingly, big developments have taken place within the financial market for all institutions and organizations, especially banks, in the monetary and capital markets. Especially banks have diversified their financial instruments, various legal regulations have been made, and a sectoral structure in harmony with the global world has been created in order to adapt to the developing financial markets.

All these global developments have taken place in Turkey as well. The importance attached to the banking sector started to increase as of 1980. That is because Turkey had an inward-oriented import-substitution economy until 1980. The banking sector exhibited non-competitive behaviors under state control in those periods. On the other hand, competitive behaviors emerged in the banking sector after the export-oriented industrialization strategy was put into practice in 1980. Entrance into the sector accelerated in 1980 due to financial liberalization. As a result, the number of banks in the Turkish banking sector started to increase as of 1990 and competitive behaviors were expected in the sector afterwards. On the other hand, some banks have left the sector and the number of banks has decreased as a result of the developments that have taken place all over the country and especially in banks after 2000. In addition to this change in the number of banks, changes have taken place in balance sheet values, capital ownership, and merger-acquisition decisions of banks (Aktaş and Kargın, 2007). These developments in the Turkish banking sector have affected the general structure, competitive power, and characteristics of the sector. Therefore, it is important to reveal the qualities of the Turkish banking sector and analyze the sector structure. That is because knowing whether the market containing the banking sector is a perfect competition market, monopoly, oligopoly, or monopolistic competition market provides information on market competition and efficient operation of the market. This information is highly important for determining policies that can be implemented in order to support the financial structure.

2 The Market Structure and Competition Analysis of the Turkish Banking Sector

The market structure consists of all qualities determining relationships between actors in a market where competitive behaviors are taken into account under current market conditions. Within this framework, the determinants of the market structure can be listed as follows: qualities of goods and services produced in industries, whether they are homogeneous, their substitutability levels, the number and characteristics of companies or buyers, actions of all decision-making units within the organization, and legal framework (Yıldırım and Eşkinat, 1996:10). In fact, all this data provide information about the market structure and enable market analyses.

This chapter analyzes the market structure of the Turkish banking sector before and after 2001 with structural and non-structural approaches within the scope of industrial organization theories. The general structure and competitive power of the sector are revealed by taking the characteristics of the market into account within this framework. The year 1990 was chosen as the starting point for the analysis. That is because it is known that activities related to a competitive banking sector started with the financial liberalization movements in 1989 along with the outward-oriented economy policies of Turkey (the export oriented industrialization strategy in 1980).

Not only the balance sheet values of the banks but also mergers and acquisitions, capital ownership of banks, and technological advances that are other important determinants of the market structure were included in the analysis. It is highly important to take into account the impact of merger and acquisition activities that have been felt more intensively since 1990 on the market structure so that healthy policies can be developed for the Turkish banking sector. In addition, there are differences in bank characteristics depending on the capital ownership (banks with domestic or foreign capital) before and after 2001 in the Turkish banking sector. These differences show their effect through policies implemented by banks. Differentiated balance sheets change the market structure and affect the competition level. Rapid technological developments affect all sectors and change decisions and applications in financial markets. Therefore, technological developments must be taken into account in analyses. In short, as you can see in Fig. 11.1, it is necessary to take into account all these characteristics, especially balance sheet values of banks, in all studies on the market structure of the Turkish banking sector so that healthier results can be obtained.

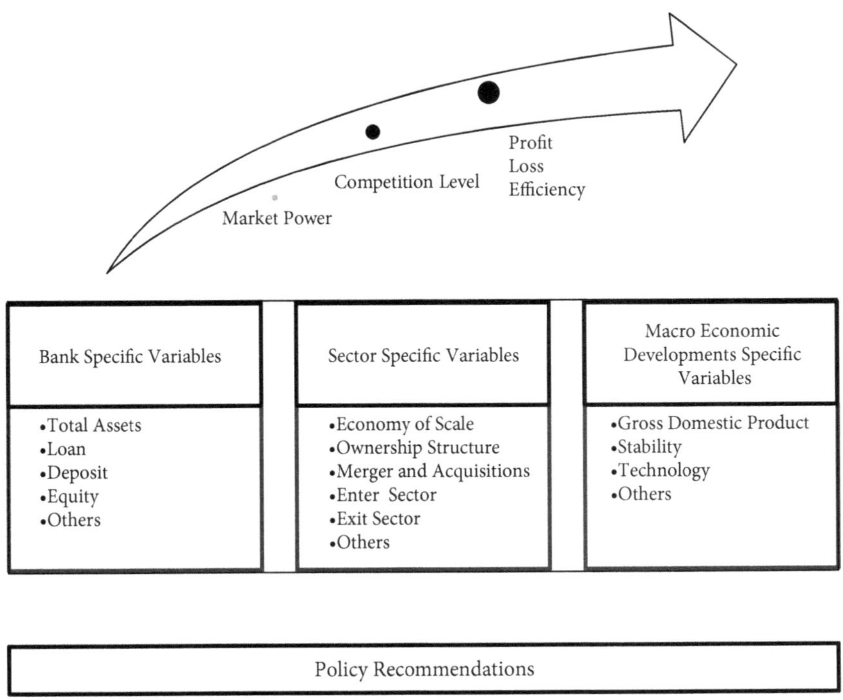

Fig. 11.1: Determinants of Market Structure in Banking Sector. Source: Created by the authors.

When we look at the international literature related to analysis of the market structure, we come across studies conducted with the Panzar Rosse H-Statistic (Panzar and Rosse, 1977), the Lerner Index (Lerner, 1934), and, more recently, Adjusted Lerner Index (Koetter, Kolari, and Spierdijk, 2008). The studies conducted in Turkey have been based mostly on the Panzer Rosse H-Statistic method. The number of studies conducted with the Lerner Index and Adjusted Lerner Index is insufficient. Although these three methods are not superior to each other, it is thought that the Adjusted Lerner Index that makes it possible to calculate separate values for each bank, takes the efficiency levels of banks into account, and performs competition analyses to produce more accurate results (Koetter, Kolari, and Spierdijk, 2012: 464–465). For this reason, evaluating the market structure of the Turkish banking sector with the Lerner Index and Adjusted Lerner Index will fill a significant deficiency.

When we look at the methods used in the literature, we see that Guevara, Maudos, and Perez (2005); Carbo, Humphrey, Maudos, and Molyneux (2009); and Agoraki, Delis, and Pasiouras (2011) found out in their studies using the Lerner Index that the banking sector in the European Union countries exhibited competitive behaviors while monopolistic competition took place in East European countries. Berger, Klapper, and Ariss (2009); Desil (2012); and Anginer, Demirgüç-Kunt, and Zhu (2014) who studied countries selected from all around the world stated that the banking sector was competitive in developed countries and non-competitive in other countries.

Yıldırım (2014) and Kasman and Kasman (2015) preferred the Lerner Index in their studies and revealed that the Turkish banking sector exhibited non-competitive market behaviors in the analysis they conducted for 2000 and later.

2.1 Model and Methodology

Formulas were used for CR_M concentration ratio and HKI (Hannah-Kay Index) (1970) that are structural approaches and panel data analysis methods were used for calculations of the Lerner Index and Adjusted Lerner Index that are non-structural approaches in order to analyze the market structure of the Turkish banking sector within the industrial organization theories. The preferred models were developed by taking the literature and the characteristics of the Turkish banking sector into account.

The translog cost function was used in the analyses conducted with the Lerner Index and Adjusted Lerner Index.

The Lerner Index and Adjusted Lerner Index

$$Lerner_{it} = \left(P_{it} - MC_{it}\right) / P_{it} \tag{1}$$

where P and MC represent the price and marginal cost, respectively. The translog cost function must be estimated in order to calculate the marginal cost. The translog cost functions used by Agoraki, Delis, and Pasiouras (2011); Delis (2012); and Anginer, Demirgüç-Kunt, and Zhu (2014) were followed for the analysis of the translog cost function and the translog cost function given in Equation 2 was obtained within the framework of the Added Value Approach and the characteristics of the Turkish banking sector.

$$\begin{aligned} lnTC_{it}^{*} = {} & a_0 + a_1 lnta_{it} + a_2 lnta_{it}^2 + a_3 lnd_{it} + a_4 lnd_{it}^2 + a_5 lnta_{it} lnd_{it} + \sum_{n=1}^{2} \alpha_n lnw_{it}^{n^*} \\ & + \sum_{n=1}^{2} \sum_{m=1}^{2} \gamma_{nm} lnw_{it}^{n^*} lnw_{it}^{m^*} + \sum_{n=1}^{2} \delta_n lnw_{it}^{n^*} lnta_{it} + \sum_{n=1}^{2} \varphi_n lnw_{it}^{n^*} lnd_{it} \\ & + m_{it} + spe_{it} + t_t + \varepsilon_{it} \end{aligned} \tag{2}$$

Equation 2 was estimated with the Ordinary Least Squares Method (OLS) (fixed effects) in order to calculate the Lerner Index. The fixed effects model in the OLS estimation was chosen through the LR Test and Hausman Test Statistic. The possible heterogeneity between the banks and the separate impacts of each bank could be taken into account by using the fixed effect model in the analysis. The annual marginal cost values of each bank were calculated.

Equation 2 was also estimated with the Stochastic Frontier Analysis in order to calculate the Adjusted Lerner Index.

2.2 Data Set

Two period analyses taking the years from 1990 to 2000 and 2001 to 2014 into account were conducted in the study. All public-financed, private-financed, and foreign-financed commercial banks including those that have branches in Turkey were taken into account in all analyses. Calculations were made for 62 commercial banks with at least four years of observation value in the first analysis period and for 40 commercial banks with the same characteristics in the second analysis period that is between 2001 and 2014. All data related to the variables used in the analyses was taken from the Banks Association of Turkey and all values were deflated.

Total assets, total credits, and total deposits were used in the CR_M and HKI calculations made in the study. Furthermore, the values of the Lerner Index and Adjusted Lerner Index that are new approaches were obtained by estimating the translog cost function. Total cost (*TC*) was used as the dependent variable in this model based on the added value approach while personnel (w_1), interest (w_2), and operating costs (w_3) that are inputs used by banks and total assets (*ta*) and total deposits (*d*) that are outputs created by banks were preferred as independent variables[1,2]. In addition, the control variables affecting the structure of the Turkish banking sector were included in the model. Mergers (*m*), trends showing technological development (*t*), and bank types according to capital (*spe*) were used. The total cost, personnel costs, and interest costs were divided by operating costs in order to avoid heterogeneity problems in the model. Moreover, the price variable that is another variable necessary for the Lerner Index and Adjusted Lerner Index cannot be directly known in each sector. Therefore, a proxy variable was used for the price variable related to the analyzed banking sector in this study. In this sense, the

1 When the Turkish banking sector is evaluated within the framework of behavior models, we see that the sector has characteristics that are more similar to the characteristics of the added value approach. The liability and asset values in the Turkish banking sector were very close to each other until 1995, and both the asset values and liabilities, especially deposits, started to increase as of 1995. This indicates that total assets and deposits can be considered to be an output of a bank in the banking sector. In other words, the Turkish banking sector has a structure that is based on deposits and total assets, most of which consist of loans. On the other hand, this approach is superior to the other approaches as it takes almost all balance sheet items of the sector into account.

2 It is not easy to determine input prices, and proxy variables are used most of the time. In this context, average wage that is the price of the labor force is accepted as the proxy price variable. That is because bank employees in a country are expected to receive similar wages. Labor payments and employee number are regarded as values necessary to calculate the labor price, and the labor price is obtained by dividing the labor payments by the total number of employees. The capital price can be accepted as the average leasing value. An assumption similar to the assumption made for labor price calculation can be used to determine the capital price. The share of total non-interest expenses within total assets or total fixed assets indicates the capital price as the proxy variable. Finally, interest rates are accepted as the deposit price, i.e., cost of borrowing and the total share obtained by interest expenses from the total deposits indicate the deposit price (Daglish, Robertson, Tripe, and Weill, 2015).

value obtained by dividing the interest income by the total assets was preferred as the proxy price variable.

2.3 Analysis Results: Structural Approaches

Exclusive CR_M analyses were conducted on three banks and ten banks for the period between 1990 and 2000 as shown in Tab. 11.1. Asset, deposit, and loan concentration results were obtained from the analyses. The results indicate that three banks with the highest amount of assets, loans, and deposits in the market owned one-third of the market while the ten banks had a share of 70 percent to 80 percent in the market. These ratios did not change much despite the developments between 1990 and 2000. The market did not have a tendency toward low concentration or a competitive market structure within this eleven-year period. It is understood from the values in the table that especially the ten banks with the biggest share had the power to lead the sector. On the other hand, some fifty banks owning the remaining 20 percent of the market are estimated to have exhibited competitive behaviors among themselves.

It is highly important to interpret the HKI index taking into account the change that took place in the sector as a result of the mergers so that the study objective can be achieved. Tab. 11.1 shows the HKI values calculated for the period between 1990 and 2000. The findings obtained when small banks were focused (α=0.6) reveal that the competition assets, deposits, and loans tended to increase for small banks. However, it is observed that the index value highlighting especially small banks decreased during the 1994 crisis, i.e., concentration increased in that year. It can be said that the increase in that period was a result of the scale effect caused by the mergers that took place in the sector. It is understood from the The First National Bank of Boston A.Ş. and Eurocredit Türk Fransız Ticaret Bankası A.Ş. examples that foreign banks made mergers through acquisition (TBB, 2018). Furthermore, Tab. 11.1 shows that there were no dramatic changes in the market structures in terms of small banks in 1994.

On the other hand, the index value for big banks (α=1.5) increased slightly throughout the 1990s. This indicates that competition tended to increase slightly among large-scale banks. Moreover, the values given in Tab. 11.1 indicate that large-scale banks might have entered the market. The HKI index values are usually in parallel with the CR concentration values.

Tab. 11.1: 1990–2000, Results of CR Concentration and HKI Indexes

	CR3			CR10			α=0,6			α=1.5		
	Asset	Loan	Deposit	Asset	Loan	Deposit	HKI Asset	HKI Loan	HKI Deposit	HKI Asset	HKI Loan	HKI Deposit
1990	0,43	0,47	0,44	0,81	0,80	0,87	39.01	38.78	35.09	0.62	0.60	0.60
1991	0,40	0,45	0,40	0,78	0,79	0,83	40.78	40.54	36.51	0.63	0.62	0.62
1992	0,40	0,47	0,42	0,75	0,79	0,82	43.69	43.58	37.10	0.64	0.60	0.62
1993	0,37	0,38	0,39	0,71	0,75	0,76	50.84	48.49	43.82	0.65	0.64	0.63
1994	0,39	0,42	0,40	0,79	0,82	0,82	44.40	41.56	40.08	0.63	0.61	0.61
1995	0,36	0,44	0,38	0,75	0,79	0,76	47.76	43.25	45.74	0.64	0.61	0.63
1996	0,35	0,39	0,38	0,71	0,73	0,73	51.83	46.85	47.94	0.65	0.63	0.63
1997	0,33	0,38	0,36	0,71	0,75	0,73	50.75	47.49	47.59	0.65	0.63	0.64
1998	0,33	0,32	0,39	0,71	0,74	0,73	52.42	49.56	47.57	0.66	0.66	0.64
1999	0,35	0,35	0,41	0,71	0,76	0,72	52.53	48.08	47.96	0.65	0.64	0.63
2000	0,35	0,33	0,38	0,73	0,78	0,72	51.68	45.68	49.34	0.65	0.64	0.64

Calculated by the authors using TBB data set.

According to concentration indexes calculated using asset values, usually the same seven banks, and mostly the five same banks among them, acquired the highest share in the market in this eleven-year period. Three of these banks are public-financed while the others are private-financed banks. The same applies to deposits and the only difference is that there are four public-financed banks. In terms of loans, two banks, one public-financed and one private-financed bank, cover the biggest share in the market. On the other hand, the same seven banks got the biggest share from the market in all years. There are no foreign-financed banks among these banks. Furthermore, the market power of T.C. Ziraat Bank in the sector does not change in any year. Türkiye Emlak Bankası that held a similar power until the mid-1990s gradually lost its power after the second half of the 1990s. Türkiye İş Bankası has a high market power among private-financed banks. In addition, it is observed that the crisis years that are assumed to have affected the sector did not affect certain banks with market power; only Akbank T.A.Ş. turned the 2001 crisis into an opportunity and became one of the biggest two powers to affect the markets (TBB, 2018). On the other hand, foreign-financed banks were among the remaining 20 percent of the market, and it is thought that competitive behaviors might have taken place between the foreign-financed banks. It is obvious that banks based on domestic capital, especially those with public capital, usually have the power to lead the market. On the other hand, banks are always changing in terms of loans. This change suggests that the biggest competition among large-scale banks take place for loans.

Tab. 11.2 shows that the period between 2001 and 2014 was not much different from the 1990s in terms of assets and loans. However, we see that fewer banks became dominant in the market. For example, the three banks with the most asset and loan value dominated more than one-third of the market in that period while ten banks dominated practically the whole sector. All these values indicate that although the number of banks decreased compared to the 1990s, more powerful and larger banks operated in the market.

On the other hand, deposits accumulated in the largest three banks, and there was a monopoly-like structure in terms of deposit banking.

According to the HKI index in Tab. 11.2, the index values increased for asset and loan values of small banks until 2005 and therefore competitive behaviors were exhibited. When we consider this together with the CR_M concentration values, we see that small-scale banks constituting a small part of the market competed with each other. The values related to deposits as of 2003 indicate that actions that did not change the market scale significantly took place within the scope of deposit banking when both small and large-scale banks entered the market. In terms of scale, it is known that foreign-financed banks dominated the market in that period (TBB, 2017). We know that these banks entered the market in order to acquire market shares until the global economic crisis or started to operate in the market after merging with private-financed banks (TBB, 2018). This change in foreign-financed banks in the market did not have the power to lead the market. On the other hand, the index values of the large-scale banks tended to increase in general. This indicates that the large-scale banks competed with each other. Furthermore, small changes in the index value for all transactions carried out between 2001 and 2014 (except deposit transactions between 2003 and 2009) show that no changes that could change the market scale took place when banks entered the market.

Tab. 11.2: 2001–2014, Results of CR Concentration and HKI Indexes

	CR3			CR10			α=0,6			α=1.5		
	Asset	Loan	Deposit	Asset	Loan	Deposit	HKI Asset	HKI Loan	HKI Deposit	HKI Asset	HKI Loan	HKI Deposit
2001	0,42	0,44	0,43	0,88	0,91	0,88	16.15	14.70	15.57	10.58	9.89	10.56
2002	0,44	0,43	0,46	0,87	0,87	0,89	16.35	16.20	15.45	10.74	11.08	10.29
2003	0,46	0,41	0,88	0,88	0,85	0,97	16.07	16.47	7.00	10.46	11.92	3.00
2004	0,44	0,37	0,88	0,87	0,83	0,97	16.97	17.08	7.14	10.98	12.63	3.22
2005	0,47	0,41	0,88	0,88	0,84	0,98	16.40	16.70	6.64	10.69	12.15	3.13
2006	0,44	0,41	0,80	0,89	0,87	0,96	16.02	15.86	8.59	10.76	11.61	4.11
2007	0,42	0,40	0,74	0,88	0,87	0,95	16.02	15.95	9.88	10.92	11.80	4.85
2008	0,43	0,40	0,75	0,89	0,88	0,96	15.85	15.62	9.85	10.83	11.50	5.08
2009	0,44	0,38	0,46	0,90	0,88	0,91	15.33	15.62	14.54	10.36	11.61	9.92
2010	0,44	0,38	0,47	0,90	0,89	0,91	15.63	15.51	14.50	10.54	11.38	9.75
2011	0,42	0,39	0,42	0,90	0,91	0,91	15.58	14.89	15.05	10.82	11.09	10.62
2012	0,40	0,39	0,41	0,91	0,91	0,92	14.67	14.43	14.28	10.71	11.07	10.60
2013	0,40	0,39	0,40	0,91	0,91	0,92	14.78	14.28	14.27	10.89	10.99	10.69
2014	0,40	0,39	0,39	0,91	0,92	0,92	14.72	14.21	14.35	10.82	10.90	10.81

Calculated by the authors using TBB dataset.

A more detailed analysis of the sector shows that the same seven banks had unchanging market power in terms of assets and loans. It is remarkable that these seven banks are public-financed and private-financed banks and all public-financed banks in the sector are included in this group. When this analysis was conducted on deposit transactions, it was found out that the market power was held by different banks, and its concentration changed during different periods (TBB, 2017). The numbers given in Tab. 11.2 indicate that only three banks led the market within the scope of deposit banking between 2003 and 2008. Furthermore, it is thought that the 2009 global economic crisis affected deposits. That is because the market power provided by deposits returned to the status before the 2003 as of 2009. In other words, the banks that had market power in terms of assets and loans between 1990 and 2014 also had market power in terms of deposit banking in the periods from 2001 to 2003 and from 2009 to 2014. However, many of these banks were not even among the first ten banks in terms of deposit banking within the period from 2003 to 2009 (TBB, 2018). Foreign-financed banks led the market in terms of deposit banking between 2003 and 2009. It is striking that foreign-financed banks that did not seem to be market leaders in the Turkish banking sector despite their numerical superiority outside these dates had the highest share only in that period. The analyses indicate

Tab. 11.3 1990–2000, Results of Lerner Index

Price = Interest Income/Total Assets											
Interest expenses and personal expenses which are homogenized by operating expenses											
	1990	1991	1992	1993	1994	1995	1996	1997	1998	1999	2000
All Banks	0,78	0,75	0,76	0,75	0,63	0,72	0,61	0,63	0,65	0,48	0,62
7 Banks	0,65	0,60	0,64	0,64	0,56	0,70	0,70	0,70	0,69	0,62	0,61

*Personal Expenses: total personal expenses/number of employees

*Operating Expenses: other expenses/total assets

*Interest Expenses: interest expenses/total deposits

Calculated by the authors using TBB data set.

that all these banks were acquired by foreign banks or international companies in those periods, or they were subject to bank mergers and acquisitions. These banks that exhibited the international fund effect also lost their market powers due to the 2009 global economic crisis.

In general, little competition is expected in this period due to the decrease in the number of banks and high concentration values. Furthermore, banks with domestic capital were dominant in the market in terms of deposits between 2003 and 2009 and in terms of assets and loans between 2001 and 2014. Private-financed banks are dominant and market leaders throughout the Turkish banking sector. Foreign-financed banks could not acquire market power except for a short period of time despite the increase in their numbers.

2.4 Analysis Results: Non-Structural Approaches

The Lerner Index and Adjusted Lerner Index that provide results for each company and each year have a very important role in market structure and competition analyses. Tab. 11.3 shows the Lerner Index and Adjusted Lerner Index values calculated in the study.

The results of the structural approach revealed that certain banks held the market power although high competition was expected in the period before 2001. As you can see in Tab. 11.3, competition was low and the monopoly power was high in the early 1990s. There was monopolistic competition in the market after 1995. According to the findings obtained from the analysis conducted on seven large-scale banks, small-scale banks operate in a market led by large-scale banks rather than a competitive environment.

Tab. 11.4: 2001–2014, Results of Lerner Index

Price = Interest Income/Total Assets														
Interest expenses and personal expenses which are homogenized by operating expenses														
	2001	2002	2003	2004	2005	2006	2007	2008	2009	2010	2011	2012	2013	2014
All Banks	0,72	0,67	0,50	0,45	0,35	0,45	0,50	0,52	0,50	0,45	0,48	0,53	0,47	0,53
7 Banks	0,63	0,56	0,40	0,45	0,31	0,45	0,44	0,41	0,44	0,46	0,42	0,44	0,39	0,40

*Personal Expenses: total personal expenses/number of employees
*Operating Expenses: other expenses/total assets
*Interest Expenses: interest expenses/total deposits

Calculated by the authors using TBB dataset.

Tab. 11.5: 1990–2000, Results of Adjusted Lerner Index

Price=Interest Income/Total Assets											
Interest expenses and personal expenses which are homogenized by operating expenses											
	1990	1991	1992	1993	1994	1995	1996	1997	1998	1999	2000
All Banks	0,85	0,83	0,83	0,82	0,80	0,80	0,80	0,80	0,80	0,79	0,92

*Personal Expenses: total personal expenses/number of employees
*Operating Expenses: other expenses/total assets
*Interest Expenses: interest expenses/total deposits

Calculated by the authors using TBB data set.

High market power and therefore low competition are expected in the 2000s. But the index values given in Tab. 11.4 are much lower than the index values calculated for the 1990s. A more detailed analysis of these values reveals that the market value that was high in the early 2000s decreased each passing year. On the other hand, 2005 is the year when most intense competitive behaviors took place. It is known that many foreign-financed banks entered the market in those periods, and it can be said that those banks increased the competition in the market especially in terms of deposits. Also Tab. 11.3 and Tab. 11.4 show the index values calculated for the seven biggest banks in terms of assets. The fact that the index values of all banks and the above mentioned seven banks were very close to each other in some years and even the index values of the seven banks were higher than the index values of all other banks is interesting. The biggest reason for this is that the Lerner Index was calculated as negative for

Tab. 11.6: 2001–2014, Results of Adjusted Lerner Index

Price=Interest Income/Total Assets														
Interest expenses and personal expenses which are homogenized by operating expenses														
	2001	2002	2003	2004	2005	2006	2007	2008	2009	2010	2011	2012	2013	2014
All Banks	0,59	0,04	0,13	0,09	0,08	0,07	0,09	0,09	0,06	0,10	0,10	0,11	0,13	0,14

*Personal Expenses: total personal expenses/number of employees
*Operating Expenses: other expenses/total assets
*Interest Expenses: interest expenses/total deposits

Calculated by the authors using TBB data set.

some banks. The Lerner Index can be negative, and this value indicates that the bank is losing money or it is not an efficient bank. In this sense, an analysis of the 1990s shows that the number of inefficient banks increased as of 1996 and a certain amount of powerful companies led the market. This is rarely observed in the 2000s. Although their number was not high, there were inefficient banks between 2004 and 2010. The number of foreign-financed banks increased, and such banks acquired the market power in deposit banking in that period. These results can indicate that these banks carried out their activities with inefficient interest rates in order to collect deposits. Although this practice made the banks acquire deposits in the short term, it might have caused them to have structural problems, thus facing costs higher than the prices. The fact that the Lerner Index was lower in the remaining years reveals that there was competition among big banks.

The results of the Adjusted Lerner Index given in Tab. 11.5 show that competition was low and monopoly power was high in the Turkish banking sector in the 1990s. The competition tended to increase after 1990, but this tendency decreased after 1999. These results are witnessed in values higher than the results of the Lerner Index. This indicates that deviant results can be obtained assuming that each bank operates efficiently.

Tab. 11.6 shows the competition level of the Turkish banking sector after 2001. The results are very low according to the results of the Lerner Index. According to the Adjusted Lerner Index, there was very high competition between 2001 and 2014. The competition was very intense especially between 2002 and 2010. It can be said that these results emerged due to high competition among foreign-financed banks even though they have created intensive market power through deposits between 2002 and 2009. These results indicate that the competition was usually high. The competition is thought to be caused by the ineffectiveness of the banks.

General Evaluation

When the market structure of the Turkish banking sector was analyzed in terms of total assets, deposits, and loans, it was found out that the concentration in the sector before 2001 was very high and competition took place among small-scale banks. The high concentration in the sector continued after 2001. Also the level of competition increased compared to the period before 2001. That is because the number of foreign-financed banks increased after 2001, and they exhibited competitive behaviors in terms of deposits. Furthermore, large-scale banks started to engage in more competitive actions in order to get higher market share after 2001. Also the mergers that took place within that period affected the market power. We think that large-scale banks and small-scale banks exhibited competitive behaviors among themselves in the period after 2001.

In conclusion, the analyses conducted with the structural and non-structural approaches support each other. The market structure of the Turkish banking sector usually reflects the characteristics of monopolistic competition. Competition took place between small-scale banks, while a certain amount of large-scale banks had the market power before 2001. Following the restructuring program implemented in 2001, the market forces of large-scale banks continued, but there was intense competition among those banks.

The results show that it is necessary to develop policies that encourage entrance into the Turkish banking sector in order to have a competitive environment similar to those in European and developed countries. In this sense, all natural and unnatural obstacles preventing entrance into the market must be eliminated and competition laws must be enforced efficiently within the sector. On the other hand, it is obvious that the number of banks is not the only determinant of the market structure and competition. Therefore, steps related to mergers and technological developments must be taken properly. Importance must be attached to production of technological products that improve competition within the sector. In addition, merger decisions that prevent competition must be painstakingly analyzed, subsidization programs must be prepared in the event that small banks perform mergers, and laws must be enforced efficiently in both cases. An environment of trust must be created for the sector and the country. Also incentive policies must be developed in order to attract foreign-financed banks that increase the competition in the Turkish banking sector. Furthermore, it must be ensured that the competitive environment in the market does not lead to inefficiency. An efficient competitive environment must be created, and losses that may be incurred by inefficient banks must be prevented.

References

Agoraki, M., Delis, M.D. & Pasiouras, F. (2011) "Regulations, Competition and Bank Risk-taking in TransitionCountries," *Journal of Financial Stability, 7*(1), 38–48.

Aktaş, H. & Kargın, M. (2007) "Türk Bankacılık Sektöründeki Yabancı ve Ulusal Bankaların Finansal Oranlar Açısından Karşılaştırılması," *Journal of Management and Economics, 14*(2), 31–46.

Anginer, D., Demirgüç-Kunt, A., & Zhu, M. (2014) "How Does Competition Affect Bank Systemic Risk?," *Journal of Financial Intermediation, 23*, 1–26.

Berger, A.N., Klapper, L.F., & Ariss, R.T. (2009) "Bank Competition and Financial Stability," *Journal of Financial Service Research, 35*, 99–118.

Carbo, S., Humphrey, D., Maudos, J., & Molyneux, P. (2009) "Cross-country Comparisons of Competition and Pricing Power in European Banking," *Journal of International Money and Finance*, 28, 115–134.

Daglish, T., Robertson, O., Tripe, D., & Weill, L. (2015) "Translog Cost Function Estimation: Banking Efficiency," Working Paper Series 4180, 1–37.

Delis, M.D. (2012) "Bank Competition, Financial Reform, and Institutions: The Importance of Being Developed," *Journal of Development Economics*, 97, 450–465.

Guevara, J.F., Maudos, J. & Perez, F. (2005) "Market Power in European Banking Sectors," *Journal of Financial Services Research, 27*(2), 109–137.

Hannah, L., & Kay, A.J. (1977) *Concentration in Modern Industry. Theory, Measurement and the UK Experience*. London: Macmillan.

Hanson, J. & Ramachandran, S. (2005) "Financial Liberalization: What Went Right, What Went Wrong?," *Economic Growth in the 1990s: Learning from a Decade of Reform* (s. 207–239). Washington, D.C.: WorldBank.

Kasman, S. & Kasman, A. (2015) "Bank Competition, Concentration and Financial Stability in the Turkish Banking Industry," *Economic System, 39*, 502–517.

Koetter, M., Kolari, J.W., & Spierdijk, L. (2008) "Efficient Competition? Testing the 'quiet life' of U.S. Banks with Adjusted Lerner Indices," Federal Reserve Bank of Chicago, 1–28.

Koetter, M., Kolari, J.W., & Spierdijk, L. (2012) "Enjoying the Quiet Life under Deregulation? Evidence from Adjusted Lerner Indices for U.S. Banks." *The Review of Economics and Statistics*, *94*(2), 462–480

Lerner, A.P. (1934) "The Concept of Monopoly and the Measurement of Monopoly Power." *Review of Economic Studies*, 157–175.

Panzar, J.C. & Rosse, J.N. (1977) "Testing for Monopoly Equilibrium." *The Journal of Industrial Economics*, *35*(4), 443–456.

TBB, T. (2017) "The Banking Sector in Turkey 1960–2016," İstanbul: TBB.

TBB (2018) https://www.tbb.org.tr/tr/bankacilik/banka-ve-sektor-bilgileri/istatistiki-raporlar/59, (1.5.2018).

Yıldırım, K. & Eşkinat, R. (1996) "Industrial Economy," (Binding 113). Eskişehir: Anadolu University Educational Health and Scientific Research Studies.

Yıldırım, C. (2014) "Competition in the Turkish Banking: Impacts of Restructuring and the Global Financial Crisis," *The Developing Economies*, *52*(2), 95–124.

İbrahim Murat Bicil and Çağatay Başarır

12 The Relationship between the Real Sector Confidence Index and Financial Indicators

Abstract: Developments in the financial system are reflected in the real sector through various channels such as real sector expectations. In this chapter, how the real sector is affected by the developments in the financial system is evaluated in the context of the causality relationship between real sector confidence index and selected financial indicators.

Keywords: Confidence Index, Financial System, Expectations, Toda-Yamamoto Causality

1 Introduction

Formation of expectations in the economy is an important factor in financial decision making. The fact that consumption, saving, and investment decisions are closely related to expectations of financial decision-making units both at the individual and company level puts expectations in a position that they both affect and are affected by many economic indicators. According to the modern portfolio theory, investors are assumed to be rational and take rational decisions. However, the behavioral finance theory that has become more important in time suggests that investor decisions are affected by psychological factors. Considering the fact that psychological factors surrounding investors affect their opinions about the future, we can say that expectations of investors about the future will have a direct impact on their investment decisions. On the other hand, positivity or negativity of expectations affect financial decisions which affect the economic performance and financial indicators.

A lot of data is collected for policy makers within the corporate structure of economy to monitor the economy, and various economic indicators emerge while preparing an economy policy. Indicators related to goods and service markets, factor markets, and the financial system are measured, consolidated, and monitored periodically. Activities related to periodical collection and publication of data for the Turkish economy are carried out by two institutions: Turkish Statistical Institute and the Central Bank of Turkey. Indicators related to economy monitoring and economic performance are not limited to market data. Investor behaviors are highly important in economy for both decision makers and those who are interested in future economic projections. Optimism in consumer confidence can increase the tendency to spend a lot and get into debt, while pessimism can cause consumers to cut down on their spending and review their financial status (Korkmaz and Çevik, 2009: 27). For this purpose, the Central Bank of Turkey (TCMB) has been developing the real sector confidence index since 1987 through surveys conducted with senior executives of private sector organizations that influence the economy. The economic tendency survey that started to be applied on a monthly basis by TCMB in 1987 is one of the significant data sources regarding expectations in Turkey. The Economic Tendency Survey (ETS) aims to create indicators reflecting tendencies related to the manufacturing industry by making sure that expectations of senior executives of workplaces operating in the manufacturing industry regarding the recent history, current status, and the future are monitored. The real sector confidence index is calculated with the data obtained from economic tendency surveys in order to reveal impressions of real sector representatives regarding the economic outlook. The real sector confidence index is an indicator that is derived from replies given to the economic tendency survey and reflects impressions of real sector representatives. The real sector confidence index is calculated as a function of the replies given to the questions in the economic tendency survey about total amount of orders, finished goods inventory, export, production, employment, fixed capital investment expenditures, and the general situation. Index values are obtained by adding 100 to the balance values of the replies that are consolidated as weighted values (TCMB).

The data collected and indexes created to monitor expectations in markets reflect impressions of the real sector about the general economic outlook. Such indicators are monitored by economic decision units and policy makers. Which financial indicators the real sector affects or is affected by is another important matter at this point. This study analyzes the causality relationship between the real sector confidence index reflecting the impressions of the real sector about the economy and the BIST industrial index, gold ounce prices, BIST 100 index, the effective Dollar exchange rate, commercial loan interest rates (Turkish Lira), commercial loan interest rates (US Dollar), and producer price index variables.

2 Literature Summary

Studies investigating the relationship between expectations and financial and macroeconomic indicators gained momentum after variables representing expectations started to be measured. There are studies analyzing the relationships of the real sector confidence index and consumer confidence index variables that are assumed to represent expectations in Turkey to chosen macroeconomic indicators, stock exchange index, and financial indicators using time-series techniques. Some of the studies conducted with confidence indexes in Turkey focus on the relationship between stock exchange index earnings and expectations, while some of them focus on the relationship between macroeconomic performance and confidence indexes. Data, methods, and findings related to some of these studies are given in the following section.

Korkmaz and Çevik (2009) analyzed the causality relationship between the BIST 100 index earnings and the real sector confidence index with the two-step method developed by Cheung and Ng (1996). The BIST 100 index earning and real sector confidence index were estimated using the EGARCH model in the first step and causality in the mean and causality in the variance tests were conducted on the variables. The findings revealed that there was a feedback effect between the index earning and real sector confidence index and the variables affected each other simultaneously.

Bildirici and Bozoklu analyzed the impacts of expectations on the economy in Turkey through the MS-VAR approach which is the multivariate version of the approach developed by Krolzig (1997) using the industrial production index, real sector production index, and BIST 100 index variables. After applying deepness, steepness, and sharpness asymmetries to the variables, the impacts of expectations and beliefs on the economy were tested using the MS-VAR model. The findings revealed a relationship between optimism and pessimism fluctuations in expectations of economic decision-making units and fluctuations in the economy.

Ekşi (2011) analyzed the relationship between bank loans and the confidence factor conducting Johansen cointegration test, the vector error correction model, and Granger causality test with monthly data related to the real sector index, VIX index and bank loans in Turkey between 2000 and 2008. The findings suggest a causality relationship from the real sector confidence index toward bank loans.

Arısoy (2012) used the VAR analysis to reveal the dynamic relationships between consumer confidence index, real sector confidence index, consumption expenditures, share market, employment, and production changes. It was found out in the study that the consumer confidence index affected developments in consumption expenditures, while the real sector confidence index affected developments in the industrial production and stock exchange index.

Köse and Akkaya (2016) investigated impacts of confidence indexes and their subcomponents on the BIST 100 index using the multiple regression, VAR analysis, and Granger causality test. The study revealed that the TCMB real sector confidence index, general situation, and three-month order subindexes affected the BIST 100 index earning.

Kale and Akkaya (2016) analyzed the relationships between consumer confidence and real sector confidence indexes and five different share indexes (total, financial, industrial, service, and technology) using VAR models. Michigan University Sentiment Index, VIX volatility index, and GFK Germany Consumer Climate Index were associated with models in order to research international impacts. The results show that there was no causality relationship between consumer confidence and share earnings, but share earnings were affected positively. On the other hand, a two-way causality was determined between the real sector index and share earnings. It was observed that the Michigan University Consumer Confidence Index and VIX volatility index were able to account for almost all share indexes in Turkey, while GFK German Consumer Climate Index did not have any impacts on any share earnings in all models. The findings indicate that the confidence climate of the USA is felt more in Turkey.

Usul, Küçüksille, and Karaoğlan (2017) analyzed the relationships between the consumer confidence index, real sector confidence index, and BIST 100 index with the KSS cointegration test and determined a cointegration relationship between the confidence indexes and the BIST 100 index. The study revealed that according to the long-term and short-term cointegration coefficients, confidence indexes had a positive impact on share markets in the short and long terms.

Canöz (2017) analyzed the macroeconomic factors affecting the Real Sector Confidence Index of the Central Bank of Turkey (TCMB) through the Johansen cointegration test and Granger causality test using the monthly data related to the period from January 2007 to March 2017. According to the analysis results, the TCMB Composite Leading Indicators Index, Capacity Usage Ratio of the Manufacturing Industry, Imputed Rate of Reference for Turkish Lira (TRLIBOR), and BIST 100 Earnings Index affect the real sector confidence index.

Eyüboğlu and Eyüboğlu investigated the relationship between the 2017 economic confidence index, BIST 100, BIST industrial and BIST services indexes through the Engle-Granger method using monthly data related to the period from January 2012 to October 2016 and determined a cointegration relationship between the confidence index and stock exchange indexes. Furthermore, the findings obtained from the error correction model suggest that the confidence index was the reason for the BIST 100, BIST industrial, and BIST services indexes.

Çağlı and Mandacı (2017) investigated whether there was a speculative bubble in the market through the recursive flexible estimation intervals algorithm using the dividend yield calculated for BIST indexes, and they used a total of twenty-one index data consisting of BIST general, BIST 100, and sector indexes for the period from November 2006 to May 2016. The analysis results showed that there were speculative bubbles for the sector and the stock exchange in general and the exchange rate, real sector confidence index, and industrial production index affected the number of speculative bubbles.

Eyüboğlu and Eyüboğlu (2018) analyzed the short-term and long-term relationships between BIST sector index earnings and the real sector confidence index with the ARDL border test approach and determined short-term and long-term relationships between the real sector confidence index and all sector indexes. Furthermore, it was observed that increases in the real sector confidence index affected stock exchange index earnings positively most of the time. On the other hand, causality findings mostly indicate a causality relationship between sector indexes and the real sector confidence index.

Küçükçaylı and Akıncı (2018) analyzed factors determining consumer confidence in the Turkish economy through the vector error correction model using monthly data related to the consumer confidence index, BIST 100 index, gold prices, foreign exchange rate, inflation, interest, oil prices, industrial production index, and unemployment rate between January 2004 and July 2016. According to the analysis results, developments in the stock exchange index and increases in the industrial production caused the consumer confidence to increase while the foreign exchange rate, inflation, oil prices, and interest rates decreased the consumer confidence.

3 Data, Method, and Findings

Monthly time-series for the period between January 2007 and June 2018 related to the real sector confidence index, BIST industrial index, gold ounce prices, BIST 100 index, the effective Dollar exchange rate, commercial loan interest rates (Turkish Lira), commercial loan interest rates (US Dollar), and producer price index variables were used in this study. The data was obtained from the Electronic Data Delivery Service of the Central Bank of Turkey and named in as Tab. 12.1 The LN (logarithm) expression was written before the variables whose logarithms were taken.

Tab. 12.1: Data Set

Real Sector Confidence Index-Level	Y
BIST industrial index	X1
Gold ounce prices Dollar	X2
BIST 100 index	X3
Effective dollar exchange rate (buying)	X4
Commercial loan interest rates TL	X5
Commercial loan interest rates USD	X6
Producer price index	X7

Considering the procedure applied to the Toda-Yamamoto causality test, the maximum order of stationarity of variables must be known. The Augmented Dickey-Fuller (ADF) Test and Phillips Perron Unit Root Test were used for stationarity analysis of the variables.

Tab. 12.2: Results of ADF and Philips Perron (PP) Unit Root Test

	Level (ADF-t statistic)				First Difference (ADF-t statistic)			
Variable	**Fixed and Trend**	**1 %**	**5 %**	**10 %**	**Fixed**	**1 %**	**5 %**	**10 %**
LNY	-4.244[1]	-4,027	-3,443	-3,146	-7.264 [0]	-3,479	-2,883	-2,578
LNX1	-2.616[1]	-4,027	-3,443	-3,146	-10.255[0]	-3,479	-2,883	-2,578
LNX2	-1.731[0]	-4,027	-3,443	-3,146	-9.452 [0]	-3,479	-2,883	-2,578
LNX3	-2.508[1]	-4,027	-3,443	-3,146	-11.264 [0]	-3,479	-2,883	-2,578
LNX4	-2.618[1]	-4,027	-3,443	-3,146	-7.841 [1]	-3,479	-2,883	-2,578
LNX5	-1.603[0]	-4,027	-3,443	-3,146	-6.181 [0]	-3,479	-2,883	-2,578
LNX6	-2.762[1]	-4,027	-3,443	-3,146	-13.940 [0]	-3,479	-2,883	-2,578
LNX7	-1.120[1]	-4,027	-3,443	-3,146	-6.719 [0]	-3,479	-2,883	-2,578
Variable	**Level (PP Test Statistic)**				**First Difference (PP Test Statistic)**			
Variable	**Fixed and Trend**	**1 %**	**5 %**	**10 %**	**Fixed**	**1 %**	**5 %**	**10 %**
LNY	-3.326[2]	-4,026	-3,443	-3,146	-7.264 [3]	-3,479	-2,883	-2,578
LNX1	-2.650[4]	-4,026	-3,443	-3,146	-10.280 [2]	-3,479	-2,883	-2,578
LNX2	-1.830[3]	-4,026	-3,443	-3,146	-9.405 [4]	-3,479	-2,883	-2,578
LNX3	-2.766[4]	-4,026	-3,443	-3,146	-11.269[2]	-3,479	-2,883	-2,578
LNX4	-2.318[2]	-4,026	-3,443	-3,146	-7.827 [6]	-3,479	-2,883	-2,578
LNX5	-1.484[5]	-4,026	-3,443	-3,146	-6.104 [4]	-3,479	-2,883	-2,578
LNX6	-2.721[7]	-4,026	-3,443	-3,146	-14.016 [6]	-3,479	-2,883	-2,578
LNX7	-0.555[4]	-4,026	-3,443	-3,146	-6.728 [2]	-3,479	-2,883	-2,578

Results of the unit root test are given in Tab. 12.2. These results show that the variables became stationary when their first differences were taken, i.e., the maximum order of stationarity was 1. The Toda-Yamamoto causality analysis was conducted after the stationarity analysis. In the Toda-Yamamoto (1995) causality analysis, the number of lags in the VAR model (k) is expanded with the order of maximum integration (d) and estimated through the order values of the variables. The VAR model at the (k+dmax) level using the order values of the variables is shown below:

$$LNY_t = \gamma_0 + \sum_{i=1}^{k} \beta_{1,i} LNY_{t-i} + \sum_{j=k+1}^{k+d_{max}} \beta_{2,i} LNY_{t-j} + \sum_{i=1}^{k} \alpha_{1,i} LNX_{t-i} + \sum_{j=k+1}^{k+d_{max}} \alpha_{2,i} LNX_{t-j} + \varepsilon_{1,t} \quad (1)$$

$$LNX_t = \delta_0 + \sum_{i=1}^{k} \varphi_{1,i} LNX_{t-i} + \sum_{j=k+1}^{k+d_{max}} \varphi_{2,i} LNX_{t-j} + \sum_{i=1}^{k} \theta_{1,i} LNY_{t-i} + \sum_{j=k+1}^{k+d_{max}} \theta_{2,i} LNY_{t-j} + \varepsilon_{2,t} \quad (2)$$

The lag duration in the VAR models were determined by taking the Schwarts Information Criterion, Hannan Quin, Final Prediction Error, and Akaike Information Criterion into account. The LM test was conducted to determine whether model with the appropriate lag order had any autocorrelation problem. It was checked whether the reverse roots of the AR characteristic polynomial of the VAR model whose lag was estimated correctly were inside the unit circle. The Y variable in the equations represents the real sector confidence index, while the X variable represents the variables from X_1 to X_7 as shown in the table. If the $H_0 = \alpha_{1,1} = \alpha_{1,2} = ... = \alpha_{1,k} = 0$ hypothesis is rejected after being tested, it means that there is a causality from the X variable to the Y variable. If the $H_0 = \theta_{1,1} = \theta_{1,2} = ... = \theta_{1,k} = 0$ hypothesis is rejected after being tested, it means that there is a causality from the Y variable to the X variable. Tab. 12.3 shows the causality test results between the real sector confidence index variable (Y) and BIST industrial index (X1), gold ounce prices (X2), BIST 100 index (X3), effective Dollar exchange rate (X4), commercial loan interest rates (Turkish Lira) (X5), commercial loan interest rates (US Dollar) (X6), and producer price index (X7).

Tab. 12.3: Toda-Yamamoto Causality Test Results

HYPOTHESES	Dmax and VAR(k)	WALD	CAUSALITY DIRECTION
From the Real Sector Confidence Index to the BIST Industrial Index	(1.2)	2.859 (0,239)	Y ⇐ X1
From the BIST Industrial Index to the Real Sector Confidence Index	(1.2)	20.088 (0.000)	
From the Real Sector Confidence Index to Gold Prices	(1.2)	1,072 (0.584)	Y ⇐ X2
From Gold Prices to the Real Sector Confidence Index	(1.2)	5,574 (0.061)	
From the Real Sector Confidence Index to the BIST 100 Index	(1.4)	3,108 (0.539)	Y ⇐ X3
From the BIST 100 Index to the Real Sector Confidence Index	(1.4)	19,505 (0.0006)	
From the Real Sector Confidence Index to Foreign Exchange Rate	(1.4)	10,209 (0.037)	Y ⇔ X4
From the Foreign Exchange Rate to the Real Sector Confidence Index	(1.4)	13,933 (0.0075)	
From the Real Sector Confidence Index to the Commercial Loan Interest Rates for Turkish Lira	(1.2)	1,352 (0.508)	Y NO X5
From the Commercial Loan Interest Rates for Turkish Lira to the Real Sector Confidence Index	(1.2)	1,066 (0.586)	
From the Real Sector Confidence Index to the Commercial Loan Interest Rates for USD	(1.5)	14,582 (0.0123)	Y ⇔ X6
From the Commercial Loan Interest Rates for USD to the Real Sector Confidence Index	(1.5)	16,043 (0.0067)	
From the Real Sector Confidence Index to the Producer Price Index	(1.3)	8,275 (0.0407)	Y ⇔ X7
From the Producer Price Index to the Real Sector Confidence Index	(1.3)	8,137 (0.0433)	

According to the causality analysis results, a one-way causality relationship was detected from the BIST industrial index, gold prices, and BIST 100 index to the real sector confidence index. A two-way causality relationship was detected between commercial loan interest rates (USD), foreign exchange rate, producer price index, and the real sector confidence index but no causality was detected between commercial loans in Turkish Lira and the real sector confidence index.

General Evaluation and Conclusion

Monitoring expectations is as important as monitoring financial indicators in the economy for economic decision-making units and policy makers. Various indicators are created in order to monitor expectations. The real sector confidence index developed from answers given to economic orientation surveys is one of the variables used as an indicator for monitoring expectations in the Turkish economy. In this study, we analyzed the causality relationship between financial indicators and the real sector confidence index reflecting the opinions of the real sector about the recent past, current situation, and the future with the Toda-Yamamato causality test. The findings revealed a one-way causality relationship from the BIST industrial index, gold prices, and BIST 100 index toward the real sector confidence index and a two-way causality relationship between commercial loan interest rates (USD), foreign exchange rate, producer price index, and the real sector confidence index.

We can conclude that developments in the stock exchange index and gold prices affect expectations of investors and therefore positive developments in such markets have a positive impact on expectations of investors. Developments related to interest rates, the foreign exchange rate, and the consumer price index first shape expectations and then assume positive or negative roles based on these expectations in such markets.

In this regard, when we take the behavioral finance theory into account, we can say that psychological states of investors affect expectations of investors; they are affected by results obtained from expectation surveys and assume positions accordingly.

References

Arısoy, İ. (2012). Türkiye Ekonomisinde İktisadi Güven Endeksleri Ve Seçilmiş Makro Değişkenler Arasındaki İlişkilerin VAR Analizi. *Journal of Finance*, 162, 304–315.

Bildirici, M., & Bozoklu, Ü. (2010). Beklentilerin Ekonomi Üzerine Etkileri: MS-VAR Yaklasimi. TÜSİAD-Koç University Economic Research Forum Working Paper Series.

Canöz, İ. (2017). An Analysis Of Macroeconomic Variables Affecting Real Sector Confidence Index: The Case Of Turkey. *International Journal of Commerce and Finance*, *3*(2), 37.

Çağli, E.Ç., & Mandaci, P.E. (2017). Borsa İstanbul'da Rasyonel Balon Varlığı: Sektör Endeksleri Üzerine Bir Analiz. *Finance, Political and Economic Reviews*, *54*(629), 63–76.

Cheung, Y. W., & Ng, L. K. (1996). A causality-in-variance test and its application to financial market prices. Journal of Econometrics, 72(1–2), 33–48.

Ekşi, İ.H. (2011). "Firmaların Banka Kredisi Kullanımında Güven Faktörünün Etkisi," *Anadolu University Journal of Social Sciences*, *11*(2), 33–42.

Eyüboğlu, K., & Eyüboğlu, S. (2017). "Ekonomik Güven Endeksi İle Hisse Senedi Fiyatları Arasındaki İlişkinin İncelenmesi: Türkiye Örneği." *Gazi University Journal of Economic and Administrative Sciences*, *19*(2), 603.

Eyüboğlu, S., & Eyüboğlu, K. (2018). "Reel Kesim Güven Endeksi ile Borsa İstanbul Sektör Endeksleri Arasındaki İlişkinin Test Edilmesi," *Business & Economics Research Journal*, *9*(1), 75–86.

Kale, S., & Akkaya, M. (2016). "The Relation between Confidence Climate and Stock Returns: The Case of Turkey." *Procedia Economics and Finance*, *38*, 150–162.

Korkmaz, T., & Çevik, E. İ. (2009). "Reel Kesim Güven Endeksi ile İMKB 100 Endeksi arasındaki dinamik nedensellik ilişkisi." *Istanbul University Journal of the School of Business Administration*, *38*(1), 24–37.

Köse, A.K., & Akkaya, M. (2016). "Beklenti ve güven anketlerinin finansal piyasalara etkisi: BIST 100 üzerine bir uygulama." *Journal of Bankers*, 99, 3–15.

Krolzig, H. M. (1997). Markov-Switching Vector Autoregressions, 454, ISBN: 978-3-642-51684-9, Springer-Verlag Berlin Heidelberg, Berlin, Doi: 10.1007/978-3-642-51684-9

Küçükçaylı, F.M. & Akıncı G.Y. (2018). "Tüketici Güveninin Makroekonomik Belirleyicileri: Bir Zaman Serisi Analizi," *International Journal of Economic and Administrative Studies*, UİİİD-IJEAS(17. UİK Özel Sayısı).

TCMB. (2017). İktisadi Yönelim İstatistikleri ve Reel Kesim Güven Endeksi, IYA-Metaveri, http://www.tcmb.gov.tr/wps/wcm/connect/TR/TCMB+TR/Main+Menu/Istatistikler/Egilim+Anketleri/Iktisadi+Yonelim+Istatistikleri+ve+Reel+Kesim+Guven+Endeksi/.

Toda, H.Y., & Yamamato, T. (1995). "Statistical Inference in Vector Autoregressions with Possibly Integrated Processes." *Journal of Econometrics 66*, 225–250.

Türkiye Cumhuriyet Merkez Bankası Elektronik Veri Dağıtım Sistemi. (2018), https://evds2.tcmb.gov.tr/index.php?/evds/archiveMarket/collapse_0/6072/DataGroup/turkish/bie_mbrkge/, (15.08.2018)

Usul, H., Küçüksille, E., & Karaoğlan, S. (2017). "Güven Endekslerindeki Değişimlerin Hisse Senedi Piyasalarına Etkileri: Borsa İstanbul Örneği." *Suleyman Demirel University Journal of Faculty of Economics & Administrative Sciences*, *22*(3), 685–695.

Ömer Faruk Biçen and Kumru Türköz

13 The Effects of Financial Development on the Real Sector in Turkish Economy

Abstract: The aim of this chapter is to test whether the developments in the financial markets give rise to crowding out effect on the real sector over the period of 2002Q1–2017Q4. The results support that financial development does not exclude the real sector, whereas it has a smaller effect on the real sector.

Keywords: Financial Development, Growth, Real Sector, Crowding Out Effect, ARDL Bound Test

1 Introduction

The economic growth phenomenon is a leading factor that draws the attention of both economists and policy makers. Many growth models have been used to look into the main resources of growth and to reveal the reasons behind it throughout history. Production increase that leads to growth results from increases in both the amount and efficiency of resources. New physical investments must be made and/or the technological advancements must be accelerated in order to achieve this.

Achieving investment increase or technological advancement requires physical endeavors, and financial resources are highly important for such investments. The main source of investments (excluding foreign capital) is domestic savings, and countries must have an effective financial sector in order to direct these savings toward investments. The role of the financial sector at this point is to establish a connection between fund holders and those who demand funds, i.e., savers and investing companies, and to ensure that the funds owned by savers are used as efficiently as possible (Cecchetti and Kharroubi, 2012: 1). The financial sector also contributes to the increases in saving amounts. For this reason, the development of the financial sector is important for economic growth.

In 1911, J. Schumpeter said that financial development played an important role in economic growth (Beck et al., 2000: 262). Bagehot mentioned the same matter in 1878, long before Schumpeter, and said that financial development would have a positive impact on growth. However, although Robinson acknowledged the correlation between financial development and growth in 1952, he argued that the variables affected each other in the opposite direction (Levine, 1997: 688). In other words, financial development does not affect growth, but economic growth affects financial developments positively.

In addition, the correlation between financial development and growth has started to be analyzed more specifically in recent years. Especially the industrial sector—more specifically, the production sub-sector of the industrial sector—is more important than the other sectors within the economic development and growth stages of countries. As economic growth takes into account the whole annual production increase in the agricultural, industrial, and service sectors, it cannot be completely revealed how and to what extent the industrial sector is affected by financial development.

The financial sector has grown to a considerable extent in many countries due to financial liberalization since the 1980s and the impacts of financial development on industrial production and labor productivity in addition to growth, i.e., its impacts on the real sector have become a research subject. Although mutual positive impacts emerged within the framework of the economic growth between the financial sector and the real sector, the analyses conducted within the framework of the industrial sector production and labor productivity in the industrial sector show that a crowding-out effect can emerge between these two sectors from time to time. Impacts distorting the resource allocation such as accumulation of trained labor force in the financial sector and accumulation of savings in the investment tools within the financial sector due to high return rates of financial development and the fact that increases in the risk levels resulting from the overgrowth of the financial sector increases economic fragility and affects the real sector negatively are among the main reasons for this (Cecchetti and Kharroubi, 2014: 3; Ductor and Grechyna, 2015: 394–395).

In the light of these developments, this study aims to analyze the impacts of the financial developments on real sector between the first quarter of 2002 and the last quarter of 2017 in Turkey that opened up to foreign countries after 1980 and faced many economic crises, the biggest of which was in 2001. This chapter consists of four sections including the Introduction. The second section first gives brief information about the theoretical and empirical studies on this matter and then discusses the development of the financial and real sectors in the Turkish economy. After the data set related to the empirical model developed to reveal the relationships between the financial and real sectors in Turkey and the findings related to the model are given, the model results are evaluated in the third section. Finally, the fourth section includes general evaluation of the analysis results.

2 The Theoretical and Empirical Framework of the Financial Sector—Real Sector Relationship and the Developments in the Turkish Economy

The relationships between the financial sector and the real sector can be analyzed in two categories as mentioned above. Some of the theoretical and empirical studies in the literature analyze the impacts of financial development on economic growth, while others discuss the impacts of financial development and growth of the financial sector especially on industrial production and labor productivity in the industrial sector, i.e., the real sector.

One of the studies in the first group that was conducted by Aslan and Küçükaksoy (2006) analyzed the causality relationship between financial development and economic growth in Turkey. The study covered the period from 1970 to 2004 and the Granger causality analysis used in the study revealed a one-way causality from financial development to economic growth.

Demir et al. (2007) analyzed the relationship between the Turkish banking system, share market, and economic growth in the period between 1995 and 2005. They used the VAR model and observed a one-way causality relationship between financial markets and growth in the long term. The error correction model revealed that financing through banks and share certificates could increase economic growth, albeit slightly in the long term.

Ağayev (2012) analyzed the correlation between financial development and economic growth in twenty transition economies for the period between 1995 and 2009. The results of the panel cointegration test revealed a long-term relationship between financial development and economic growth. The panel causality analysis revealed one-way causality from financial development to economic growth.

Bozoklu and Yılancı (2013) analyzed the correlation between financial development and economic growth in fourteen developing economies for the period between 1988 and 2011. They used the Panel Granger causality analysis and found out that financial development was the reason for economic growth.

Kaya et al. (2013) analyzed the impact of financial development on economic growth between the first quarter of 1998 and the last quarter of 2009 in the Turkish economy. The Least Squares Method, Johansen-Juselius Cointegration Test, and Granger causality analysis showed that financial development had a positive impact on economic growth and the real sector and there was a long-term correlation between the variables in the Turkish economy.

Law and Singh (2014) analyzed the relationship between financial development and growth in eighty-seven developed and developing countries in the period from 1980 to 2010. The findings indicated a level effect between the two variables. Accordingly, financial development affects growth positively to a certain level but it starts to have negative impacts on growth once this level is past. As a result, an optimal financial development is necessary for economic growth.

Finally, Karahan et al. (2018) analyzed the impact of bank credits on growth in Turkish economy between the first quarter of 2002 and the last quarter of 2016. The empirical results indicate a two-way causality between bank credits and growth.

There are studies analyzing the relationships between financial development and the real sector in addition to studies analyzing the impacts of financial development on economic growth. First, King and Levine (1993) conducted a study in which they analyzed the correlations between financial development and GDP per capita, physical capital accumulation ratio, and economic efficiency level for eighty countries in the period from 1960 to 1989. The results revealed a strong correlation between financial development and growth rate, physical capital accumulation, and the developments in the efficiency level.

Beck et al. (2000) performed an empirical analysis on the impacts of developments at financial intermediaries on economic growth, growth in the total factor productivity, physical capital accumulation, and the private sector savings ratio in sixty-three countries between 1960 and 1995. The findings showed that developments at financial intermediaries would feed economic growth and therefore have a positive impact on the total factor productivity, whereas there was no clear correlation between developments at financial intermediaries and physical capital stock and private sector saving ratios.

Beck and Levine (2002) analyzed the impacts of financial development on the growth of the industrial sector, foundation of new companies and capital allocation to new branches of industry between 1980 and 1995 using data related to 42 countries and 36 branches of industry. The study results indicated that financial development brought about foundation of new companies and more efficient resource allocation in addition to having a positive impact on the growth of the industrial sector.

Cecchetti and Kharroubi (2012) analyzed the impacts of financial development on the total factor productivity using data related to fifty developed and developing countries between 1980 and 2009. The share of private sector loans in the national income, the share of bank loans in the national income and the share of financial sector labor force in total employment, and the growth rate of the financial sector were used as criteria of financial development. The real GDP growth rate per capital is the variable representing the productivity level. According to the results, financial development supports economic growth to a certain degree but has a negative impact on it afterwards. Financial development has a negative impact on productivity. In short, an extremely growing financial sector brings about negative impacts on resource allocation.

Cecchetti and Kharroubi (2014) analyzed the correlation between the growth rate of the financial sector and the total factor productivity in fifteen developed OECD countries for the period between 2000 and 2008. The variables representing the growth rate of the financial sector are as follows: the share of the banking sector assets in the GDP, the share of the private sector loans in the GDP, and the share of private sector bank loans in the GDP. It was observed in the study that emergence of factors disrupting resource allocation caused the growth in the financial sector to have a negative impact on the total factor productivity.

Ductor and Grechyna (2015) analyzed the relationships among financial development, real sector production ratio, and economic growth in 101 developed and developing countries for the period between 1970 and 2010. The results showed that the impacts of financial development on economic growth depended on the growth rates of the loans provided for the private sector compared to the growth of the real production level, and financial development could affect economic growth negatively in the event that loans provided for the private sector increased more compared to the growth rate of the real sector. In other words, it was concluded that the real sector and financial sector must grow in a balanced manner so that economic growth could take place smoothly.

Tomaskovic-Devey et al. (2015) analyzed the correlation between the investments of the non-financial sector and the increases in the added value of the same sector in the USA between 1970 and 2008. According to the results, the financial investments of the non-financial sector decreased the added value of the same sector by approximately 3.9 percent.

Finally, Aizenman et al. (2015) analyzed the relationships among financial depth, financial efficiency, and value-added growth rate using data related to forty-one countries and ten sub-sectors between 1996 and 2011, and the empirical results showed that financial depth and financial efficiency produced different results for different sectors. Accordingly, there is a negative correlation between financial depth and production industry for East Asian economies, whereas there is a positive correlation between financial depth and finance, insurance, and real estate sectors for Latin American economies. Furthermore, it was observed that the correlation between financial efficiency and the construction sector was negative for the East Asian countries and positive for the Latin America economies.

Studies indicate that results related to correlations between financial development and economic growth, and correlations between financial development

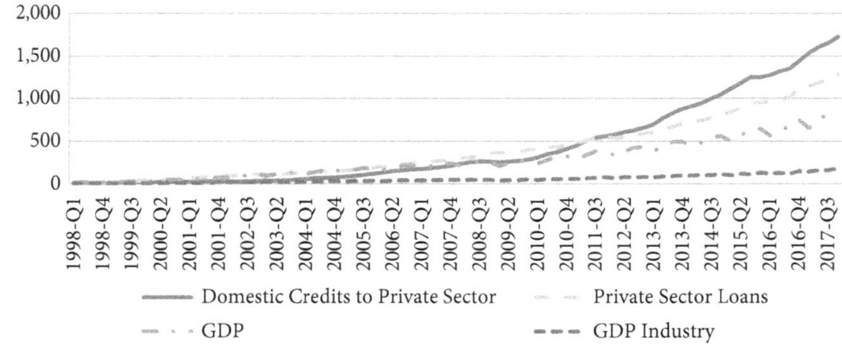

Fig. 13.1: Financial sector and real sector indicators in Turkey (billion TL).
Source: CBRT, 2018)

and real sector growth, can differ. Financial development accelerates economic growth by enabling increased saving, but excessive growth of the financial sector can have negative impacts on economic growth. Similarly, the financial sector affects the real sector positively to a certain extent whereas the negative impacts of the financial sector on the real sector can emerge afterwards. Overgrowth of the financial sector creates problems in risk perception, and accumulation of resources in the financial sector is reflected negatively in the other sectors. Decreasing savings in the real sector will affect investments and technological advancement negatively (Ductor and Grechyna, 2015: 394). This is an indication that the excessively growing financial sector can have a crowding-out effect on other sectors, particularly the real sector.

The relationships between the financial sector and the real sector can be analyzed within the framework of the Turkish economy as well. Turkey aimed for a more liberal economic structure after 1980, and this liberalization manifested itself in the financial sector. Turkey benefited from the positive impacts of financial developments during this period, but it was negatively affected by economic crises that took place from time to time.

Fig. 13.1 summarizes the relations between the Turkish financial and real sector starting from 1998 using quarterly data. The loan amounts provided for the real sector in Turkish Liras and the deposits of the real sector were used as indicators related to the financial sector while the GDP in Turkish Liras and the GDP level of the industrial sector were used as indicators related to the real sector. All the data was linear, and the data related to the financial sector after the 2001 crisis and the GDP level had an increasing trend. The problems related to the asset-liability balance in the banking system before the crisis in February 2001 constituted one of the main causes of the crisis. Serious precautions were taken to restructure the economy within the framework of the Transition to the Strong Economy Program that was put into effect immediately after the crisis. Those serious precautions included restructuring of the financial sector and foundation of the Banking Regulation and Supervision Agency in order to audit the banking rector more closely (Kepenek, 2012: 215–216; Pamuk, 2014: 286). The restructuring of the financial sector is also important for the development of the financial sector in the following period.

Although the private sector loans and deposits increased to a great extent especially after the 2008 crisis, the GDP level did not increase in the same way. The GDP level of the industrial sector was linear throughout the analyzed period. This especially indicates that some level of financial development took place in Turkey, but the industrial sector could not benefit from this financial development sufficiently.

3 Data and the Econometric Method

3.1 Model and Data set

The theoretical literature discusses various variables for indicators related to financial development and the real sector. This study was based on the studies conducted by Back and Levine (2002), Cecchetti and Kharroubi (2012 and 2014), and Ductor and Grechyna (2015). The volume of the total domestic loans provided for the private sector and the chain volume index related to the production industry were used as indicators of financial development and the developments in the real sector, respectively, and the correlation between these variables are modeled as in Equation 1.

$$LOGIMS_t = \alpha_1 + \alpha_2 \, LOGKRD_t + u_t \quad (1)$$

In Equation 1, LOGIMS represents the production industry chain volume index and LOGKRD represents the logarithmic values of the total domestic loans provided for the private sector. The study analyzes the period between the first quarter of 2002 and the last quarter of 2017 in Turkey, and the data set regarding the variables was obtained from the Electronic Data Delivery System of the Central Bank of the Republic of Turkey (CBRT-EVDS). The quarterly series was seasonally adjusted using the moving averages method. The correlation between the variables was estimated with the ARDL Bounds Test approach using the econometric package program.

First, the stationarity of the series was tested in order to determine the cointegration relationship between the series in Equation 1.

3.2 Unit Root Analysis

Non-stationarity of series in time series analysis causes a spurious regression problem (Granger and Newbold, 1974). The stationarity of the series was analyzed with the Augmented Dickey-Fuller (ADF), Phillips-Perron (PP), and Zivot-Andrews (ZA) unit root tests. Tab. 13.1 shows the results of the ADF and PP unit root tests.

Tab. 13.1: Results of ADF and PP Unit Root Test

Variables	ADF		PP	
	Intercept	**Trend and Intercept**	**Intercept**	**Trend and Intercept**
LOGIMS	-0.62	-3,21	0,00	-3,22
LOGKRD	-3.44**	-2,18	-2,21	-1,08
ΔLOGIMS	-10,10*	-10,01*	-11,07*	-10,94*
ΔLOGKRD	-6,02*	-7,08*	-6,21*	-7,06*

Note: (*) and (**) indicates statistical significance at the 5 % and 10 % levels respectively.

According to the ADF and PP test results, the LOGIMS dependent variable is stationary in the intercept model at level at the 5 percent significance level, and the LOGKRD independent variable is stationary in both intercept and intercept and trend models in the first difference at 1 percent significance level. The integration levels of the series were investigated in the study using the Zivot and Andrews (ZA) (1992) unit root test taking into account the structural change in the series in addition to the traditional unit root tests.

Tab. 13.2: Results of the ZA Unit Root Test

Variables	Model A Intercept		Model B Trend		Model C Trend and Intercept	
LOGIMS						
Test Statistics	-4,62 I(1)**		- 2,84 I(1)**		-4,84 I(1)**	
Break Date	2008Q3		2010Q3		2008Q2	
LOGKRD						
Test Statistics	-3,49 I(1)**		-3,62 I(1)*		-3,68 I(1)*	
Break Date	2005Q1		2006Q1		2005Q4	
Critical Values	%1	%5	%1	%5	%1	%5
	-5,34	-4,93	-4,80	-4,42	-5,57	-5,08

Note: (*) and (**) indicate statistical significance at the %5 and %10 levels, respectively. Critical values are taken from Zivot and Andrews (1992).

According to the ZA unit root test results given with the breaking date and test statistics in Tab. 13.2, both LOGIMS and LOGKRD series were determined to be stationary.

3.3 Cointegration Analysis

The Bounds Testing approach developed by Pesaran et al. (2001) was preferred in order to test whether there was a long-term correlation between the series after the stationary testing. This approach was preferred because the number of observations was limited (n=64), and the series integrate at different levels in the traditional unit root tests. In this context, the equation formed to determine the cointegration relationship is as follows:

$$\Delta LOGIMS = \alpha_1 + \sum_{i=1}^{k} \alpha_{2i} \Delta LOGIMS_{t-i} + \sum_{i=0}^{k} \alpha_{3i} \Delta LOGKRD_{t-i} + \alpha_4 LOGIMS_{t-1} + \alpha_5 LOGKRD_{t-1} + \varepsilon_1 \quad (2)$$

The suitable lag number (k) must be determined in order to detect a cointegration relationship between the series included in the model. The k value minimizing the Akaike Information Criterion (AIC) is considered to be the best lag. The maximum lag length was determined as eight for the series included in the models and the best lag value was calculated according to minimum AIC for the cointegration model.

Tab. 13.3: Test Results for Determining the Lag Length

Lag Length	AIC	Serial Correlation Test (LM)
(1.1)	-3,177	0,51(0,77)
(2.2)	-3,094	12,41(0,00)
(3.3)	-3,309	6,08 (0,04)
(4.4)	-3,365	3,89 (0,14)
(5.5)	-3,317	0,71 (0,69)
(6.6)*	-3,415	1,33 (0,51)
(7.7)	-3,395	5,93(0,05)
(8.8)	-3,403	3,27(0,19)

Note: (*) shows the lag length with the lowest AIC value without autocorrelation problem, and the values in brackets show the probability values of the test results.

The suitable lag was determined as 6.6 within the scope of AIC for the cointegration analysis in Tab. 13.3. Tab. 13.4 shows the F statistic value calculated according to this lag and the descriptive statistics related to the model.

Tab. 13.4 Bound Test Results

Number of Observations	k	F Statistics	%1 Level of Significant		%5 Level of Significant		%10 Level of Significant	
			Lower Bound I(0)	Upper Bound I(1)	Lower Bound I(0)	Upper Bound I(1)	Lower Bound I(0)	Upper Bound I(1)
64	1	6.19	7.32	8.43	5.13	5.98	4.17	4.93
R^2: 0,61 Adj R^2:0,47 $\chi 2_{SER}$: 0,51 $\chi 2_{HET:}$ 0,66 $\chi 2_{NOR:}$0,56 DW: 1.87								

Note: Critical lower and upper bound values are taken from Narayan (2005). k; the number of independent variable in the model, χ2NOR; Jarque-Bera normality test statistic, χ2SER Breusch-Godfrey test statistic, and $\chi 2_{HET}$ show Breusch-Pagan-Godfrey test statistics probability value.

As you can see in Tab. 13.4, the value of the F statistic testing of the long-term correlation is 6.19. Here the variables passed all descriptive tests. The F statistic value was compared with the lower and upper critical values in the unrestricted fixed term and no-trend models created by Narayan (2005) for thirty to eighty observations, as the number of observations included in the study was low. The F statistic value that was calculated accordingly was higher than the upper critical value at the 5 percent significance level. So, a cointegration relationship was determined between the variables.

Tab. 13.5: ARDL (5,7) Long Run Coefficients

Dependent Variable: LOGIMS		
Variables	**Coefficients**	**T Statistic**
LOGKRD	0,31*	0.00
C	11,26*	0.00
Descriptive Statistics		
R^2: 0,98 Adj R^2: 0,97 $\chi2_{SER}$: 0,30 $\chi2_{HET:}$ 0,46 $\chi2_{NOR:}$ 0,63 DW:1,81		

Note: (*) indicates statistical significance at the %1 level.

3.3.1 Long-Term Estimation Results

The equation formed in order to test the long-term relationship between the variables after determining the cointegration relationship is given below:

$$LOGIMS = \alpha_1 + \sum_{i=1}^{k} \alpha_{2i} LOGIMS_{t-i} + \sum_{i=0}^{l} \alpha_{3i} LOGKRD_{t-i} + \varepsilon_t \qquad (3)$$

The most suitable model for the long term according to the AIC criterion without the autocorrelation problem was determined as (5, 7) and this model passed all diagnostic tests. According to the results in Tab. 13.5, the LOGKRD coefficient and fixed term are statistically significant at 1 percent significance level. Within the scope of these results, a 1 percent increase in the domestic loans provided for the private sector in the relevant period causes the production in the manufacturing sector to increase by 0.31 percent. In other words, financial development has a crowding-out effect on the real sector in the long term.

3.3.2 Short-Term Estimation Results

The short-term correlation between the variables was analyzed with the error correction model based on the ARDL approach. Equation 4 shows the model formed in this scope:

$$\Delta LOGIMS = \alpha_1 + \alpha_2 ECT_{t-1} + \sum_{i=1}^{k} \alpha_{3i} \Delta LOGIMS_{t-i} + \sum_{i=0}^{l} \alpha_{4i} \Delta LOGKRD_{t-i} + \varepsilon_t$$

(4)

The ECT_{t-1} term in the model represents the value of the error terms series obtained from the long-term correlation lagged for one period. The coefficient and t statistic are expected to be negative and significant respectively. The maximum lag length was determined as 8 again for the variables in the model and

Tab. 13.6: ARDL (5,7) Short Run Coefficients

Dependent Variable: ΔLOGIMS		
Variables	**Coefficients**	**T Statistic**
ΔLOGKRD	0.19	0.52
C	-0.001	0.93
ECT	-0.76**	0.02
Descriptive Statistics		
R2: 0.63 ADJ R2: 0.51 χ2SER: 0.09 χ2HET: 0.42 χ2NOR: 0.65 DW: 1.83		

Note: (*) indicates statistical significance at the %5 level.

the most suitable model for the short-term correlation was determined as ARDL (5,7) with the help of the values making the AIC minimum. Tab. 13.6 shows the estimation results related to the error correction mechanism.

According to the error correction model results in Tab. 13.6, the coefficient of the ΔLOGKRD variable and the fixed term are statistically insignificant. According to these results, an increase in the domestic loans provided for the private sector does not have a significant impact on the production in the manufacturing sector in the short term as opposed to the long term. The error correction term (ECT) in the equation indicates how much the imbalance in the short term will be corrected in the long term. This coefficient is negative and statistically significant as expected. This coefficient indicates that about 76 percent of a deviation in period t-1 will be corrected in period t.

Conclusion and General Evaluation

The literature contains many empirical and theoretical studies on the correlation between financial development and economic growth. However, the direct impact of the financial sector on the real sector has started to be analyzed recently. The main reason for this is the aim to investigate whether the financial system resulting from the financial liberalization process that emerged in Turkey as in many other countries especially as of the 1980s has had any crowding-out effect on the real sector. The period between the first quarter of 2002 and the last quarter of 2017 in Turkey was analyzed in order to find out this crowding-out effect in this study. As the share of the industrial sector within the real sector and the share of the manufacturing sub-sector within the industrial sector were high, the production level of the manufacturing sector was used to represent the real sector, and the total amount of loans provided for the private sector was used to represent the financial development.

The results of the ARDL Bounds Test revealed a cointegration relationship between the variables in the long term. The long-term analysis results showed that financial development caused the real sector production to increase significantly but less than itself, while the short-term analysis results showed that financial development did not have any statistically significant impacts on the real sector. Accordingly, financial development does not have a crowding-out effect on the real sector either on the short or the long term. These results are similar to the findings obtained by Beck and Levine (2002). On the other hand, as shown in Graphic-1, financial development increased throughout the analyzed period, while the GDP in the industrial sector was linear in all periods. This indicates that the industrial sector cannot benefit enough from the developments in the financial markets in Turkey as supported by the analysis results. The fact that the impact of financial development on the real sector was weak although it did not have a crowding-out effect during the analyzed period indicates that Turkey can have problems in industrial production, added value, growth, and employment, etc., in the future. As pointed out by Ductor and Grechyna (2015), the real sector and financial sector must grow in a balanced manner so that economic growth can take place smoothly. That is because financial risks increase, and resource allocation gets even worse for the real sector when the growth of the financial sector is above the optimal level.

References

Ağayev, Ş. (2012) "Geçiş Ekonomilerinde Finansal Gelişme ve Ekonomik Büyüme İlişkisi," *Marmara University Journal of Economic and Administrative Sciences*, *XXXII* (I):155–164.

Aizenman, J., Jinjarak, Y., & Park, D. (2015) "Financial Development and Output Growth in Developing Asia and Latin America: A Comparative Sectoral Analysis," National Bureau of Economic Research, No. w20917.

Aslan, Ö. & Küçükaksoy, İ. (2006) "Finansal Gelişme ve Ekonomik Büyüme İlişkisi: Türkiye Ekonomisi Üzerine Ekonometrik Bir Uygulama", İstanbul University Faculty of Economics Journal of Econometrics and Statistics, 4: 12–28.

Beck, T., Levine, R., & Loayza, N. (2000) "Finance and the Sources of Growth," *Journal of Financial Economics*, *58*(1–2), 261–300.

Beck, T. & Levine, R. (2002) "Industry Growth and Capital Allocation: Does Having a Market-or Bank-Based System Matter?," *Journal of Financial Economics*, *64*(2): 147–180.

Bozoklu, Ş. & Yılancı, V. (2013) "Finansal Gelişme ve İktisadi Büyüme Arasındaki Nedensellik İlişkisi: Gelişmekte Olan Ekonomiler İçin Analiz,"

Dokuz Eylül University Journal of Economic and Administrative Sciences, 28(2): 161–187.

Cecchetti, S.G. & Kharroubi, E. (2012) "Reassessing the Impact of Finance on Growth," BIS Working Paper, 381.

Cecchetti, S.G. & Kharroubi, E. (2014) "Why Does Financial Sector Growth Crowd Out Real Economic Growth?," BIS Working Paper, 490.

Demir, Y., Öztürk, E., & Albeni, M. (2007) "Türkiye'de Finansal Piyasalar ile Ekonomik Büyüme İlişkisi," *Karamanoğlu Mehmetbey University Journal of Social and Economic Research, 2*: 438–455.

Ductor, L. & Grechyna, D. (2015) "Financial Development, Real Sector, and Economic Growth," *International Review of Economics & Finance, 37*: 393–405.

Granger, C.W.J. & Newbold, P. (1974) "Spurious Regressions in Econometrics", Journal of Econometrics, 2 (2): 111–120.

Karahan, Ö., Yılgör, M., & Özekin, A.A. (2018) "Türkiye'de Banka Kredilerindeki Genişleme ile Ekonomik Büyüme Arasındaki İlişki," *Finance, Political and Economic Reviews, 55*(636): 25–36.

Kaya, A., Gülhan, Ü., & Güngör, B. (2013) "Türkiye Ekonomisinde Finans Sektörü ve Reel Sektör Etkileşimi," *Journal of Academic Research and Studies*, 5(8): 1–15.

Kepenek, Y. (2012) *Turkish Economy*, Remzi Kitabevi: İstanbul.

King, R.G. & Levine, R. (1993) "Finance and Growth: Schumpeter Might Be Right," *The Quarterly Journal of Economics, 108*(3): 717–737.

Law, S.H. & Singh, N. (2014) "Does Too Much Finance Harm Economic Growth?," *Journal of Banking & Finance, 41*: 36–44.

Levine, R. (1997) "Financial Development and Economic Growth: Views and Agenda," *Journal of Economic Literature, 35*(2): 688–726.

Narayan, P.K. (2005) "The Saving and Investment Nexus for China: Evidence from Cointegration Tests," *Applied Economics, 37*(17): 1979–1990.

Pamuk, Ş. (2014) Türkiye'nin 200 Yıllık İktisadi Tarihi, *Turkey Business Bank Culture Publications*: İstanbul.

Pesaran, M.H., Shin, Y., & Smith, R.J. (2001) "Bounds Testing Approaches to the Analysis of Level Relationship," *Journal of Applied Econometrics, 16*(3): 289–326.

Tomaskovic-Devey, D., Lin, K.H., & Meyers, N. (2015) "Did Financialization Reduce Economic Growth?," *Socio-Economic Review, 13*(3): 525–548.

Türkiye Cumhuriyet Merkez Bankası Elektronik Veri Dağıtım Sistemi (CBRT) (2018) https://evds2.tcmb.gov.tr/index.php?/evds/serieMarket, (10.04.2018).

Zivot, E. & Andrews, D.W.K. (1992) "Further Evidence on the Great Crash, the Oil Price Shock and the Unit Root Hypothesis," *Journal of Business and Economic Statistics. 10*(3), 251–270.

Umut Uyar and Özlem İnce

Examining the Relationship between Market Information and Buy-Sell Decisions by PIN Values

Abstract: The *Probability of Informed Trading (PIN)* term refers to the possibility of any transaction decision made by investors who have special information about any specific share. In this chapter, twelve bank stocks of BIST are analyzed regarding PIN framework. Also, linear models are run between macroeconomic variables and stocks' PIN values. The results show the dynamic relation of buy-sell decisions for investors in BIST.

Keywords: PIN Value, Risk Behaviour, Intra-Day Data, Borsa Istanbul, BIST Banks

1 Introduction

There is extensive finance literature dealing with risk assessment and a return of stocks, bonds, and other assets. For a long time, academia widely focused on the risk premium of assets, risk relation with prices and optimal portfolio selection of investors in order to minimize hazards and/or maximize profits. Conventional finance theories explain price changes with the stock amount of assets (Ho and Stoll, 1981; O'hara and Oldfield, 1986). For instance, if one share is highly demanded in the market, the number of shares decreases more than predicted. This situation may lead to a sudden leap in its price and a significant difference in margins. However, for some (Easley and O'hara, 1987), this point of view is a rather static way of evaluating stock markets. Each and every day all around the world, financial markets experience hundreds of new events which cause stocks to be bought and sold excessively; stock values to accelerate, decelerate to a large extent. It means abrupt changes in transaction frequency and sudden price movements. In this respect, the base price effects on volume and transaction number, but beyond this perspective, there is a diverse and novel standpoint. It can be explained as buying extensive amounts of a particular stock makes other investors believe that the share will appreciate. As a result, many investors who do not have any knowledge about the current situation buy the share which soon causes the price to increase in reality. Uninformed trader transactions in this plotline create the concept of reverse choice or "adverse selection" behavior as it is named in the literature. This perception management having vital effects on information flow reveals rather young literature of "Probability of Information Trading (PIN)" (Easley and O'hara, 1987). The term refers to the possibility of any transaction decision made by investors who have particular information about any specific share. In other words, PIN values demonstrate the percentage of transaction orders coming from informed traders. Easley and O'hara's (1987) article about the fundamentals of PIN theory gave rise to a large number of applications with different PIN models. The main application research was conducted by Easley, Kiefer, O'hara, and Paperman in 1996. With the estimation of PIN indicators, they appraise two critical findings: first, because they are mostly stable and very risky, the rate of informed trading is higher for less traded shares. It means that if a trader invests in assets with low transaction volume, he probably has private information; otherwise, he would not be willing to bear the risk. The second outstanding implication is that the number of informed traders is considerable in high transaction volume shares, but more interestingly; this high number of informed traders is compensated with a much higher number of uninformed traders (Easley et al., 1996).

PIN literature is dominated by the classic EKOP model (Easley et al., 1996) which is used to analyze microstructure variables and estimate PIN values by the use of these variables. EKOP Model is followed by Fama and French (Fama, French, and MacBeth, 1973; Fama and French, 1992) and Markow Switching Models (Hamilton, 1994). Many scholars improve mentioned models by adding a wide range of indicators like investor types, reverse choices as endogenous variables, or exchange rates and oil prices as exogenous variables (Cepoi and Toma, 2016). According to Gan, Wei, and Johnstone (2017), since PIN estimators are not exogenous variables, the model's adaption level must be taken into consideration.

The main purpose of this chapter is to calculate the PIN values for twelve banking stocks which are being traded in Borsa Istanbul (BIST) and to investigate the relationship between the market information and buy-sell decisions. An additional purpose of this chapter is to regress a linear model between macroeconomic variables (exchange rate of USD/TRY and interest rate of Turkey) and PIN values as Cepoi and Toma (2016) suggest in their study. In the next sections, first, the probability of informed trading and the details of EKOP model are explained. In the second part, the PIN literature is reviewed starting from the fundamental article of Easley and O'hara (1987). After a short explanation of Borsa Istanbul and Turkish banking sector, the data is presented. In the fifth section, according to the framework, findings of EKOP model and regression results of macroeconomic variables are demonstrated. Finally, the discussion of estimation results and conclusion parts will be stated.

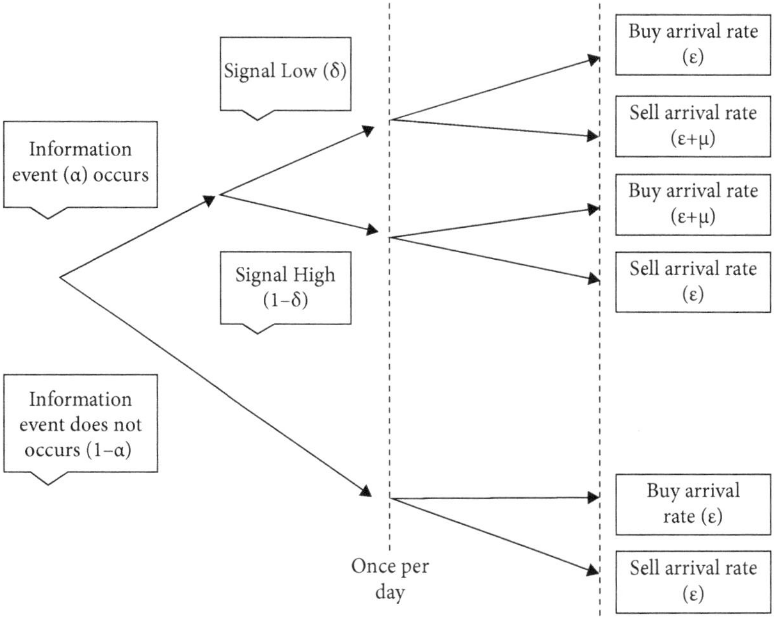

Fig. 14.1: PIN diagram. *Source: Easley, Kiefer, O'hara, and Paperman (1996: 1409)*

2 The Probability of Informed Trading

In their pioneering article, Easley, Kiefer, O'hara, and Paperman (1996) set out a sequential model (EKOP model) which analyses the trading process by using microstructure indicators and give rise to extended PIN literature in the following years. They segment trade decisions as coming from informed and uninformed traders in any given trading day ($t_i = t_1, \ldots, t_N$ days) and presume that any trading day is independent of the other. In this study, we estimate microstructure indicators, as well as PIN numbers for different stocks by using EKOP model. A brief explanation of the trading process in each independent trading day can be found in the diagram below (Fig. 14.1).

As seen on the left-hand side of the diagram, in each day information enters the market or no information arrives. The probability of an information entry is shown by α. Naturally, the probability of no information days will be 1-α. In the model, trading decisions coming from uninformed traders are represented with ε while μ displays informed traders' decisions. Thus, during no information days, both buy and sell decisions are assumed to have come from uninformed traders and both numbers are equal to ε. However, when any information enters the market there are two alternatives: Either this information is a bad one or a good one. If the information is bad, in other words, the signal is low, (δ), buy decisions are assumed to have come from uninformed traders (ε) while sell decisions are assumed to have come from both uninformed and informed traders (ε+μ). Finally, if information entry is toward good news or if the signal is high (1-δ), then sell decisions are considered to have come from uninformed traders (ε) while both informed and uninformed traders may decide to buy (ε+μ).

The probability of buy and sell decisions over N days can be reached through a daily basis function of maximum likelihoods,

$$L(\theta M)\prod_{i=1}^{N} L(\theta B_i, S_i) \tag{1}$$

By applying poisson distribution to the function of order types (B for buys and S for sells), the likelihood becomes,

$$\begin{aligned} L(B,S)\theta = (1-\alpha) * e^{-\varepsilon}\frac{\varepsilon^B}{B!} * e^{-\varepsilon}\frac{\varepsilon^S}{S!} + \alpha\delta * e^{-\varepsilon}\frac{\varepsilon^B}{B!} * e^{-(\varepsilon+\mu)}\frac{(\mu+\varepsilon)^S}{S!} \\ + \alpha(1-\delta) * e^{-(\varepsilon+\mu)} * \frac{(\mu+\varepsilon)^B}{B!} * e^{-\varepsilon}\frac{\varepsilon^S}{S!} \end{aligned} \tag{2}$$

Likelihood equation allows researchers to analyse no event days $(1-\alpha)$ as well as other trading days including bad $(\alpha\delta)$ and good news $\left[\alpha(1-\delta)\right]$. For no information days, α will be zero, as well as second and third parts. With bad information days, the second part will be valid to estimate the parameters. Finally, for good information days, the last part of the function will give the likelihood of buy and sell decisions coming both from informed and uninformed traders as along with the probability whether the trading day includes information entry or not. After estimating microstructure parameters $\theta = \{\alpha, \delta, \varepsilon, \mu\}$ PIN variables for each interval can be calculated with the formula below (Easley et al., 1996):

$$\text{PIN} = \frac{\alpha\mu}{\alpha\mu + 2\varepsilon} \tag{3}$$

In this formula, "$\alpha\mu$" is the percentage of information arrival days times arrival rates coming from informed traders and represents the rate of decisions of informed traders. "$\alpha\mu + 2\varepsilon$" shows all trading decisions coming from all traders.

3 Literature Review

Many scholars estimate PIN values and conclude that PIN value is significantly high for low volume shares compared to high volumes. Due to volume and PIN correlation, price margins are expected to be substantially higher for low and medium volume shares. In conformity with Easley et al.'s (1996) results, Nyholm (2002) also observes a positive correlation between spreads and PIN by using NYSE data with high and low trading amounts. Another notable finding of his study is that stocks with low trading amount are more subject to informed trading, and it needs more arrival rates for new information to be realized in low trading stocks compared to high trading ones. It means that new information is internalized much sooner in high-trade-volume stocks compared to stocks with less volume. As having a narrow and low volume market, Argentina stocks have significantly high PIN values; the high tendency of returns to information imbalance and also high margins of spreads (Agudelo, et al., 2015). By using three different portfolios from the Hong Kong stock exchange including blue and red chips and H-shares, Brockman and Chung (2008) also find out PIN values and reverse choices are increasing in the portfolios. The finding that low volume stocks are more exposed to informed trading and the impacts of informed trading is larger for them point out a very critical implication: less traded shares are much riskier (Easley et al., 1996).

Besides as corporate trades rise in the market, margins are also increasing due to fluctuant and unstable conditions of the marketplace (Dey and Radhakrishna, 2013). Paiardini (2015) also indicates institutional traders have a knowledge advantage over individual traders and the necessity of transparency regulations to protect disadvantageous traders. As a further indication, Easley et al., (2002) state that this risk can be considered as a type of systematic risk, since it may not be avoided by portfolio selection. Even they choose a large variety of shares having distinct risk premiums; uninformed traders get harm from this type of informed imbalances. Thus, as many scholars do, to decrease information imbalances policy implications for effective regulatory actions are required in financial markets, especially for the ones in developing economies.

There has been a consensus that regulations such as increasing information channels and explanatory public announcements to decrease information asymmetry between traders are necessary. Idier and Nardelli (2011) point out that asymmetric information has been continuously decreasing due to regulatory actions being taken as a consequence of the Euro market reform in 2005 and the financial crisis in 2008 and 2009. Their study implies that financial regulations, as well as policy implementations, have a certain effect on PIN values by influencing the level of information differences in the market. Lin (2016) analyzes Taiwan stock exchange which is dominated by individual traders before and after disclosure regulations and has revealed that information imbalances, as well as PIN values, reduce in regulated markets in terms of transparency. However, it depends on the case, but the debt scenario of a company may worsen after the new terms of restructuring agreements have been realized. So, transparency regulations may cause more complex results in terms of information asymmetry. While aiming to create fair market rules, more uninformed or confused traders seem to occur in the market. The positive relation between quarterly report disclosure variable and PIN values in Brown and Hillegeist's (2007) analysis supports the issue. Also, as a result of Zhu and Gippel's (2017) work demonstrates information differences among trades significantly increase in announcement days. As a solution, they suggest that regulatory authorities or market makers should put more informing channels into use or provide more informative content in announced reports for ordinary traders. Likewise, Brown and Hillegeist (2007) demonstrate that there is less information imbalance and fewer liquidity costs for companies in correctly regulated markets. Thus, the authors emphasize with more transparency and controls over the market, liquidity risk decreases and accurate information flow leads to economic development through financial deepening.

Having rather young literature, PIN models need to be improved and consist of a wide range of potential work for academics to progress the subject. Deficiencies in PIN models are dealt with many scholars in many aspects. First of all, incorrect categorization of stocks may lead to miscalculation of PIN values, and some errors may occur in PIN models. Errors generally occur as underassessment of PIN values, i.e., calculations may show substantially lower PIN data than the accurate ones (Boehmer et al., 2007). Sometimes errors may occur as insignificant estimations of the stock data (Lin, 2016). In order to overcome the problem, Boehmer et al. (2007) propose a kind of input fixing mechanism, and this process reduces the bias of PIN values significantly. Others select to segment the data set due to criteria such as volume, size, frequency, etc., and in this way reach significant results (Easley et al., 1996; Lin, 2016). Aktas et al. (2007) applied the PIN model by using mergers and acquisitions data and found out that PIN assessments do not fit with the information dissemination phase before arrival decisions. In order to inform traders about any price shock that might happen beforehand, Easley et al. (2011) disclosed a measure called "VPIN metric." It determines the level of information pollution in the market and reaches its highest levels during specific events influencing the market to a large extent. Thus, as a pre-alerting mechanism, some formulations can be used to check the market conditions continuously and take the appropriate position or amend the decisions accordingly both for traders and regulators. However, Chang and Whang (2015) imply another shortcoming of PIN model: When private information comes into the market, informed traders generally tend to hide their investing decisions by demonstrating a reverse behavior. They either buy/sell against sell/buy decisions of uninformed traders or separate their block transactions into smaller pieces. In order to adapt the reverse decisions of traders into PIN model, Ormos and Timotity (2016) included "PH-probability of heuristic driven investing," while Chang and Whang (2015) added two more variables called "PC-probability of contrarian trading" and "PCL-the probability of contrarian trading in low volumes." Some researches make current projections for improvement of the PIN model. For further research, Agudelo et al. (2015) suggest analyzing the effects of other variables such as market structures, information resources, and investor types on PIN values and information dissemination. For us, the novel progress came from Cepoi and Toma (2016) by adding macroeconomic variables into the PIN model. By testing the top three stocks data from the Bucharest stock exchange, they estimated the correlation between macroindicators and PIN values. They found a significant relation between information included investing and macroeconomic conditions. In consideration of the fact that macroeconomic developments are always influential on market conditions, especially on the information flow and investors' decisions, we will add macroindicators to PIN model in further parts of this chapter.

4 Data

Borsa Istanbul Stock Index (BIST) which were formerly named Istanbul Stock Exchange (ISE) started operating in 1985. In 2012, Borsa Istanbul was founded and brought together all the exchanges operating in the Turkish capital markets under a single roof. By the end of 2017, while the traded value of the market is approximately 324 million dollars, the number of shares traded in the market were 475. The main index of Borsa Istanbul is BIST 100; however, it has some submarkets which are BIST 50, BIST 30, BIST ALL SHARES, BIST INDUSTRIALS, BIST MINING, BIST BANKS, etc[1]. According to the Public Disclosure Platform, there are thirteen stocks of banks trading in BIST BANKS Index. Turkish financial market has strategic importance for many banks. Because of the investment potentials of Borsa Istanbul, many private and government oriented banks are operating in this market. Domestic and foreign investors remark the investment

1 For further information, please visit www.kap.gov.tr

Tab. 14.1: The List of Banks. Source: Bloomberg Terminal Database

NO	STOCK CODES	STOCK NAMES
1	AKBNK	AKBANK TA.S.
2	ALBRK	ALBARAKATURK KATILIM BANKASI A.S.
3	DENIZ	DENIZBANK A.S.
4	FINBN	FINANSBANK A.S.
5	GARAN	TURKIYE GARANTI BANKASI A.S.
6	HALKB	TURKIYE HALK BANKASI A.S.
7	ICBCT	ICBC TURKEY BANK A.S.
8	ISCTR	TURKIYE IS BANKASI A.S.
9	SKBNK	SEKERBANK T.A.S.
10	TSKB	TURKIYE SINAI KALKINMA BANKASI A.S.
11	VAKBN	TURKIYE VAKIFLAR BANKASI T.A.O.
12	YKBNK	YAPI VE KREDI BANKASI A.S.

opportunities for many years. Although there are a total of forty-seven banks operating in the Turkish banking sector and thirteen of them are trading in the BIST 100 Index. By the end of 2017, the traded value of BIST BANKS market is nearly 100 million dollars.

In our analysis, we use EKOP model to estimate microstructure indicators and PIN variables for each stock independently. Data set is obtained from the BIST 100 Index in our analysis and can be seen in Tab. 14.1. We analyze twelve stocks for a six-month period from October 22nd, 2016 to May 5th, 2017. Only one bank named Turkiye Kalkinma Bankasi is excluded from analysis because of data unavailability. All of the shares are from the banking sector including state banks, private banks, and one participation bank. We divided each trading day into 104 five-minute intervals starting from 09:30 am and ending at 6:05 pm. The total observation number is 20,384 for each stock.

Then we grouped our sample concerning trading volume and categorized them as low and high volume stocks by taking their mod and median (Sample mod=182,781.00 and Sample median=226,950.00) as seen in Tab. 14.2. The first part of the analysis depends on the estimation of microstructure variables and PIN values due to high and low volume segmentation. Exchange and interest rates as explanatory macroeconomic variables are added to PIN equation in the second part, and results are given regardless of the volume segmentation. As macroeconomic data, market last USD/TRY and TR LIBOR rates sourced by Bloomberg Professional Terminal Database are regressed with PIN values. The descriptive statistics of all series are provided in Tab. 14.2.

Tab. 14.2: The Descriptive Statistics of Data Set. Source: Authors' Own Calculations

STOCK CODES		AKBNK	ALBRK	DENIZ	FINBN	GARAN	HALKB	TR LIBOR
PRICE	MEAN	8.3709	1.2114	3.7082	5.0283	8.3646	10.3828	3.5618
	MEDIAN	8.3700	1.2200	3.6700	5.1900	8.3500	10.4900	3.6169
	ST. DEV.	0.6159	0.0415	0.2136	0.3693	0.7405	1.0632	0.1926
VOLUME	MEAN	295,952	34,234	5,114	2,933	961,884	337,732	-
	MEDIAN	194,028	3,063	1,284	501	657,093	217,848	-
	ST. DEV.	364,131	119,163	13,573	10,753	1,040,495	455,843	-
STOCK CODES		**ICBCT**	**ISCTR**	**SKBNK**	**TSKB**	**VAKBN**	**YKBNK**	**USD TRY**
PRICE	MEAN	1.7547	5.8066	1.1828	1.4082	4.9550	3.6914	11.1423
	MEDIAN	1.8060	5.6900	1.1900	1.4100	4.7500	3.7700	11.2739
	ST. DEV.	0.2641	0.7877	0.0443	0.0795	0.6103	0.3183	0.9661
VOLUME	MEAN	15,951	284,093	26,255	81,470	297,914	379,871	-
	MEDIAN	3,718	170,932	3,503	10,015	168,506	154,229	-
	ST. DEV.	46,378	366,597	82,425	236,870	372,984	533,809	-

5 Findings

According to the aim of the chapter and EKOP model methodology, the analyses run and the first findings are shown in Tab. 14.3 and Fig. 14.2. The second step of analysis contains macroeconomic variables and the findings demonstrated in Tab. 14.4 and 14.5. As seen in Tab. 14.3, information entry days do not fall under 7 percent and do not exceed 21 percent of all trading days in the banking sector in Turkey. Sector average for info including days (α) is 15.9 percent, and it means three of each twenty days includes the possibility of informed trades. This possibility is the highest for HALKB and lowest for FINBN stocks for the sample period. Almost 62 percent of this information entry has a low signal in Turkey's finance industry. This bad-news-entry variable (δ) is lowest for HALKB and highest for FINBN. Except for HALKB, more than half of the information entries infer bad news for all stocks.

When it comes to PIN values, it can be observed in Tab. 14.3 that sector PIN average is 7 percent, which means that 7 percent of trading days has a risk of informed trading or information inequalities seem to occur almost twice a month in Turkey's finance market. The second important finding here is that PIN values considerably change among low and high-volume stocks. There is no negative correlation between PIN and volume for BIST's finance stocks in contrast with most of the literature. Another contradiction is that all finance stocks

Tab. 14.3: PIN Variables, Volume, and PIN-Volume Correlations. Source: Authors' Own Calculations

		ε	μ	α	δ	PIN	DAILY AVR. VOLUME	PIN-VOLUME CORRELATION
HIGH VOLUME SHARES	**HALKB**	99.07 %	99.91 %	21.01 %	47.96 %	9.10 %	337,732	50.67 %
	ISCTR	98.67 %	99.86 %	19.01 %	52.17 %	8.31 %	284,093	41.93 %
	VAKBN	98.44 %	99.88 %	18.68 %	55.23 %	8.11 %	297,914	33.30 %
	AKBNK	98.25 %	99.85 %	18.11 %	56.43 %	7.88 %	295,952	33.80 %
	GARAN	98.07 %	99.86 %	16.89 %	59.40 %	7.40 %	961,884	32.89 %
	YKBNK	97.71 %	99.84 %	15.21 %	62.62 %	6.74 %	379,871	26.98 %
LOW VOLUME SHARES	**SKBNK**	98.67 %	99.88 %	18.20 %	54.32 %	7.98 %	26,255	51.07 %
	TSKB	98.46 %	99.86 %	18.20 %	55.10 %	7.95 %	81,470	45.46 %
	DENIZ	99.70 %	99.94 %	16.53 %	62.04 %	7.16 %	5,114	48.07 %
	ALBRK	96.65 %	99.73 %	11.34 %	73.63 %	5.12 %	34,234	46.78 %
	ICBCT	96.04 %	99.80 %	10.40 %	76.47 %	4.73 %	15,951	41.86 %
	FINBN	95.44 %	99.68 %	7.75 %	84.83 %	3.60 %	2,933	44.34 %
SECTOR AVERAGE		97.93 %	99.84 %	15.94 %	61.68 %	7.01 %	226,950	41.43 %

in our sample have positively correlated PIN values with their trading volume. This finding leads us to infer that volume is directly proportional to the probability of informed trading. In Tab. 14.2, both in high volume and in low volume stock groups, PIN values are sorted from highest to lowest. HALKB has the highest PIN value again and PIN values of the following eight stocks are between 7 percent–8 percent margins and very close to each other. However, as having less volume, PIN values are below 6 percent for ALBRK, ICBCT, and FINBN.

In Fig. 14.2, PIN graphs for all of the 12 finance stocks are shown for the period from Nov 2016 to April 2017. It is obvious that ICBT, ALBRK, and FINBN have considerably lower PIN values compared to others. Volumes of these stocks are also lower in contrast to other high-volume stocks. DENIZ's, SKBNK's, and TSKB's daily average volumes are also relatively very few with 5114 ; 26,255 and 81,470. Apart from these six private banks' stocks with low volumes, it can be observed that remaining six stocks have similar trends in the Nov–Apr period. PIN values of highly traded stocks are increasing from Nov to Dec and decreasing again in Jan. Some of them start to increase in Feb while others have a lagged effect and start to rise in Mar. Thus, it can be said that high volume stocks (HALKB, ISCTR, VAKBN, AKBNK, GARAN, and YKBNK) have a kind of U-shape pattern within the period (between December '16 and March '17). Finally, it can be seen that PIN variable decreases for most of the stocks in

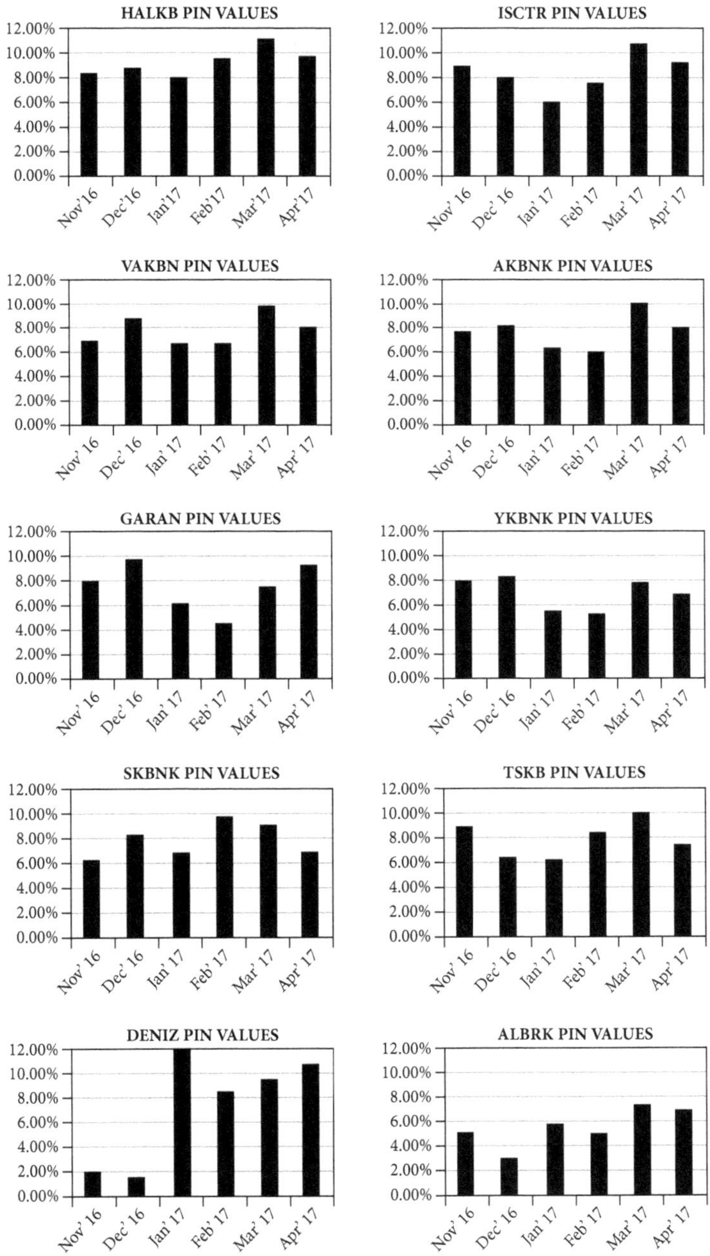

Fig. 14.2: PIN values of 12 stocks in the sample. *Source: Authors' own calculation*

Tab. 14.4: PIN and USD/TRY Regression Coefficients. Source: Authors' Own Calculations

Dependent Variable:		**PIN Values**	**Observation:**	**196**
Independent Variable:		**USD/TRY**		
Period:		**Oct 22, 2016 – May 5, 2017 (Daily)**		
	Coefficient	**Std. Error**	**t-Statistic**	**Prob.**
AKBNK	-0.0037	0.0231	-0.1613	0.8720
ALBRK	0.0403	0.0182	2.2152	0.0279**
DENIZ	0.1651	0.0210	7.8738	0.0000*
FINBN	0.0579	0.0141	4.0952	0.0001*
GARAN	-0.0149	0.0221	-0.6740	0.5011
HALKB	0.0479	0.0221	2.1682	0.0314**
ICBCT	0.0138	0.0174	0.7948	0.4277
ISCTR	-0.0018	0.0218	-0.0817	0.9349
SKBNK	0.0221	0.0213	1.0369	0.3011
TSKB	0.0104	0.0223	0.4644	0.6429
VAKBN	-0.0036	0.0233	-0.1550	0.8770
YKBNK	-0.0248	0.0208	-1.1947	0.2337

*0,01, **0.05, ***0.10 statistically significance levels respectively

April 2017. When PIN trends are observed, DENIZ has the highest variation among our data set consisting of twelve finance stocks. PIN value of DENIZ makes a peak in January, and it is nearly six times higher than December's PIN. Likewise, the increase in HALKB's PIN values from January to March also refers to a remarkable finding and deserves an explanation.

In the last part of our analysis, we estimate macroeconomic variables with PIN values, as Cepoi and Toma (2016) suggest in their study. We used the model which they suggested in their study (Equation 4).

$$PIN_t = \alpha + \theta_1 MACRO_t + \varepsilon_t . \tag{4}$$

where, PIN_t is the daily PIN value of each banking stock; $MACRO_t$ is the explanatory variables which are USD/TRY exchange rate and interest rate (6 Months TR Libor). As seen in Tab. 14.4 and Tab. 14.5, PIN values are in a significant positive relationship with the exchange rate (USD/TRY) for four stocks while five of them have a significant positive relation with interest rate (6 Months TR Libor) again. Results show that as exchange rate rises 1 percent the risk of informed trades or information imbalance increases by 16 percent for DENIZ and by 4–5 percent intervals for ALBRK, FINBN, and HALKB. When it comes to interest rate, it can

Tab. 14.5: PIN and TRLIB6M Regression Coefficients. Source: Authors' Own Calculations

Dependent Variable:		**PIN Values**	**Observation:**	**196**
Independent Variable:		**TRLIB6M Index**		
Period:		**Oct 22, 2016 – May 5, 2017 (Daily)**		
	Coefficient	**Std. Error**	**t-Statistic**	**Prob.**
AKBNK	0.0035	0.0046	0.7600	0.4482
ALBRK	0.0092	0.0036	2.5391	0.0119**
DENIZ	0.0313	0.0042	7.3606	0.0000*
FINBN	0.0083	0.0029	2.8826	0.0044*
GARAN	-0.0015	0.0044	-0.3347	0.7382
HALKB	0.0115	0.0044	2.6211	0.0095*
ICBCT	-0.0019	0.0035	-0.5464	0.5854
ISCTR	0.0059	0.0043	1.3583	0.1759
SKBNK	0.0073	0.0042	1.7307	0.0851***
TSKB	0.0072	0.0044	1.6299	0.1047
VAKBN	0.0044	0.0046	0.9531	0.3417
YKBNK	-0.0025	0.0041	-0.6015	0.5482

*0.01, **0.05, ***0.10 statistically significance levels respectively

be said that compared to the exchange rate, the interest rate has less impact on PIN values that is less than 1 percent. Other stocks do not have a significant PIN correlation with macroeconomic variables.

6 Discussion of Results

Researchers who conducted studies in PIN literature widely share the view that the risk of informed trading increases as volume decreases as a result of the higher risk included by low volume stocks (Easley and O'hara, 1987; Easley et al., 1996; Nyholm, 2002; Brockman and Chung, 2008; Agudelo et al., 2015). However, our study shows that PIN values vary among all stocks regardless of their volume category. For instance, some of the low volume stocks (SKBNK, TSKB) have higher PINs than some of the high volume stocks (GARAN, YKBNK). Moreover, there is no negative correlation; in contrast, as volume increases, PIN values also increase within the same stock data. This implies a positive correlation between volume and PIN for each one. In Turkey, the banking sector has been started to be intensely regulated over the last decade, since the speculations and manipulations created a very risky environment for investors in the past. Risk tests conducted to traders and other investors, financial leverage restrictions, and transaction limitations are all examples of the mentioned regulations. Related to these improvements, public bodies make either informed traders invest in stock markets or uninformed traders invest through institutions that have adequate information about the current developments and knowledge about procedures applied in the stock market. Thus, we can assume that as volume increases most parts of the transactions probably come from block traders or individual informed traders and so PIN value also rises. This explanation is also valid for finance stocks in BIST. Related to its structure, the banking sector is dominated by a wide range of information flow from financial statements to macroeconomic data or from Central Bank's policy announcements to score updates of credit rating agencies. In order to invest in a single manufacturing company stock, traders need to be informed about a limited number of sector and company developments or just follow informed traders. However, to invest in a finance stock, they need to possess an intense and wide range of information flow both in the domestic sector and in foreign markets. Besides, due to block trades of large institutions and informed traders' price margins being utilized in a short time span; return expectations of uninformed traders are lessened for high volume stocks. Many individual traders who are risk takers but have limited information tend to invest more in low volume stocks in Turkey. However, this assessment needs to be tested for other sector stocks in BIST, and future research may be conducted to analyze the correlation between the probability of informed trading, information imbalances, and the risk behavior of traders and volumes.

When the monthly PIN values are analyzed, a sharp increase in the Jan-Mar period in HALKB, ISCTR, VAKBN, and TSKB stocks can be observed. These are public banks shares, which are partially or fully state-owned. This increase is possibly related to a public announcement stating that all state banks and public-owned companies will be transferred to Turkey Wealth Fund, a newly founded institution established in Aug 2016. Transfer news is released on January 23rd, and some of the companies have been handed over in February and some of them have been passed on in March officially. This announcement has been perceived as a bad signal by traders since the transfers will be done in order to provide collateral for foreign obligations. Thus, sell transactions from informed traders (μ) as well as PIN values of the four public banks stocks increased in this period. Second conspicuous implication derived from graphs is the decline in most of the PIN values in April. This might be because of the Constitutional Referendum held on April 16th, 2017. Before the Referendum, uncertainty seems to have contributed to high PIN values in March. However, afterward in April, especially for state banks again, PIN values decrease noticeably most likely because of leaving the uncertainty environment behind.

Besides upside and downside movements of twelve finance stocks in Fig. 14.2, one movement is worthy of paying attention to in a deeper sense: DENIZ with its highest fluctuation in PIN values (from 1.61 percent to 11.84 percent) between Dec and Jan. It seems a remarkable increase and needs an explanation. Public Disclosure Platform (KAP) is an electronic system through which electronically signed notifications required by the capital markets and BIST regulations are publicly disclosed. KAP is the first place to find any evidence about that fluctuation; however, there is no unusual news from Dec to Jan for DENIZ. The second place which may find any evidence is the newspapers. After a broad search in national newspapers' archives, some important news came out in Jan. Primary news about a syndicated loan for commercial firms. The news indicated that DENIZ was a part of the huge syndicated loan and provided loans at a lower interest rate than the market. Also, another news about Sberbank, which was the biggest shareholder of DENIZ, was found. The vice chairman of the Sberbank announced that they were expecting more cyberattacks in 2017 against their systems by hackers. These two developments are essential with reference to the risk perception of the investors. While the first of them might be increased default risk of the stock, the second one creates a mistrustful situation for investors. Although there are bad news in the market about DENIZ, there is also another perspective for explaining that abnormal peak. According to the regression results in Tab. 14.3, DENIZ has the highest relationship with the USD/TRY exchange rate. This result may show that DENIZ has a tie with exchange rate due to its capital structure. When the exchange rate of USD/TRY was analyzed in Dec and Jan, a significant fluctuation between 3.40 and 3.90 TL per dollar was observed. Taking into consideration that serious increase in exchange rate, DENIZ might be affected by USD/TRY due to its capital structure.

Like the study conducted by Cepoi and Toma (2016), as a further step in our analysis, we test the impact of USD/TL and six months-TRLIBOR as macroeconomic indicators on PIN values. It is expected that as exchange rate increases risk of informed trades and information imbalances also rise because traders conceive this upheaval effect as a bad signal in the stock market, and their decisions will be toward selling their stocks and buying foreign exchange instead. This means an exact increase in informed traders' selling decision rate (μ). The same effect is also valid for the interest rate and informed traders' decisions. Our estimate confirms this prediction. Especially exchange rate impact on DENIZ's PIN value is remarkably higher than others. As the exchange rate appreciates by 1 percent, informed traders are inclined to sell by 16 percent. This will increase sell decisions and information imbalances 16 percent more. This number alters between 4 and 5 percent for other significantly correlated stocks. On the other part, the interest rate has a very less impact on PIN values in Turkey's banking sector. This might be because of the fact that deposit account investors are different from stock traders in terms of investing patterns, risk-taking decisions and information level. This simply means that most of the time deposit investors do not invest in stocks in Turkey because of not having the required level of knowledge about the stock market; the procedures need to hold transactions and also because they perceive stock market as a hazardous investment type due to substantial fluctuations depending on economic and political conjuncture. Time deposit holders are generally the risk-averse type of investors. Thus, any fluctuation in interest rates may not necessarily have a significant effect on the possibility of informed trading volumes.

Conclusion

In our study, twelve financial sector stocks of BIST were analyzed. PIN indicators were calculated, and also the PIN volume correlation was examined in the first part. Based on the results, it can be said that the BIST financial market receives information entry for more than four days each month. More than half of these information entries are comprised of bad signals. When public news and announcements are examined, the bad signal percentage is expected to be more than the good signals. Announcements from credit rating agencies about cutting down financial institutions' scores or news about macroeconomic indicators such as unemployment, inflation current account deficit are all perceived as bad signals by the stock exchange market. It is also found that as the volume increases for each stock, the PIN value rises as well; i.e., PIN and volume correlations for finance stocks are found to be positive, unlike findings that are common in the literature. It is thought that this result is due to BIST and the banking sector stock market showing diversified and unique characteristics from international markets. While international stock exchanges are deeper markets and more dominated by deregulation facilities, BIST has a developing market structure, and many regulations are put into practice to exert control over the market to some extent. Since uninformed traders suffered significant capital losses in the past, public bodies put a series of regulatory actions in use. These actions will aim that especially informed traders to enter the market and uninformed traders are required to make transactions through institutional traders. From this point of view, a positive correlation between transaction volume and PIN values can be identified as a normal result for BIST. However, in addition to these measures, it is beneficial to increase the sources of information and to make them more transparent for individual traders who prefer to make investments on their own. These measures include providing individual investor training, continually presenting informative short notes about the market in the digital environment, establishing media channels that solely broadcast about the stock market, providing clearer explanations for KAP info notes. In this way, uninformed traders will be protected as well as BIST, as an emerging market, can be deepened. In the last part of our study, the relationship between macrovariables and PIN data were analyzed. As expected, exchange rate and interest rate data were found to be positively and significantly correlated with PIN values for some of the stocks. However, interest rate-PIN coefficients were very low and did not imply a clear correlation.

Consequently, the findings imply that correlations between many other stocks are insignificant and again the fact that many significant correlations are very low indicate a very critical point: The difference between traders who invest in stock exchange market and other investors investing in other financial instruments is deepened in Turkey. The most significant factor here is the fact that traders and investors show many diversified characteristics from one another, and these two markets do not constitute complete alternatives to each other in Turkey. In future studies, it is thought that it will be possible to make more in-depth interpretations by analyzing the relationship between PIN and macrovariables in other sectors other than finance.

Acknowledgments

We are grateful to George Pennacchi who is a Professor of Finance in University of Illinois at Urbana-Champaign for many pertinent comments and helpful suggestions.

References

Agudelo, D.A., Giraldo S., & Villarraga, E. (2015) "Does PIN Measure Information? Informed Trading Effects on Returns and Liquidity in Six Emerging Markets," International Review of Economics and Finance, *39*: 149–161.

Aktas, N., De Bodt, E., Declerck, F., & Van Oppens, H. (2007) "The PIN Anomaly around M&A Announcements," *Journal of Financial Markets*, *10*(2): 169–191.

Boehmer E, Grammig J., & Thiessen E. (2007) "Estimating the Probability of Informed Trading, Does Trade Misclassification Matter?," *Journal of Financial Markets*, *10*: 26–47.

Brockman, P. & Chung Y.C. (2008) "Investor Protection, Adverse Selection, and the Probability of Informed Trading," *Rev Quant Finan Acc*, *30*: 111–131.

Brown, S. & Hillegeist S.A. (2007) "How Disclosure Quality Affects the Level of Information Asymmetry", Rev Acc Stud, *12*: 443–477.

Cepoi, C.O. & Toma F.M. (2016) "Estimating Probability of Informed Trading on the Bucharest Stock Exchange," *Czech Journal of Economics and Finance*, *66*(2): 140–160.

Chang, S.C. & Whang, A.W. (2015) "Adverse Selection and the Presence of Informed Trading," *Journal of Empirical Finance*, *33*: 19–33.

Dey, M.K. & Radhakrishna, B. (2015) "Informed Trading, Institutional Trading, and Spread," *J Econ. Finan*, *39*: 288–307.

Easley, D. & O'hara, M. (1987) "Price, Trade Size and Information in Securities Market," *Journal of Financial Economics*, *19*: 69–90.

Easley, D., Hvidkjaer, S., & O'hara, M. (2002) "Is Information Risk a Determinant of Asset Returns?," *The Journal of Finance*, *5*: 2185–2221.

Easley, D., Kiefer, N.M., O'hara, M., & Paperman, J.B. (1996) "Liquidity, Information, and Infrequently Traded Stocks," *The Journal of Finance*, 4: 1405–1436.

Easley, D., Prado,M.M.L., & O'hara, M. (2011) "The Microstructure of the 'Flash Crash': Flow Toxicity, Liquidity Crashes and the Probability of Informed Trading," *The Journal of Portfolio Management*, Winter: 118–128.

Fama, E.F. & French K.R. (1992) "The Cross Section of Expected Stock Returns," *The Journal of Finance*, 47: 427–465.

Fama, E.F., & MacBeth, J.D. (1973) "Risk, Return, and Equilibrium: Empirical Tests," *Journal of Political Economy*, *81*: 607–636.

Gan, Q., Wei, W.C., & Johnstone, D. (2017) "Does the Probability of Informed Trading Model Fit Empirical Data?," *The* financial *Review*, *52*: 5–35.

Goldstein, M.A., Ness, B.F.V., & Ness, R.A.V. (2005) "The Intraday Probability of Informed Trading," WSPC/B351, *11*: 139–158.

Gozluklu, A.E. (2016) "Pre-Trade Transparency and Informed Trading: Experimental Evidence on Undisclosed Orders," *Journal of Financial Markets*, *28*: 91–115.

Hamilton, J.D. (1994) *Time Series Analysis*, Princeton University Press, Princeton, NJ.

Ho, T. & Stohl, S. (1981) "Optimal Dealer Pricing under Transactions and Return Uncertainty," *Journal of Financial Economics*, *9*: 47–73.

Idier, J. & Nardelli, S. (2011) "Probability of Informed Trading on the Euro Overnight Market Rate," *International Journal of Finance and Economics*, *16*: 131–145.

Lin, Y. (2016) "Does Greater Market Transparency Reduce Information Asymmetry?," *Emerging Markets Finance & Trade*, *52*: 2565–2584.

Nyholm, K. (2002) "Estimating the Probability of Informed Trading," *The Journal of Financial Research*, *4*: 485–505.

O'hara, M. & Oldfield, G. (1986) "The Microeconomics of Market Making," *Journal of Financial and Quantitative Analysis*, *21*: 361–376.

Ormos, M. & Timotity, D. (2016) "Market Microstructure during financial Crisis: Dynamics of Informed and Heuristic-Driven Trading," *Finance Research Letters*, *19*: 60–66.

Paiardini, P. (2015) "Informed Trading in Parallel Bond Markets," *Journal of Financial Markets*, *26*: 103–121.

Zhu, Y. & Gippel, J. (2017) "Informed Trading on Debt Covenant Violations: The Long and Short of It", *Accounting and Finance*, *57*: 289–315.

Sezer Bozkus Kahyaoğlu

15 Generalized Autoregressive Score (Gas) Model: An Applied Analysis on the BIST 100 Index

Abstract: In general, volatility has been used as a parameter for measuring risk in the literature. However, there are various approaches to calculate risk. In this work, Generalized Autoregressive Score (GAS) model is introduced as a new technique to calculate down side risk of Borsa Istanbul BIST100 index in order to contribute relevant literature.

Keywords: GAS Model, Down Side Risk, Tail Effect, BIST 100 Index

1 Introduction

The latest advancement in information technologies and rapid increase in data accumulation (big data) create new approaches and techniques to be developed with the aim of modeling and estimating the core components in financial markets. Especially the high frequency natures of financial time series increase the costs of operations for financial institutions. In that sense, there is trade-off for financial institutions to decide while they are applying the accurate tools and techniques in down side risk calculations. On the one hand, they need to consider using true predictors which are consistent and efficient parameters of risk to be more competitive in the market; on the other hand they face increasing amount of costs related to information technology infrastructure and risk management professionals to recruit. After the global financial crisis and failures which have had long lasting impacts on the world economy, there are lessons to be learnt for the market players and stakeholders. Hence, these events have changed the point of view toward corporate risk management and lead transparency to gain importance as an instrument. It is a fact that corporate governance principles, and especially the transparency, make enormous contribution to the finance theory, along with the requirement for detailed explanation of techniques used to estimate risks. In general, volatility has been used as a parameter for measuring risk in the literature. However, there are various techniques and approaches to calculate risk. In this work, GAS model is introduced as a new technique to calculate down side risk in order to contribute relevant literature.

Decision makers face many risks that emerge in the economic life based on globalized competition. Such decision makers make different position and/or portfolio choices depending on their financial status in order to manage these risks. In practice, sudden changes in markets, policies, interest rates, share prices, and foreign exchange rates resulting from financial developments are regarded as indicators of risk. It is assumed that distributions used to create parameters in analyses conducted to estimate such indicators have not changed depending on the previous and new information. This causes parameters to be estimated as fixed across time. The fact that time series have high frequencies makes it necessary to arrange possibility functions according to new data in a way that they are consistent and efficient for new parameter estimations. This has shifted the attention from techniques related to a parameter-based estimation process to techniques related to an observation-based estimation process. Observation-based estimation processes offer an approach that enables parameters to change depending on time. This way, parameters can be estimated depending on differences in distribution. As a result, the Generalized Autoregressive Score (GAS) that is a scoring technique giving tail and scale values that are main parameters of the distribution used to estimate financial risks was used in this study. The GAS model enables parameters to change according to time while analyzing the dynamic structures of univariate and multivariate time series. In addition, it is possible to make estimations using the lagged values of the dependent variable and other external variables that can affect the system. This technique enables time dependence. The GAS approach brings innovations to the literature as an "observation-based" modeling technique. The most important feature of this approach is that it is a technique making it possible to predict time-dependent parameters perfectly for the next period. In this context, the earning series derived from the BIST 100 index, the value at risk in the analyzed period, and the expected shortfall value are estimated through the GAS approach within the framework of log-likelihood in the application part of this chapter.

The first part of this chapter gives information about the newly emerging literature related to the GAS model. The differences and similarities between the GAS model and GARCH models are explained and the advantages of the GAS model are revealed in this part. The GAS model is introduced as a method, and the main hypothesis is stated with the assumptions on which the model is based in the second section. The data, descriptive statistics, and empirical findings obtained from the GAS model are discussed in the third section. The estimated parameters of the GAS model related to the return series of the BIST 100 index are financially interpreted. In the Conclusion, policy suggestions are made based on the empirical findings related to the GAS model, thus aiming to make a contribution to the newly emerging literature.

2 Literature Review

Inter-temporal dependence between data in financial time series is the memory of the series in time dimension. Estimation processes are stochastic in this memory structure. The most important feature of this process is that the sources of errors are "themselves." Therefore, parameters of a stochastic process can change depending on time (Blasques et al., 2016: 1–2). GAS approaches take into account parametric distribution characteristics of observations in addition to the above mentioned process. This way, it is possible to estimate a model that enables parameters to change depending on time. Due to the abovementioned characteristics, the GAS approach can be expressed as a "special case" of estimations to be obtained through changes in distribution parameters of the GARCH family.

The most important feature of modeling techniques with time-dependent parameters is that they have a dynamic nature. In this context, the equation structures to be based on observations can be divided into two main groups as observation-driven and parameter-driven (Cos, 1981: 94–95). The time-dependent parameter is defined in observation-driven models, and a functional structure is established based on observation values of the previous periods. Score-based techniques were first discussed by Creal et al. (2011, 2013) and Harvey (2013) in the literature, and they drew a lot of attention thanks to their advantages. The main reason why GAS models have gained importance is that score-based models are more flexible compared to other approaches and estimations complying with distribution characteristics of the analyzed data are robust (Blasques et al., 2017:3–4). Harvey and Luati (2014) used the GAS approach and modeled data with a thick-tail structure according to location and scale parameters. They found out that data with a skew distribution in GAS models were more effective in analysis of thick-tail structure compared to data with a normal distribution, thus providing advantages for estimation and modeling of financial risks. Creal et al. (2014) conducted a dynamic factor modeling based on mixed scales. The latest applications based on scoring contributing to the literature were applied to the existing techniques. Salvatierra and Patton (2015), Makatjane et al. (2017), Oh and Patton (2017), and Buccheri et al. (2018) adapted GAS to copula and spatial econometric techniques. The studies conducted by those authors revealed that score-based GAS model approaches were more effective in modeling conditional distribution characteristics of correlations and volatilities. Blasques et al. (2016) found out that the GAS model yielded perfect results in times of financial distress. They found out that estimating risk measurement techniques related to value at risk, and expected shortfall based on the GAS model would make it possible to obtain more consistent results. It was determined in empirical studies; for example, the studies conducted by Harvey and Sucarrat (2014) on market risk, Oh and Patton (2013) on systematic risk, Creal et al. (2014) on credit risk analysis, Harvey and Thiele (2015) and Janus et al. (2014) on dependence modeling, Blasques et al. (2014) and Catania and Bill (2016) on spatial econometrics that the estimation power of the GAS model was more effective and consistent compared to GARCH in periods of very high or very low volatility in financial markets. Therefore, the GAS model has been a new approach preferred for estimation and modeling of financial risks recently.

3 The GAS Model

The GAS model has *Nx1* vectors. Y_t, f_t, and x_t represent the dependent variables determined by subject, the time-dependent parameter vector, and the vector of external variables, respectively, while *t* and *teta* (θ) represent the vector of the static parameters. Accordingly, the vectorial representation of the variables in the GAS model is as follows (Creal et al., 2012: 38–40).

$$Y^t = \{y_1, y_2, \ldots y_t\}$$

$$F^t = \{f_1, f_2, \ldots f_t\}$$

$$X^t = \{x_1, x_2, \ldots x_t\}$$

Data set owned in the t time period $\{f_t, F_t\}$

$$F_t = \{Y^{t-1}, F^{t-1}l, X^t\}$$

It is assumed that the observation values of y_t are obtained from density functions.

$$y_t \sim p((y_t | f_t, F_t)) \tag{1}$$

The function defining the update of the time-dependent parameter in Equation 1 is as follows:

$$f_{t+1} = \kappa + \sum_{i=1}^{p} A_i s_{t-i+1} + \sum_{j=1}^{q} B_j f_{t-j+1} \tag{2}$$

κ represents the matrix of fixed values, while A and B represent the coefficient matrix for the relevant dimensions. Unknown coefficients are shown with teta (θ). Accordingly; $\kappa = \kappa(\theta)$, $\kappa = \kappa(\theta)$, $A_i = A_i(\theta)$ ve $\kappa = \kappa(\theta)$, $A_i = A_i(\theta)$ ve $B_j = B_j(\theta)$ and *i=1, 2,.....p* ve *j=1, 2,....q*. Estimations are made according to the observation density function specified in Equation 1 in the GAS model. In this regard, the time-dependent parameter (f_t) is shown as follows for the *t+1* time period when the y_t observation takes place.

$$s_t = S_t . \nabla_t, \quad s_t = S_t . \nabla_t \quad \nabla_t = \frac{\partial lnp(y_t | f_t, F_t; \theta)}{\partial f_t} \tag{3}$$

It is defined as positive in Equation 3 and $S_t = S(t, f_t, F_t; \theta)$ is a scale matrix function. When a diagonal form is used in St=JxJ representation, it transforms into the "Jacobian" matrix as a special form. A scale matrix is obtained from the observation-dependent mechanism in Equation 2, and it helps to define p and q orders in the GAS model in Equation 1 and Equation 3. In general, *P=q=1 in the GAS (p,q) representation.*

$$\kappa \equiv (\kappa_\mu, \kappa_\varphi, \kappa_\vartheta)' \ \kappa \equiv (\kappa_\mu, \kappa_\varphi, \kappa_\vartheta)' \ A \equiv diag(a_\mu, a_\varphi, a_\vartheta) \quad and \quad \kappa \equiv (\kappa_\mu, \kappa_\varphi, \kappa_\vartheta)'$$
$$A \equiv diag(a_\mu, a_\varphi, a_\vartheta) \text{ve} \, B \equiv diag(b_\mu, b_\varphi, b_\vartheta)$$

$$J(\widetilde{\theta_t}) = \begin{vmatrix} 1 & 0 & 0 \\ 0 & exp(\widetilde{\varphi_t}) & 0 \\ 0 & 0 & exp(\widetilde{\vartheta_t}) \end{vmatrix} \tag{4}$$

$$\rho_{hk,t} = c_{h1,t} c_{k1,t} + \sum_{m=2}^{h-1} c_{hm,t} c_{km,t} \prod_{l=1}^{m-1} s_{hl,t} s_{kl,t} + c_{hk,t} \prod_{l=1}^{h-1} s_{hl,t} s_{kl,t}$$

$1 \leq h < k \leq N$ is assumed to be valid for all values. Accordingly,

$$c_{hk,t} \equiv cos(\widetilde{\rho_{hk,t}}) \ c_{hk,t} \equiv cos(\widetilde{\rho_{hk,t}}) \ s_{hk,t} \equiv sin(\widetilde{\rho_{hk,t}})$$

$$R_t \equiv \{\rho_{ij,t}\}_{i,j=1}^{N} \ \text{is a correlation matrix} \tag{5}$$

f_t is used intuitively in the scoring applied in the GAS model. Values of the existing parameters in *t* time are defined according to the steepest part of the probability and density function. This way, the parameter update is estimated in a way that is most compatible with its natural aspect. On the other hand, the scores are determined according to not only the first and second moments of the observation but also the total density function. This is possible with the help of S_t scale

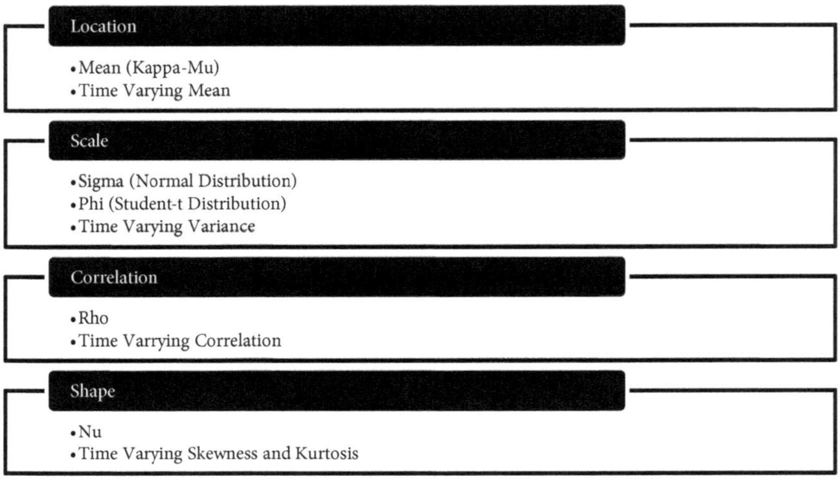

Fig. 15.1: Main parameters related to the GAS model. *Source: Ardia et al., 2016*

matrix applied in the GAS model. The outlook of the scaling is determined by the variance of the score. The GAS model is estimated with the maximum likelihood model that makes the parameters suitable. Therefore, the GAS model is also defined as a score-driven or dynamic conditional score model in the literature (Ardia et al., 2016: 2–6). Explanations are given below about location, scale, correlation, and shape that are the main parameters of the GAS model.

Parameters estimated in the GAS model are calculated according to distribution characteristics of data. Names and numbers of parameters on the basis of distribution characteristics suggested for univariate and multivariate analyses are as shown in Tab. 15.1. The GAS model was prepared as univariate in this study taking three different types of distribution into account. Parameters related to the BIST 100 index series are estimated in R program as an application example and empirical findings obtained from this are explained in the following sections.

4 Data and Empirical Findings

A return series was created in this study using the closing prices data of the BIST 100 index between 04.01.2010 and 03.07.2018. This data is listed by working days in accordance with the time-series approach. Fig. 15.1 shows the data used in the analysis.

Tab. 15.1: Parameter Estimations Depending on Distribution Characteristics in the GAS Model

Distribution Name	Type	Parameters	No of Parameters
Gaussian	Univariate	Location, Scale	2
Student t	Univariate	Location, Scale, Shape	3
Skewed Student t	Univariate	Location, Scale, Shape, Skewness	4
Asymmetric Laplace	Univariate	Scale, Shape, Skewness	3
Poisson	Univariate	Location	1
Gamma	Univariate	Scale, Shape	2
Exponential	Univariate	Location	1
Multivariate Gaussian	Multivariate	Location, Scale, Correlation	3
Multivariate Student t	Multivariate	Location, Scale, Shape, Correlation	4

R Program (2017)

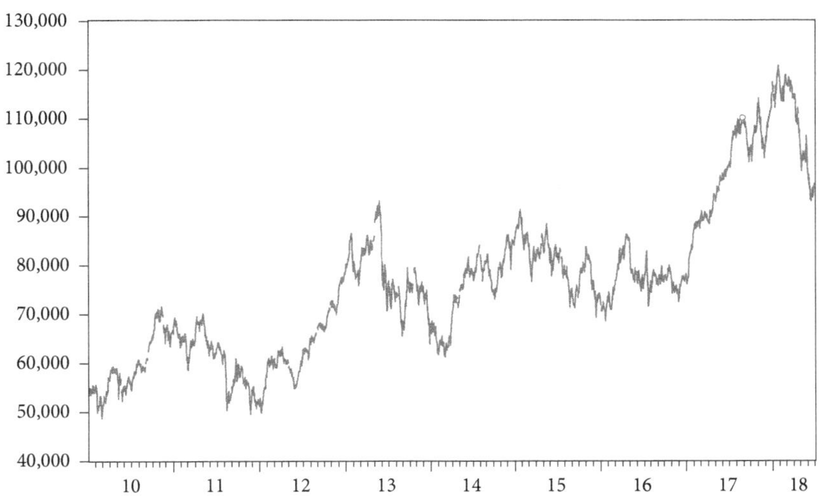

Fig. 15.2: Closing price data of the BIST 100 index (2010–2018)

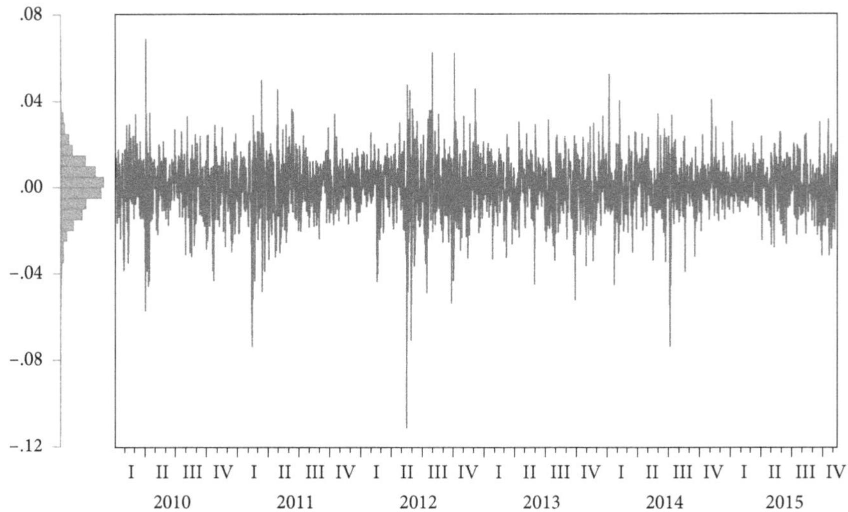

Fig. 15.3: BIST 100 index return series (2010–2018)

Fig. 15.2 shows data about the BIST 100 return series calculated according to the BIST 100 data.

The probability related to the return series is presented together with normal distribution in fig. 15.3 in order to make a comparison for the density function. According to the data obtained from Fig. 15.3, the blue line represents the geometric locations of the points when the data has normal distribution. The fact that the returns in the tail are outside the blue area indicates that the returns differ from normal distribution and have thick tails.

The visual information in Fig. 15.3 is a finding showing that the BIST 100 index does not have a normal distribution on the return series. This finding is also supported by the descriptive statistics results shown in Tab. 15.2. According to the Jarque-Bera value in the descriptive statistics, the null hypothesis suggesting that the returns have a normal distribution is rejected (Jarque and Bera, 1987).

The ADF unit root test was conducted for stationary analysis of the BIST 100 index returns according to the mean value (Dickey and Fuller, 1979). The test result was -13 at 0.01 significant level and 12 lag length. Accordingly, the null hypothesis suggesting that the returns have "weakly stationary" could not be rejected. As the level of integration with the memory structure was below 1, the KPSS stationarity test was conducted in addition to the ADF test (Kwiatkowski et al., 1992). The KPSS test value was calculated as 0,032. This means that the null

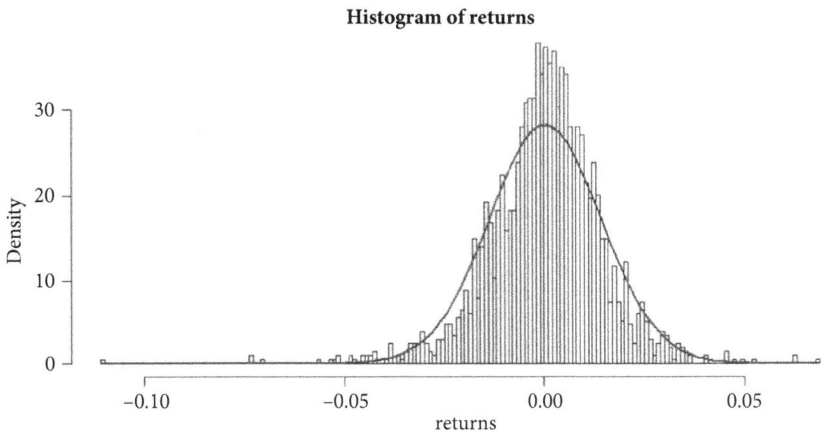

Fig. 15.4: Comparison of the BIST 100 index returns and normal distribution

Tab. 15.2: BIST 100 Index Returns—Jarque-Bera Test Result

Mean	0.000278
Median	0.000792
Maximum	0.068952
Minimum	-0.110638
Std. Dev.	0.014117
Skewness	-0.515966
Kurtosis	6.919481
Jarque-Bera	1462.707
Probability	0.000000
Sum	0.593242
Sum Sq. Dev.	0.425710
Observations	2137

hypothesis defining the series as stationary at the 0.1 significance level cannot be rejected.

It was found out that the BIST 100 index returns were weakly stationary according to the above mentioned unit root test results. As the GAS model was used in the study, the returns must not be linear. For this purpose, the Teraesvirta Neural Network Test was conducted to find out whether the returns were linear. This test was estimated within the scope of the Rmetrics — Nonlinear and

Chaotic Time Series Modeling obtained from the R Program (2017). According to the estimation results, it was concluded that the returns were not statistically linear in average at 10,703 Chi-square value and 0.004 significance level.

The prerequisites for the GAS model estimation were provided. The value at risk (VaR) was estimated with the GAS approach for the BIST 100 index return series. The value at risk approach is a technique developed to calculate possible down side risks (shortfall) in financial markets. New approaches have been emerging in addition to the new techniques developed in the literature in order to calculate values at risk. The failure to take the tail structure into account while making estimations according to the VaR method is criticized in the literature (Yamai and Yoshiba: 2002, 57–59). The tail effect is usually called "tail risk" in financial markets. Prices and shocks causing this tail effect in financial markets determine and change distributions of returns. The standard VaR method provides values calculated with the assumption that the data distribution is in line with normal distribution without taking the above mentioned impacts into account. However, the analysis for stationarity of tail, scale, shape, and location parameters indicating the changes in the distribution as mentioned earlier has become an important process. Therefore, it has become important to use methods related to analysis tools such as VaR taking distribution changes into account (Gonzalez-Rivera et al., 2004).

Firstly, possible impacts of rare incidents started to be analyzed in connection with the impacts of returns on distribution. In general, impacts of rare incidents on distribution of returns are discussed within the scope of tail effect, which is also called "tail risk" in the literature. As the presence of tail effects affects expected shortfall more than realized shortfall risks, the developed techniques are called Expected Shortfall (ES) techniques in the literature. This way, possible shortfall risks can be estimated in accordance with tail risks and impacts of data on distribution thanks to this method (Artzner et al., 1997: 68–70). The GAS model is taken into account while estimating the impacts of return series on the distribution. As a result, methods used to calculate shortfall risks have become methods used to test whether the GAS parameters are consistent and effective predictors in risk management. So a cross-check method has emerged for stages in which model and risk levels are calculated in financial risk management. In other words, the calculated VaR values have become an indicator providing information about "model risk" and possible risk levels. Accordingly, this indicator provides information that can be used by decision makers in the market while setting the "stop-lost" risk limit. Techniques used to calculate shortfall risks usually enable us to perform evaluations about validity of models used to calculate such risks. In addition,

Tab. 15.3: Results of VaR Parameter Estimations Based on the BIST 100 Index Returns and GAS Model

Estimates	Normal Distribution	Student t Distribution	Skewed Student t Distribution
Kappa1	4.555e-05 (1,470)	0.0004098 (3.706)*	3.271e-04 (2.29)*
Kappa2	-7.345e-01 (-9.712)*	-0.3219668 (-9.524)*	-8.522e-02 NaN
Kappa3		-0.9032528 (-9.020)*	-7.450e-07 (-6.190)*
Kappa4			-4.703e-02 (-2.744)*
A1	1.000e-06 (2.872.663)*	0,0000010 (3.444.071)*	1.000e-06 (872.9)*
A2	1.898e-01 (9.656)*	0,1897517 (6.407)*	1.000e-04 (6.739)*
A3		2.2759207 (202.653)*	
A4			5.500e+00 (68.26)*
B1	9.303e-01 (9.974.986)*	0,5993104 (3.938.804)*	5.331e-01 (3.641)*
B2	9.138e-01 (103.137)*	0,9634483 (252.179)*	9.800e-01 NaN
B3		0.6158621 (52.032)*	
B4			9.800e-01 (197.7)*
Location	0.0006539	0,0010227	0,0007005
Scale	0.0001993	0,0001495	0,0141095
Shape		7.9999960	7,9992890
Skewness			0.999999
Information Criteria	AIC BIC -12316 -12282	AIC BIC -12437 -12386	AIC BIC -12332 -12275

(*) is statistically significant at 1 %.

using shortfall risks together with the GAS model makes it a technique providing additional information about which effects (tail risks) will have a determining role in risk calculation.

The VaR values calculated for the BIST 100 index returns were estimated in this study within the framework of the GAS model. The results are listed in Tab. 15.3. The VaR parameters estimated with the GAS model were calculated for three different types of distribution: Normal Distribution, Student *t* Distribution, and Skewed Student *t* Distribution. The results in Tab. 15.3 show the time-dependent parameters obtained through the BIST 100 index returns and the distributions from which these parameters were obtained. The results in Tab. 15.3 show that the parameters calculated according to the Student *t* distribution and Skewed Student *t* distribution are significant. These two distributions provide information about thick (fat) tails and asymmetric effect in case of fat tails, respectively.

The "shape" value determining the shape of the distribution in Tab. 15.3 was approximately equal and higher than three (>3) in both distributions. This value provides information about estimations made in the presence of possible tail effects in the period in which the BIST 100 index returns were analyzed. The fact that the "skewness" value calculated according to the Skewed Student *t* distribution for the BIST 100 index returns was determined as 0.999999 indicates that the parameters were estimated in the presence of asymmetry.

In order to show that these estimated values are consistent and effective predictors in terms of risk management, the VaR of the BIST 100 index returns was calculated using the parameters. There is a difference between the realized risk level and calculated risk levels due to the fact that the calculated VaR values are affected by deviations caused by the estimation model. In practice, this can cause the realized shortfalls to be higher than the calculated amount of shortfalls. This makes the effectiveness of this method controversial against extreme shocks in risk management based on the VaR approach.

It is usually accepted that risk management techniques providing the lowest number of deviations are the most effective and consistent approaches (Bolgün and Akçay, 2005). This study tests whether there is a statistical difference between expected deviations and those resulting from the calculated VaR values in order to prove that the estimation results obtained in this study using the GAS model are estimation parameters that determine the number of deviations is a consistent and effective manner. For this purpose, firstly some backtesting approaches were used to determine whether there were any statistical differences between realized and expected deviations. These approaches are: the unconditional coverage test of Kupiec (1995), the conditional coverage test of Christoffesen (LRcc) (1998), and the Dynamic Quantile test of Engle and Manganelli (DQ) (2004). The Kupiec test can be insufficient in terms of reliability of models due to leaps that can cause excessive deviations, volatility accumulations with bubbles, and time-dependent effects emerging in time.

Tab. 15.4: VaR Backtesting Results of the BIST 100 Index Returns

Distribution Type	Test Type	1 % Confidence Level	5 % Confidence Level
Normal Distribution	LRuc	4.09097 (0.04311)	1,8120 (0.1783)
	LRcc	4.67960 (0.09635)	1,8737 (0.3919)
	DQ	9.337 (0.2294)	7,317 (0.3966)
Student *t* Distribution	LRuc	0.3798 (0.5377)	0,02119 (0.88427)
	LRcc	0.6716 (0.7148)	0,1002 (0.9511)
	DQ	3.09 (0.8765)	5,809 (0.5622)
Skewed Student *t* Distribution	LRuc	0 (1)	3,29374 (0.06954)
	LRcc	0.2022 (0.9038)	3,4588 (0.1774)
	DQ	14.38 (0.04478)	14,65 (0.04081)

The conditional coverage test of Christoffesen (1998) is used in the literature for a more effective measurement of the differentiation between realized and expected shocks resulting from the fact that the impacts are time-dependent. The above mentioned techniques can create biased results based on the impacts defined as tail effects. The Dynamic Quantile test of Engle and Manganelli (2004) is a more effective technique for evaluation of results in the presence of tail effects.

Tab. 15.4 shows the results of the back tests of the VaR calculations based on the GAS parameters obtained through the above mentioned backtesting techniques.

When we analyze the results in Tab. 15.4 according to the 1 percent and 5 percent significance levels, we see that the Kupiec test (LRuc) result is 4.09 according to normal distribution at 1 percent significance level. This reveals a difference between expected shortfalls and shortfalls based on normal distribution at the 1 percent significance level. The other two tests (LRcc and DQ) do not support this result according to this distribution. This result suggests that impacts caused time dependence and tail effects in the calculated values.

It is observed that the results provided by the GAS model other than those in the DQ test based on the Skewed Student *t* distribution were consistent and effective. However, the result of the DQ test proves presence of tail effects. This is caused by the impacts resulting from presence of tail effects on the BIST 100 index returns within the analyzed period. Accordingly, the null hypothesis suggesting that there is no difference between realized shortfalls and expected shortfalls in general is rejected according to the DQ test.

Conclusion

This chapter shows that the GAS model is not effective and consistent while calculating differences between realized shortfall risks and expected shortfall risks even though it takes time-dependent parameters into account. A deviation is observed in the shortfall risk calculated by the DQ test due to the tail effect between the realized shortfalls and expected shortfalls in the period analyzed for the BIST 100 index returns.

Considering the BIST 100 index returns, it can be said that this is caused by the tail effects determined in back tests. From this point of view, this does not support the result that the GAS model generates consistent and effective predictors emphasized in the literature for the developing financial markets. Therefore, it must be paid attention that improving this estimation technique with different approaches can make a significant contribution to the literature. Especially research analyzing presence of tail effects during development of the GAS model by taking the frequency and time characteristics into account can make more contributions to the literature.

References

Artzner, P., Delbaen, F., Eber, J.M. and Heath, D. (1997), “Thinking Coherently,” *Risk*, *10* (11), 68–71.

Ardia D., Boudt, K., and Catania L. (2016), “Generalized Autoregressive Score Models in R: The GAS Package,” https://arxiv.org/pdf/1609.02354.pdf.

Blasques, F., Lucas, A., and Vlodrop A. (2017), “Finite Sample Optimality of Score Driven Volatility Models,” *Tinbergen Institute Discussion Paper*, TI 2017-111/III. https://papers.tinbergen.nl/17111.pdf

Blasques, F., Gorgi, P., and S.J. Koopman (2016), “Accelerating Score-Driven Models: Optimality, Estimation and Forecasting,” https://feb.kuleuven.be/drc/Economics/misc/nesg2016/papers/blasques-gorgi-koopman.pdf.

Blasques F, Koopman S.J., and Lucas, A. (2014), “Maximum Likelihood Estimation for Correctly Specified Generalized Autoregressive Score Models: Feedback Effects, Contraction Conditions and Asymptotic Properties” techreport TI 14-074/III, Tinbergen Institute. URL http://www.tinbergen.nl/discussionpaper/?paper=2332.

Bolgün, K.E. and Akçay M.B. (2005), Risk Yönetimi-Gelişlmekte Olan Türk Finans Piyasasında Entegre Risk Ölçüm ve Yönetim Uygulamaları. İstanbul, Scala Yayıncılık.

Buccheri G., G. Bormetti, F. Corsi and F. Lillo, (2018), "A Score Driven Conditional Correlation Model for Noisy and Asynchronous Data: an Application to High Frequency Covariance Dynamics," Cornell University, https://arxiv.org/abs/1803.04894.

Catania L., and Bill´e A.G. (2016), "Dynamic Spatial Autoregressive Models with Autoregressive and Heteroskedastic Disturbances," Working Paper, URL http://arxiv.org/abs/1602.02542.

Christoffersen P.F. (1998), "Evaluating Interval Rorecasts." *International Economic Review*, *39* (4), 841–862. doi: 10.2307/2527341.

Cox, D.R. (1981), "Statistical Analysis of Time Series: Some Recent Developments," *Scandinavian Journal of Statistics*, *8*, 93–115.

Creal, D., Koopman, J., and Lucas, A. (2011), "A Dynamic Multivariate Heavy-Tailed Model for Time-Varying Volatilities and Correlations," *Journal of Business & Economic Statistics*, *29* (4), 552–563.

Creal, D., Koopman, J., and Lucas, A. (2012), "Generalized Autoregressive Score Models," *AENORM*, *20* (75), May 2012.

Creal, D., Koopman, J., and Lucas, A. (2013), "Generalized Autoregressive Score Models with Applications," *Journal of Applied Econometrics*, *28* (5), 777–795.

Creal, D., Schwaab, B., Koopman, S.J., and Lucas, A. (2014), "Observation Driven Mixed Measurement Dynamic Factor Models with an Application to Credit Risk," *Review of Economics and Statistics*, *96* (5), 898–915.

Dickey, D.A. and Fuller, W.A. (1979), "Distribution of the Estimators for Autoregressive Time Series with a Unit Root," *Journal of the American Statistical Association*, *74*, 427–31.

Engle, R.F. and Manganelli, S. (2004), "CAViaR: Conditional Autoregressive Value at Risk by Regression Quantiles." *Journal of Business & Economic Statistics*, *22* (4), 367–381. doi: 10.1198/073500104000000370.

Gonzalez-Rivera, G., Lee, T.H., and Mishra, S. (2004), "Forecasting Volatility: A Reality Check Based on Option Pricing, Utility Function, Value-at-Risk, and Predictive Likelihood." *International Journal of Forecasting*, *20* (4), 629–645. doi: 10.1016/j.ijforecast.2003.10.003.

Harvey, A.C. (2013), *Dynamic Models for Volatility and Heavy Tails: With Applications to Financial and Economic Time Series* Volume *52*. Cambridge University Press.

Harvey, A. and Luati, A. (2014), "Filtering with Heavy Tails," *Journal of the American Statistical Association*, *109* (507), 1112–1122.

Harvey, A.C. and Sucarrat, G. (2014), "EGARCH Models with Fat Tails, Skewness and Leverage," Computational Statistics & Data Analysis, *76*, 320–338. doi:10.1016/j.csda.2013.09.022.

Harvey, A.C. and Thiele, S. (2015), "Testing against Changing Correlation," doi:10.1016/j. jempfin.2015.09.003. *Journal of Empirical Finance*, *38*, Part B, September 2016, 575–589.

Janus, P., Koopman, S.J., and Lucas, A. (2014), "Long Memory Dynamics for Multivariate Dependence under Heavy Tails," *Journal of Empirical Finance*, *29*, 187–206. doi:10.1016/j.jempfin. 2014.09.007.

Jarque Carlos M. and Anil K.B. (1987), "A Test for Normality of Observations and Regression Residuals," *International Statistical Review / Revue Internationale de Statistique*, *55* (2) (Aug., 1987), 163–172. https://www.jstor.org/stable/1403192?seq=1#page_scan_tab_contents.

Kupiec, P.H. (1995), "Techniques for Verifying the Accuracy of Risk Measurement Models." *The Journal of Derivatives*, *3*(2), 73–84. doi: 10.3905/jod.1995.407942.

Kwiatkowski, D., Phillips, P.C.B., Schmidt, P., and Shin, Y. (1992), "Testing the Null Hypothesis of Stationarity against the Alternative of a Unit Root," *Journal of Econometrics*, *54*, 159–178.

Makatjane, K.D., Xaba, D.L., and Moroke, N.D. (2017), "Application of Generalized Autoregressive Score Model to Stock Returns," World Economy of Science, Engineering and Technology, *International Journal of Economics and Management Engineering*, *11* (11), 2017.

Oh, D.H. and Patton A.J. (2013), "Time Varying Systematic Risk: Evidence from a Dynamic Copula Model of CDS Spreads," Duke University, http://public.econ.duke.edu/~ap172/Oh_Patton_GAS_factor_copula_CDS_23may13.pdf.

R Program (2017), "Rmetrics - Nonlinear and Chaotic Time Series Modelling," https://cran.r-project.org/web/packages/fNonlinear/fNonlinear.pdf.

Yamai, Y. and Yoshiba, T. (2002), "On the Validity of Value-at-Risk: Comparative Analysis with Expected Shortfall," *Monetary and Economic Studies*, *20* (1), Bank of Japan, 57–86.

Haşim Bağcı and Burhan Günay

16 The Effect of Basel Accords on Economic Value Added and Market Value Added

Abstract: This chapter compares and analyzes the market structure of the Turkish banking sector before and after 2001 with structural and non-structural approaches within the frame of industrial organization theories. It differs from other studies considering not only the balance sheet values of banks but also the other important determinants of the market structure such as the mergers, capital ownership of banks, and technology.

Keywords: Basel Criteria, Economic Value Added, Market Value Added, Banking Sector, Panel Data Analysis

1 Introduction

Banking is the primary sector that has an important place in developing economies. Today, banking sector is one of the most basic sources of income for economies. Therefore, positive and negative developments in the banking sector directly affect national economies. The banking sector needs to be supervised in order to ensure that economies are not adversely affected by the banking market, or they are affected to the minimum extent. The reason is because banking is a sector that contains risks.

In 1975, the Basel Committee was set up within the Bank for International Settlements to ensure supervision and control of the banking sector. The twelve founding member states of the Basel Committee included Belgium, Canada, France, Germany, Italy, Japan, Luxembourg, the Netherlands, Switzerland, Sweden, Spain, the United Kingdom, and the United States (USA). The number of member states increased throughout years. Turkey became a member of the committee on January 1, 2002. Institutions responsible for representing these countries in the Basel Committee are central banks and bank supervisory authorities of the countries. This committee aims not to change the rules of the member states, but rather to create standards as a whole, to enable the world to achieve these standards, to exchange ideas between countries, and to minimize the risks arising from the banking sector. The Basel Committee has the right to submit proposals and suggestions, although it does not have power to enact a law. Nevertheless, member states that do not comply with the Basel standards will be overlooked at the international arena and the risk levels of these countries will be negatively affected (Tanyıldız, 2007: 80–81; Turgut, 2007: 30–31).

The functioning of the Basel process is divided into classes, and these classes consist of standard setters, a standard disseminator, and other groups. The duties and functions of the institutions that make up these classes are very different. Standard setters consist of the Basel Committee on Banking Supervision, International Association of Insurance Supervisors, International Association of Deposit Insurers and Committee on Payment and Settlement Systems. The standard disseminator is the Financial Stability Institute. Other groups consist of the Committee on the Global Financial System, the Markets Committee, and the financial Stability Forum (The Banks Association of Turkey, 2005: 37). Standards called Basel accords were issued to ensure the functioning of this process and to achieve the objectives.

Basel I was the first Basel standard issued. Basel I accords were issued in 1988. The main purpose of these accords is to determine the minimum capital adequacy ratio. By means of this ratio, banks would have the opportunity to be prepared for potential adverse effects through risk controlling. According to the Basel I accords, this ratio should have been ≥ 8 percent. As time passed, the Basel I accords remained inadequate in the face of the conditions and the necessity of issuing a new standard emerged. Therefore, the process of transition to the Basel II started in 2004. According to the Basel II accords, capital ratio must be no lower than 8 percent; however, in addition to the risk in Basel I, operational risk was added into the calculation of the risk. Although the Basel II accords were a set of standards that could solve and control many problems and that could ensure efficiency of the banking sector, it was revealed that they must be updated after the financial crisis that started in 2007. Therefore, the Basel III accords were issued in 2009. Basel III is a regulatory accord that introduced a set of reforms which make up for the inadequacies of Basel II. Under Basel III, the minimum capital adequacy ratio is 10.5 percent. The difference of 2.5 percent is due to the addition of capital conservation buffer. Capital buffer is one of the concepts introduced in addition to the Basel II accords. It is argued that the Basel III accords are inadequate today; therefore, preparations for the transition to Basel IV accords are made. These regulations are expected to be completed and published in 2018–2019 (Atiker, 2005: 2; Babuşcu, 2005: 262; Gürel et al., 2012: 17; Erdogan, 2014: 169; The Banks Association of Turkey, 2016: 1–12).

The main aim of companies is to maximize the market value. In line with this aim, they use different techniques to calculate their market value. These techniques allow for performance measurement and calculation of market value. Since the performance measurement does not come up with a net result while determining the market value of companies, the concept of value is important for firms.

The concept of "value" is one of the fundamental problems of companies. The reason is because there are many different approaches to measuring value due to its abstract nature. The primary goal of the firms adopting a value-based management approach is to ensure that all decisions are taken with an eye on value creation. Companies' goal of creating value has been encouraging all employees and partners and has become the primary goal for all (Ercan and Ban, 2005: 334; Sakarya, 2008: 176–177). The points that need to be taken into consideration by firms while creating values and measuring them are as follows (Chambers, 2009: 24):

- The return on an investment in an asset in the real market must be higher than the investment's alternative (opportunity) cost; value can only be created in this way.
- The higher the return on capital is than the cost, the higher the value is.
- Tactics that will maximize the present value and economic profit of cash flows should be preferred.
- The value of a stock is equal to the actual value of that stock depending on the estimates on its future performance.
- When calculating the shareholder yield, the changes in the estimates rather than the actual performance of a stock play a decisive role.

This study examined the effects of the Basel accords on economic value added and market value added in thirteen banks registered at the public disclosure platform of Borsa Istanbul. The capital adequacy ratios of banks were used as a measure of the Basel accords.

2 Economic Value Added

There are many different methods used for value calculation in the literature. Some of these methods are economic value added (EVA), market value added (MVA), shareholder value added (SVA), cash value added (CVA), and refined economic value added (REVA) (Sümer Göğüş, 2011: 10).

The EVA method was developed by bringing new arrangements to the concept of residual income. This method was introduced by Stern Stewart & Co in 1980. The main purpose of this method is to create a measurement method between the value and performance of the discounted cash flows. The EVA method is different from the accounting profit in that it takes account of both the weighted average cost of capital and the cost of debt. EVA has a strong correlation with the current market value, since it considers the future costs and returns on investments (Ünlü and Saygın, 2014: 142). In sum, EVA is the difference between the net operating profit after tax and the risk-adjusted cost of equities and foreign assets on the debit side of the balance. Therefore, EVA calculates the company value in amount. A positive EVA indicates that the economic value of a company is high and the wealth of the partners is increasing. A negative EVA indicates that the company is not generating economic value and that the partners are losing money. It is stated that companies should create positive EVA in line with the main goal of maximizing their market value (Akbaş, 2011: 119).

Although there are different approaches in the literature to calculating EVA, the generally accepted formula is as follows: EVA = Net Operating Profit after Tax - Cost of Invested Capital. The detailed version of the formula is as follows (Prober, 2000: 27; Damodaran, 2002: 864; Sparling and Turvey, 2003: 256):

- Net Sales - Operating Expenses = Operating Profit
- Operating Profit - Taxes = Net Operating Profit after Tax
- Invested Capital * Weighted Average Cost of Capital = Cost of Capital
- Net Operating Profit after Tax - Cost of Capital = **Economic Value Added (EVA).**

3 Market Value Added

In order to achieve their main goal of maximizing their market values, companies need to consider the market value added. Therefore, firms learn the status of the capital they provided via market value added (MVA). MVA is directly related to EVA. Therefore, economic profitability is also linked to MVA. MVA is the method used to determine the efficiency of capital. It refers to the difference between the market value of a company and the capital, and it measures the effective resource utilization. MVA is used to measure how much value is created or destroyed by the company in relation to the investment of shareholders. A low MVA indicates that the capital is used inefficiently (Stewart, 1991: 169; Sullivan and Needy, 2000: 11).

There are different views on the calculation of MVA. In sum, MVA is calculated as follows (Gapenski, 1996: 56):

MVA = Present Value of Future EVAs
MVA = Market Value - Invested Capital
MVA = Market Value - Total Equity (Market Value = Paid-Up Capital * Lot Value).

Calculated by using these formulas, MVA equals the market value of the company minus sum of the book value. It is a good method to measure effective resource utilization and company success (Stern, Shiely, and Ross, 2001: 23).

4 Background

The literature review shows that there are various studies on EVA and MVA. However, the number of studies examining the impacts of the Basel accords on EVA and MVA is very limited.

Akyüz (2013) investigated the relationship between EVA and MVA by using the financial data on ceramic companies included in the BIST 100 index. He found that none of the companies created positive EVA and MVA, and they always decreased in value. He also reported that there was relationship between EVA and MVA in general.

Demirgüneş et al. (2009) tested the effect of the EVAs of companies in Borsa Istanbul on their company value using econometric methods. The data set of the sample covered the years 2006–2007. They found that EVA has a very high capacity and power to explain the company value compared to other criteria.

Bayrakdaroğlu and Ünlü (2009) conducted a comparative analysis of Borsa Istanbul and New York Stock Exchange for EVA and MVA. They proved that Borsa Istanbul was not able to achieve a positive performance for EVA and MVA.

Topal (2008) investigated the relationship between EVA and MVA values of the manufacturing companies in the BIST and found no relationship between certain sub-sectors, despite the high correlation found between EVA and MVA in general.

In another study, Şamiloğlu (2005) measured the effects MVA and stock returns had on each other. Similarly, a study involving manufacturing industry reported that stock prices were affected by the beta of the stock; however, there was no interaction between MVA and stock prices.

Şamiloğlu (2004) examined the mutual interaction of EVA and stock returns. Covering the period between 1995 and 2002, the study revealed that 7.9 percent of the manufacturing companies listed in Borsa Istanbul were explained by EVA.

Abdeen and Haight (2002) examined the relationship between EVA and MVA and revealed that this relationship should be established not for the company as a whole, but for each of its subsidiaries, divisions, or business units individually.

Fernandez (2002) investigated the relationship between EVA and MVA of 582 American companies for a period of eighteen years and found a low correlation between EVA and MVA. The relationship between EVA and NOPAT variable was found to be relatively higher compared to MVA.

Lehn and Makhija (1996) examined the relationship of EVA and MVA to stock prices. They used 241 firms operating in the manufacturing industry as a sample. As a result of their research, they concluded that all variables were related to stock prices; but the strongest relationship was found to be with EVA.

Stewart (1991) aimed to rank the top 1000 US companies by their EVA and MVA, but examined only 613 companies due to the problems in the data set. It was found that a positive EVA score led to a strong relationship between EVA and MVA, whereas a negative EVA did not lead to a significant relationship between EVA and MVA.

5 Solutions

In this study, we calculated EVA, MVA, and capital adequacy ratios of thirteen banks operating in the Banks and Special Finance Institutions sector registered to Borsa Istanbul for the period between 2000 and 2016. We aimed to identify the relationship of the Basel accords adopted by the banks studied with EVA and MVA. The relationship was examined using panel data analysis. We used panel data analysis because we had multiple years and multiple variables in our data. Panel data analysis is an econometric analysis technique that examines the interaction among multiple variables across multiple periods. Panel data analysis is performed using Stata and EViews. In this study, the analysis was performed by using the EViews 9 package program. The model analyzed was as follows:

$$\text{Basel Accords (Capital Adequacy)}_{it} = \beta_{0it} + \beta_{1it}\,\text{EVA}_{it} + \beta_{2it}\,\text{MVA}_{it} + \mu_{it}.$$

Some preliminary tests need to be performed before creating a panel data model. Panel models should be constructed based on the results of these preliminary tests. These preliminary tests are autocorrelation test, cross-section dependence test, and heteroscedasticity test. Autocorrelation is the deviation showing that error terms are correlated in a regression model. This prevents constructing regression equations correctly. Cross-section dependence refers to the correlation between the units in regression models. Heteroscedasticity refers to the problem that occurs when the error terms in a regression equation do not have constant variance. If any or all of these preliminary tests yield a negative result, the model to be constructed should be corrected using resistance estimation methods. In this study, we performed these preliminary tests and constructed a panel model based on the test results.

First, we performed the Hausman test to determine which panel data analysis method was used to construct the model. Tab. 16.1 shows the results of the Hausman test.

Tab. 16.1: Results of the Hausman Test

Test Name	Test Statistics	P Value (5 %)
Hausman	89.628	0.000

Tab. 16.2: Cross-Sectional Dependence Test Results

Test Name	Test Statistics	P Value (5 %)
Pesaran CD	18.134	0.000

Tab. 16.3: Panel Unit Root Test Results

Variables	CIPS Test Statistics	
	With Constant	With Constant and Trend
SUSTAINABLE	-4.72	-4.88
EVA	-5.84	-5.13
MVA	-4.12	-4.18

As shown in Tab. 16.1, since the p value was below 5 percent , the null hypothesis H_0 assuming the existence of random effects was rejected and the hypothesis H_1 assuming that the model was fixed effects model was accepted.

In the second stage, the Pesaran CD test was performed to see whether there was cross-sectional dependence between the variables. Tab. 16.2 shows the results of the test.

As shown in Tab. 16.2, since the p value was below 5 percent , the null hypothesis H_0 assuming that there was no cross-sectional dependence was rejected and the hypothesis H_1 assuming the existence of cross-sectional dependence was accepted. In cases where there is a correlation across units, i.e., cross-sectional dependence, stability of the series should be tested using unit root tests. Due to the presence of cross-sectional dependence in this study, the use of a second-generation unit root test is needed. Therefore, stability of the series was tested by the Pesaran's CADF test, which is a second generation unit root test. Tab. 16.3 shows the results of the test.

CIPS critical values shown in Tab. 16.3 were obtained from the annexes of Pesaran's article dated 2007 titled "A Simple Panel Unit Root Test in the Presence of Cross Section Dependence." Since the CIPS test values are lower than the critical values in the article as shown in Tab. 16.3, the hypothesis H_0 assuming that

Tab. 16.4: Heteroscedasticity Test Results

Test Name	**Test Statistics**	**P Value (5 %)**
Wald Test	1.8e+34	0.000

Tab. 16.5: Autocorrelation Test Results

Test Name	**Test Statistics**
Durbin-Watson Test	1.236

the series contained a root was rejected. It was found that the series did not have a unit root and that they were all stationary. Therefore, there was no need to make them stationary.

Then the Wald test was performed to test whether there was heteroscedasticity among the variables. Tab. 16.4 shows the test results.

As shown in Tab. 16.4, since the p value was below 5 percent, the null hypothesis H_0 assuming that there was no heteroscedasticity was rejected and the hypothesis H_1 assuming the existence of heteroscedasticity was accepted. We used the Durbin-Watson test to find out whether there was autocorrelation between the variables. Tab. 16.5 shows the test results.

As shown in Tab. 16.5, we found that the test statistic was below two, so there was autocorrelation between the variables. All problems found as a result of these preliminary tests were solved by using the Driscoll Kraay Resistance Estimator. Tab. 16.6 shows the model which constituted the primary aim of the study.

Tab. 16.6 shows the results of the panel regression test which describes the relationship between variables. The results revealed that the probe value of the whole model was 0. Since this score was 0 <0.05, the model was significant at 5 percent level. The R-squared value of the model was found to be 0.0975. This means that the model explains 9 percent of the "Basel Accords" which was titled sustainability. This score is very low. The reason is because the R-squared coefficient of the model is expected to be above 50 percent for the relationship between them to be strong. In addition, probe values of independent variables must be examined to see the relationship between the dependent and independent variables of the model. The probe value of the MVA was found to be 0.9273, whereas the probe value of the EVA was found to be 0.4624. These probe values show that there is no correlation between the dependent and independent variables. This is because the probe values show no relationship between them at 1 percent, 5 percent, and 10 percent significance levels.

Tab. 16.6: Panel Regression Results

Dependent Variable: SURDURULEBİLiR
Method: Panel Least Squares
Date: 04/05/18 Time: 16:41
Sample: 2000 2016
Periods included:
Cross-sections included: 16
Total panel (unbalanced) observations: 232

Variable	Coefficient	Std. Error	t-Statistic	Prob.
C	5.54E+08	23776000	23.32115	0.0000
MVA	7.79E-06	8.53E-05	0.091220	0.9273
EVA	3.399300	0.183691	18.50554	0.4624

Effects Specification

Cross-section fixed (dummy variables)

R-squared	0.0975	Mean dependent var	7.54E+08
Adjusted R-squared	0.0264	S.D. dependent var	1.99E+09
S.E. of regression	8.28E+08	Akaike info criterion	44.01209
Sum squared resid	9.29E+20	Schwarz criterion	44.60940
Log likelihood	-33410.22	Hannan-Quinn criter.	44.23442
F-statistic	75.99573	Durbin-Watson stat	1.149086
Prob (F-statistic)	0.000000		

Conclusion and Future Research Directions

Risk monitoring and performance control is crucial for the banking sector to achieve a stable progress and development. There are a number of regulations to ensure such monitoring and control. There are Basel accords that constantly monitor risk and prevent it from falling below a certain level. These accords regulate the risk level of banks at the international level. Compliance with these accords is one of the most important investment criteria taken into consideration by both local and foreign sectors because a banking sector that does not comply with the Basel accords carries a risk for the investor. Another issue is the performance of banks. Although performance analysis can be performed using many different methods, EVA and MVA are the most reliable ones. EVA and MVA can be used to calculate the market value of a company. The primary goal of a company is to maximize its market value. In line with this goal, values of companies are measured using EVA and MVA.

In this chapter, we calculated EVA, MVA, and capital adequacy ratios of thirteen banks operating in the Turkish banking sector and registered to Borsa Istanbul for the period between 2000 and 2016. The purpose of this calculation is to examine the relationship between EVA, MVA, and capital adequacy ratios. In order to perform this study, we used the panel data analysis method and performed a panel regression test. As a result of the regression test, we found no relationship between EVA, MVA, and capital adequacy ratios in the Turkish banking sector for the period between 2000 and 2016. We also found that the Basel accords did not affect EVA and MVA.

Further studies may be conducted by expanding the period and adding different variables of the banking sector. Besides, the banking sector may be compared with another sector, or the study may be turned into a more universal study by including a comparison of sectors in more than one country. However, in its current form, this study still serves as a reference for investors.

References

Abdeen, A.M. and Haight, G.T. (2002). "A Fresh Look at Economic Value Added: Empirical Study of the Fortune Five-Hundred Companies," *Journal of Applied Business Research*, *18*(2-Spring): 27–36.

Akbaş, H.E. (2011). "Ekonomik Katma Değer Yaklaşımı ve Hissedar Değeri," *Journal of Financial Solution*, *21*(July–August): 115–133.

Akyüz, Y. (2013). "Ekonomik Katma Değer (EVA) ve Pazar Katma Değer (MVA) Analizi: İMKB'de İşlem Gören Seramik İşletmelerinde Bir Uygulama," Süleyman Demirel University, *Journal of Economic and Administrative Sciences*, *18*(2): 339–356.

Atiker, M. (2005). "Basel I ve Basel II," Konya Chamber of Commerce Survey Research Service, *41*(08): 1–15.

Babuşcu, Ş. (2005). *Basel II Düzenlemeleri Çerçevesinde Bankalarda Risk Yönetimi*, Ankara: Academy Consulting & Training Publications.

Bayrakdaroğlu, A. and Ünlü, U. (2009). "Performans Değerlemede EVA ve MVA Ölçütleri: Bu Ölçütler Açısından İMKB ve NYSE'nin Karşılaştırılmalı Analizi," Süleyman Demirel University, *Journal of Economic and Administrative Sciences*, *14*(1): 287–312.

Chambers, N. (2009). *Firma Değerlemesi*, İstanbul: Beta Yayınları.

Damodaran, A. (2002). *Investment Valuation: Tool and Techniques for Determining The Value of Any Asset* (Second Edition), New York: John Wiley & Sons, Inc.

Demirgüneş, K., Öztürk M.B., Şamiloğlu, F., Ban, Ü., and ve Güzel, A. (2009). "Ekonomik Katma Dğerin Bilgi Verme İçeriğinin Analiz Edilmesine Yönelik Bir Ampirik Çalışma," *Journal of Trade and Tourism Education Faculty, 1*: 1–24.

Ercan, M.K. and Ban, Ü. (2005). *Financial Management*, Ankara: Gazi Kitabevi.

Erdoğan, A. (2014). "Basel Kriterlerinin Bankacılık Sektörüne Etkisi ve Türkiye'de Bankacılık Sektörünün Basel Kriterlerine Uyum Süreci," Trakya University, *Journal of Social Science*, *16*(1): 141–182.

Fernandez, P. (2002). Valuation Methods and Shareholder Value Creation, IESE Business School.

Gapenski, L.C. (1996). "Using MVA and EVA to Measure Financial Performance," *Healthcare Financial Management*, *50*(3): 56–60.

Gürel, E., Bulgurcu Gürel, E.B., and Demir, N. (2012). "Basel III Kriterleri," *Journal of Banking and Insurance Research*, 1(3–4): 16–28.

Lehn, K. and Makhija, A.K. (1996). "EVA & MVA: As Performance Measures and Signals for Strategic Change," *Strategy & Leadership*, *24*(3-May-Jun): 34–38.

Pesaran, H.M. (2007). "A Simple Panel Unit Root Test in the Presence of Cross-Section Dependence," *Journal of Applied Econometrıcs*, *22*(2): 265–312.

Prober, L.M. (2000). "EVA: A Better Financial Reporting Tool", Pennsylvania CPA Journal, *71*(3): 27–33.

Sakarya, Ş. (2008). "Hissedar Değeri ve Hesaplanması Üzerine Bir Uygulama," *Journal of Accounting and Financing*, *40*(October): 175–184.

Şamiloğlu, F. (2004). "Ekonomik Katma Değer: İstanbul Menkul Kıymetler Borsası'nda Örnek Olay İncelemesi," *Journal of Accounting and Financing*, *24*(October): 150–157.

Şamiloğlu, F. (2005). "Piyasa Katma Değeri ve Hisse Getirileri: İMKB'deki İmalat Sanayi Şirketlerinde Ampirik Bir Uygulama," *Journal of Accounting and Financing*, *25*(January): 79–88.

Sparling, D. and Turvey, C.G. (2003). "Further Thoughts on the Relationship between Economic Value Added and Stock Market Performance," *Agribusiness*, *19*(2-Spring): 255–267.

Stern, J.M., Shiely, J.S., and Ross, I. (2001). *The EVA Challenge Implementing Value-Added Change in an Organization*, New York: John Wiley & Sons Inc.

Stewart, G.B. (1991). *The EVA Management Guide: The Quest for Value*, New York: Harper Business Publishers.

Sullivan, W.G. and Needy, K.L. (2000). "Determination of Economic Value Added for a Proposed Investment in New Manufacturing," *Engineering Economist*, *45*(29): 11–24.

Sümer Göğüş, E.H. (2011). "Ekonomik Katma Değer ve HesaplanışI," *Journal of Management*, *22*(69): 9–23.

Tanyıldız, H. (2007). "Türk Bankacılık Sisteminde Basel II Kriterleri Çerçevesinde Risk Yönetimi," Balıkesir University Social Science İnstitute Department of Business Master's Thesis, Balıkesir.

Topal, Y. (2008). "Ekonomik Katma Değer (EVA) ve Pazar Katma Değer (MVA) Arasındaki İlişki İMKB İmalat İşletmelerinden Örnek," Süleyman Demirel University, *Journal of Economic and Administrative Sciences*, *13*(2): 249–261.

Turgut, A. (2007). "Bankalar ve KOBİ'ler İçin Dönüm Noktası: Basel II Standartları", Karamanoğlu Mehmetbey University, *Journal of Social and Economic Research*, 2: 29–44.

The Banks Association of Turkey, (2005). "Finansal İstikrar ve Basel II'nin Etkileri" 16–18 Mayıs 2005 İstanbul Konferansı FSI Başkanı Josef Tosovsky'nin Konuşması," https://www.tbb.org.tr/Dosyalar/Araştırma_ve_Raporlar/finansal istikrar.pdf (Erişim Tarihi: 15.05.2018).

The Banks Association of Turkey, (2016). "Basel IV Bankaları Bekleyen Zorluklar," İstanbul.

Ünlü, U. and Saygın, O. (2014). "Arındırılmış Ekonomik Katma Değer (REVA) Yöntemiyle Performans Ölçümü: Turizm Sektörü Uygulaması," *Journal of Accounting and Financing*, *63*(July): 139–150.

List of Figures

Fig. 3.1: Nominal and real oil prices ($ /barrel). *Source: US Energy Information Administration* 42
Fig. 3.2: OPEC oil exports (billion dollars). *Source: OPEC Annual Statistical Bulletin* 43
Fig. 3.3: OPEC real export and imports (2017 Dollars). *Source: OPEC Annual Statistical Bulletin* 45
Fig. 3.4: OPEC current account balance (2017 Dollars). *Source: OPEC Annual Statistical Bulletin* 47
Fig. 3.5: OPEC international reserves (2017 Dollars). *Source: Worldbank* . 49
Fig. 4.1: Levels of Time Series 55
Fig. 4.2: Impulse Responses for the Model-1 (1990:Q1–2016:Q3) 59
Fig. 5.1: The Bitcoin-USD exchange rates time series 67
Fig. 5.2: Inverse roots for the VAR model 69
Fig. 5.3: Impulse response functions 71
Fig. 6.1: Fat and Non-Fat Measures of Liquidity Creation in US 84
Fig. 6.2: The ratio of liquidity creation measures in US 84
Fig. 6.3: The ratio of liquidity creation measures in US for small banks 85
Fig. 6.4: Fat and Non-Fat measures of liquidity creation in US for small banks 85
Fig. 6.5: Fat and Nonfat measures of liquidity creation in Turkey 86
Fig. 6.6: The ratio of liquidity creation measures in Turkey 87
Fig. 6.7: Decomposition of liquidity creation in US 88
Fig. 6.8: Decomposition of liquidity creation in Turkey 89
Fig. 6.9: Decomposition of liquidity creation for small banks in US 89
Fig. 6.10: Decomposition of off-balance sheet items in Turkey 91
Fig. 6.11: Decomposition of derivatives in Turkey 91
Fig. 7.1: Bank-related parties (stakeholders). *Source: Jeucken, 2001* 99
Fig. 7.2: Green investment types 101
Fig. 7.3: Green loan cycle. *Source: Peralta, 2016.* 103
Fig. 7.4: A pyramid of national development banking activity. *Source: United Nations (2005: 11)* 103
Fig. 7.5: Objectives of environmental and social protection measures. *Source: Kiss, 2011* 104
Fig. 7.6: Risks for trade banks caused by environmental costs. *Source: ICBC, 2016: 10* 108

Fig. 9.1: Development of non-performing loans. *Source: Compiled from the reports published by BDDK about the Overview of the Turkish Banking Sector* ... 132
Fig. 9.2: CUSUM test ... 138
Fig. 11.1: Determinants of market structure in banking sector. *Source: Created by the authors* ... 159
Fig. 13.1: Financial sector and real sector indicators in Turkey (billion TL) (1998Q1–2017Q4). *Source: Central Bank of the Republic of Turkey. Electronical Data Delivery System (2018).* https://evds2.tcmb.gov.tr/index.php?/evds/serieMarket (10.04.2018) ... 188
Fig. 14.1: PIN diagram. *Source: Easley, Kiefer, O'hara, and Paperman (1996: 1409)* ... 199
Fig. 14.2: PIN values of 12 stocks in the sample. *Source: Authors' own calculation* ... 207
Fig. 15.1: Main parameters related to the GAS model. *Source: Ardia et al., 2016* ... 222
Fig. 15.2: Closing price data of the BIST 100 index (2010–2018) ... 223
Fig. 15.3: BIST 100 index return series (2010–2018) ... 224
Fig. 15.4: Comparison of the BIST 100 index returns and normal distribution ... 225

List of Tables

Tab. 1.1: Indicator-Based Measurement Method. Source: Basel Committee on Banking Supervision (BCBS, 2013: 6) 16
Tab. 3.1: Recycling of Exports Windfall (In 2017 Dollars). Source: OPEC Annual Statistical Bulletin 45
Tab. 3.2: Current and financial Accounts Windfall (Billion Dollars, 2017 Prices). Source: OPEC Annual Statistical Bulletin 48
Tab. 4.1: Results of Unit Root Tests 56
Tab. 4.2: Correlation Coefficients 56
Tab. 4.3: Rank of Cointegration Tests 57
Tab. 4.4: The BoE and the FED Short-Term Dynamics Equation Result for the Period 1990:Q1 to 2016:Q3 58
Tab. 4.5: Ramsey Reset Test for the Model-1 59
Tab. 5.1: The Correlation Matrix between the Variables 68
Tab. 5.2: Granger Causality Test Results 69
Tab. 5.3: Variance Decomposition Analysis Results 72
Tab. 7.1: Global Risks and Their Effects. Source: World Economic Forum 2018, Global Risks Reports 97
Tab. 8.1: Other Strategies That Can Help Relationship Marketing Strategies. Reference: Tinsley (2002), 71 122
Tab. 9.1: Results of Stationarity Tests 135
Tab. 9.2: Bound Test (F Statistic) Results 136
Tab. 9.3: Long-Term ARDL Model Estimations Based on the HQ Criterion 137
Tab. 9.4: ARDL Model Long-Term Coefficients 138
Tab. 9.5: Short-Term ECM Estimation Results Based on the ARDL Model 140
Tab. 10.1: Research Hypotheses 151
Tab. 10.2: Research Variables 151
Tab. 10.3: Simple Logistic Analysis Results 152
Tab. 10.4: The Correlation between the Net Profit for the Period and GUD 154
Tab. 11.1: 1990–2000, Results of CR Concentration and HKI Indexes 163
Tab. 11.2: 2001–2014, Results of CR Concentration and HKI Indexes 166
Tab. 11.3: 1990–2000, Results of Lerner Index 167
Tab. 11.4: 2001–2014, Results of Lerner Index 168
Tab. 11.5: 1990–2000, Results of Adjusted Lerner Index 168
Tab. 11.6: 2001–2014, Results of Adjusted Lerner Index 169

Tab. 12.1: Data Set ... 177
Tab. 12.2: Results of ADF and Philips Perron (PP) Unit Root Test ... 178
Tab. 12.3: Toda-Yamamoto Causality Test Results ... 180
Tab. 13.1: Results of ADF and PP Unit Root Test ... 190
Tab. 13.2: Results of the ZA Unit Root Test ... 191
Tab. 13.3: Test Results for Determining the Lag Length ... 192
Tab. 13.4: Bound Test Results ... 192
Tab. 13.5: ARDL (5,7) Long Run Coefficients ... 193
Tab. 13.6: ARDL (5,7) Short Run Coefficients ... 194
Tab. 14.1: The List of Banks. Source: Bloomberg Terminal Database ... 204
Tab. 14.2: The Descriptive Statistics of Data Set. Source: Authors' Own Calculations ... 205
Tab. 14.3: PIN Variables, Volume, and PIN-Volume Correlations. Source: Authors' Own Calculations ... 206
Tab. 14.4: PIN and USD/TRY Regression Coefficients. Source: Authors' Own Calculations ... 208
Tab. 14.5: PIN and TRLIB6M Regression Coefficients. Source: Authors' Own Calculations ... 209
Tab. 15.1: Parameter Estimations Depending on Distribution Characteristics in the GAS Model ... 223
Tab. 15.2: BIST 100 Index Returns— Jarque-Bera Test Result ... 225
Tab. 15.3: Results of VaR Parameter Estimations Based on the BIST 100 Index Returns and GAS Model ... 227
Tab. 15.4: VaR Backtesting Results of the BIST 100 Index Returns ... 229
Tab. 16.1: Results of the Hausman Test ... 239
Tab. 16.2: Cross-Sectional Dependence Test Results ... 239
Tab. 16.3: Panel Unit Root Test Results ... 239
Tab. 16.4: Heteroscedasticity Test Results ... 240
Tab. 16.5: Autocorrelation Test Results ... 240
Tab. 16.6: Panel Regression Results ... 241

www.ingramcontent.com/pod-product-compliance
Ingram Content Group UK Ltd.
Pitfield, Milton Keynes, MK11 3LW, UK
UKHW020153290926
15471UKWH00005B/845

9 783631 779866